DOMESTIC VIOLENCE

DOMESTIC VIOLENCE

Assessment and Treatment

Edited by
Rafael Art. Javier, Ph.D.
William G. Herron, Ph.D.
and Andrea J. Bergman, Ph.D.

JASON ARONSON INC.
Northvale, New Jersey
London

Production Editor: Elaine Lindenblatt

This book was printed and bound by Book-mart Press of North Bergen, New Jersey.

Copyright © 1996 by Jason Aronson Inc.
            1994 by Human Sciences Press, Inc.

10 9 8 7 6 5 4 3

All rights reserved. Printed in the United States of America. No part of this book may be used or reproduced in any manner whatsoever without written permission from Jason Aronson Inc. except in the case of brief quotations in reviews for inclusion in a magazine, newspaper, or broadcast.

Library of Congress Cataloging-in-Publication Data

Domestic violence : assessment and treatment / edited by Rafael Art. Javier,
   William G. Herron, and Andrea J. Bergman.
       p.   cm.
     "The material in this book originally appeared in the Journal of social
distress and the homeless, vol. 3, nos. 1 and 3, January and July, 1994"—
T.p. verso.
     Includes bibliographical references and index.
     ISBN 1-56821-851-6 (sc : alk. paper)
     1. Family violence—Treatment. 2. Family violence—Cross-cultur-
al studies. 3. Family violence—Social aspects. I. Javier, Rafael Art.
II. Herron, William G. III. Bergman, Andrea J.
RC569.5.F3D65 1996
616.85'822—dc20   96–11818

Manufactured in the United States of America. Jason Aronson Inc. offers books and cassettes. For information and catalog write to Jason Aronson Inc., 230 Livingston Street, Northvale, New Jersey 07647.

To the memories of my father
and younger brother, Luis
Rafael Art. Javier

To my wife, Mary Jane
William G. Herron

To my parents
Andrea J. Bergman

Contents

Foreword

Recently there has been a public outcry about violence, particularly domestic violence, in the United States. Charges and countercharges fly back and forth. There are those who blame violence on the family; there are those who blame family violence on society. There are those within the family who point fingers at each other. There are self-anointed pundits who propose to explain domestic violence and make it go away. They often suggest remedies that seem to coincide with their own personal, ethnic, religious, or political agendas. Unfortunately, despite all of the rhetoric, domestic violence continues to maim and destroy families and family members, psychologically and physically. Further, its ramifications spread throughout our communities and society.

There is an oft-quoted view that nature is "red in tooth and claw." However, the survival of individuals, societies, and our species rests more on prosocial impulses such as caring, sharing, helping, and sacrificing for others than on violence. The mark of civilized societies is that their people have learned to constrain their violent impulses and build on their prosocial impulses. That is, their citizens advocate that people, individually and collectively, contain their violence and direct their energies into prosocial, civilized channels. Such positive, constructive characteristics are as much or more a part of our human natures than is violence.

The organizers of the dialogue that produced this volume deserve our respect for their mature and civilized approach to this epidemic. The thought and effort they have devoted to the issue of domestic violence have produced admirable results. They have begun the process of mapping out the interrelated factors we must consider in order to understand and control domestic violence.

That is, these chapters outline for us the many ways in which societies, families, and individuals have fallen short of using civilized approaches with each other, but instead have resorted to personal and institutional violence. They have identified a range of social and individual factors that contribute to domestic violence as well as to the selection of its most common victims. They have likewise made it clear that there is much that can be done to reduce violence.

Not surprisingly, since most of the contributors are working in social, behavioral, and health-oriented fields, their approaches and recommendations embody the values of these fields and focus more directly on therapeutic-type interventions. As important as such therapeutic contributions are, there are other equally important factors contributing to domestic violence that cannot be addressed therapeutically. Fortunately, the ideas and analyses contained in this book also provide a basis for identifying and facing these other issues we have not yet faced.

It is evident from what has been written here that therapy can never be enough. As professionals and as citizens we need also to begin to focus our expertise on changing our society's investment in power, oppression, and violence. For example, a recent cross-cultural book reporting on domestic violence concluded that there is less domestic violence/spouse abuse in societies which provide cultural sanctions against such behavior and sanctuary for real and potential victims. We do need to provide sanctions and sanctuary for victims of violence. We also need to provide alternatives to violence as a solution to problems. We must develop prosocial ways of building harmony and cohesiveness within a framework of acceptance for diversity so that there is less occasion to turn to violence.

We need to restrain people's violence, but it is also crucial that we help people learn to curb their violence. To accomplish these twin goals we need a better understanding of how we can acknowledge the humanity and prosocial strengths of violent people. We also need to develop ways to help them build on their own better impulses. To do that, we must involve ourselves in correcting the social injustices and exploitations that both fuel violent impulses and provide their social justification.

As we seek to accomplish such goals, it is vital that we remember several points. At any level, there is no one way of living or understanding or dealing with violence that is the best or only approach for everyone. Families from different ethnic, cultural, and racial heritages have formed different ethnically based ways of organizing their relationships. These individuals, their families, and their communities have strengths as well as limitations. It is not just the individuals in violent families but our entire society that needs to recognize the importance of working out ways for all of us to survive and nurture ourselves in a heterogeneous cultural context such as that of the United States.

The organizers of and contributors to this book have provided an invaluable service by laying out the groundwork and stimulating this enormously important dialogue about domestic violence. It is up to all of us to build on it.

Forrest B. Tyler, Ph.D.
Professor Emeritus
Department of Psychology
University of Maryland

Acknowledgements

Many individuals responsible for putting together this volume are deserving of our deepest gratitude. Margaret Schwartz and Carolyn DeCesare provided essential secretarial assistance, while Maura McDonald-Gomez helped to review many of the manuscripts and made important contributions in that regard. The contribution made by Philip Yanos in the preparation of the book is also acknowledged. Finally, we recognize the support and encouragement of Willard Gingerich and Jeffrey Fagen, in making possible the conference structure facilitating the manuscripts.

About the Editors

Rafael Art. Javier, Ph.D., is Clinical Professor of Psychology and Director of the Center for Psychological Services and Clinical Studies, St. John's University, Jamaica, NY. He is also a faculty member and supervisor at New York University Medical Center and the Object Relations Institute. A graduate of the NYU clinical psychology program and postdoctoral program in psychotherapy and psychoanalysis, Dr. Javier has presented in national and international meetings on bilingualism, cognition, memory, aggression, and moral reasoning, and has published extensively on psycholinguistic issues in treatment and on ethnic and cultural issues in psychoanalytic theories and practice. He is in private practice.

William G. Herron, Ph.D., is Professor of Psychology, St. John's University, and Senior Supervisor and Training Analyst, Contemporary Center for Advanced Psychoanalytic Studies. He is in private practice in Woodcliff Lake, NJ, and the coauthor of *Narcissism and the Psychotherapist* and *Money Matters: The Fee in Psychotherapy and Psychoanalysis.*

Andrea J. Bergman, Ph.D., is Assistant Professor of Psychology at St. John's University, where she teaches courses in the area of psychopathology. She received her bachelor's degree from Cornell University and her Ph.D. from Emory University. Dr. Bergman, formerly a senior psychologist at Elmhurst Hospital Center in New York City, has published several scientific papers on schizophrenia and continues to do research in developmental psychopathology, with a focus on schizophrenia spectrum disorders.

Contributors

Lydia K. Adlerstein, doctoral candidate, St. John's University, Jamaica, NY.

Caren Baruch, doctoral candidate, St. John's University.

Janet R. Brice-Baker, Ph.D., Assistant Professor, Ferkauf Graduate School, Yeshiva University, New York, NY.

Elizabeth Brondolo, Ph.D., Assistant Professor of Psychology, St. John's University.

Susan Chan, C.S.W., Hamilton-Madison House, New York, NY.

Elizabeth Conway, C.S.W., Philadelphia, PA.

Raymond DiGiuseppe, Ph.D., ABPP, Professor of Psychology, St. John's University; Institute for Rational Emotive Therapy.

Christopher Eckhardt, Ph.D., Assistant Professor, University of North Carolina, Wilmington, NC; Institute for Rational Emotive Therapy.

Beverly Greene, Ph.D., Professor of Psychology, St. John's University.

Clare G. Holzman, Ph.D., in private practice, New York, NY.

Cynthia W. Leong, doctoral candidate, St. John's University.

Lawrence Marsh, C.S.W., Mental Health Corporation of Denver, Denver, CO.

Maura McDonald-Gomez, doctoral candidate, St. John's University.

Arthur G. Mones, Ph.D., ABPP, Adjunct Supervisor, St. John's University Center of Psychological Services and Clinical Studies.

Pamela E. Panitz, Ph.D., St. John's University.

Daniel Pilowsky, M.D., Assistant Clinical Professor of Psychiatry, Johns Hopkins University; Medical Director of the Kennedy Krieger Family Center, Baltimore, MD.

Mitchell Robin, Ph.D., Professor, New York City Technical College, New York, NY.

Raymond Tafrate, Ph.D., Assistant Professor, Hofstra University, Hempstead, NY; Institute for Rational Emotive Therapy.

Gail Elizabeth Wyatt, Ph.D., Professor, Dept. of Psychiatry and Biobehavioral Sciences, University of California, Los Angeles, CA.

Introduction

Recently, there was an explosion of media coverage about the issue of domestic violence, partly precipitated by the O.J. Simpson story. Following the sensational television coverage of the minute details of that incident, it appears that the number of reports of domestic violence increased substantially and that society experienced a period of greater sensitivity to the pervasiveness and seriousness of the problem. It was truly a desperate call for action as we all became poignantly aware that even our superheroes are not immune to the heinous impact of domestic violence; and that we can no longer afford to bury our heads in the sand or to turn our backs on this problem, if we are going to restore our heroes to their righteous position in our lives. As a twelve-year-old boy said in response to the O.J. Simpson story, "I just have to take them [athletes] for what they are, human." It is, precisely, a human problem in need of a more human response.

It is not unusual that a situation involving a highly visible individual can serve as a catalyst for a whole society to mobilize itself from stagnation and indifference. But will this call be sufficient for our legal, educational, religious, government, health, and mental health institutions to become more systematically responsive to victims of domestic violence? Will this lead to a systematic development of policies and programs from all these institutions working separately and in concert with one another to find practical and effective responses to this problem?

There are many reports of victim spouses whose desperate cries for help to the police and legal system or even to family members have fallen on deaf ears, gone unanswered, or, if a response is given, been responded to with disbelief of the critical nature of the dilemma confronted by the victim. As a result, many have become reluctant to discuss abuse and have opted instead to live with a sense of helplessness and hopelessness about society's ability to protect them.

Domestic violence is, indeed, a troublesome issue because, unlike other types of violence, violence perpetuated by one member of a family against another can leave the most devastating and indelible psychological marks in individuals. With the proliferation of violence in most other aspects of society frequently reported by the media (*Newsweek*, April 1, 1991, March 9, 1992; *Time*, August 23, 1993), one expects the family to serve as a safe haven, a buffer against a hostile environment. However, what kind of explanation can be provided when violence is not only close to home, but is perpetuated at home by those one expects to be protected by?

According to most statistics reported, violence in the family has reached epidemic proportions, with an act of domestic violence being committed every 18 seconds. John Aponte, who for several years has worked very closely with Victim Services in New York City, suggests in this regard that six million wives and 280,000 husbands are beaten annually in the United States. He tells us that the battering of women is the single major cause of injury, more frequent than auto accident, mugging, and rape combined (Aponte, 1993). These statistics are even more alarming if child abuse and neglect are also included (Alpert & Green, 1992; Tseng, 1992). The reader is referred to a special issue published by the *Journal of Social Distress and the Homeless* (1992, vol. 1, nos. 3/4) dedicated entirely to the exploration of the issue of child abuse and neglect.

Statistics on violence, however, may be problematic due to variations in individuals' perspectives and tolerance of violence. It is thus very likely that violence is under-reported in some groups and over-reported in others. This is particularly the case for the lower class abused victims who are likely to find themselves in a public agency after a violent incident where reporting may be mandatory. In contrast, more privileged individuals may be protected from the report of violence by their private physicians. This phenomenon was previously discussed by Rubin (1992) with regard to child abuse and neglect. Brice-Baker's contribution in this book discusses the issue with regard to domestic violence in African-American and African-Caribbean families.

Thus, a major problem facing behavioral scientists and mental health providers has to do with how to assess the nature of violence in a society populated by different ethnic, cultural, and linguistic groups. What constitutes a violent act and what is the most appropriate method of intervention may depend on the context of the specific characteristics of our multicultural communities. Although we can all agree that any aggressive behavior that results in physical and/or psychological damage to an individual can be construed as violence, where it may become problematic is in the perception of the degree of seriousness and consequently the need for intervention. This may be coupled by the culturally sanctioned need for privacy from families whose members then suffer in silence the effect of violence and abuse in their midst in hopes of retaining some semblance of family cohesion. The challenges to behavioral scientists and mental health service providers are indeed enormous.

We are left with the question as to why it has been so difficult for our society to come to terms with such an abhorrent phenomenon. Why have we tolerated the proliferation of violence in our own family, the expected cradle of safety for our children, in the name of the right to privacy? These are some of the questions that St. John's University probed in the context of its annual conference in May of 1993, dedicated to the systematic exploration of issues related to domestic violence from a multicultural perspective. The purpose of this publication is to continue our discussion on the issue and to shed some additional light on this complex phenomenon. We are particularly concerned with introducing a theoretical framework and introducing explanatory models that could help us to address some of the problems we have discussed. We are also interested in providing a diagnostic framework that could serve as guidance for the assessment and treatment of this phenomenon in a multicultural context.

It is difficult to assemble contributions that can exhaustively address the enormous issues related to violence and domestic violence. The present chapters have been organized under the premise that the impact of violence is felt not only in the family but also in the street and in the school setting among our youth. With that in mind, we have included adaptations of contributions to the third annual conference (May, 1993) sponsored by St. John's University on domestic violence as well as additional contributions, so as to provide the reader with a wider range of related topics than otherwise possible. Our hope is that these contributions will serve as points of discussion about the complex factors concerning violence in general and domestic violence in particular.

In Part I, we have included contributions addressing a wide range of conceptual issues. The first chapter by Gail Wyatt, for instance, provides an overview of the sociocultural and epidemiological factors to be considered in the assessment of domestic violence. She believes that traditional research on this subject suffers from what she calls a "cross sectional, broken down chain approach." Data obtained by such a process cannot explain the complex factors involved in the occurrence of violence in the multicultural society. She suggests that a more appropriate research approach should incorporate ethnic and culturally based information related to the nature of the family dynamic regarding violence, including the resolution of violence and historical information about the perception and tolerance of violence. Thus, a sociocultural assessment should include a thorough assessment of the "ethnic self," "the ethnic community," "attitudes and interaction of the larger community," the role of the nuclear and extended family, as well as the socioeconomic stressors often affecting the multicultural society.

The contribution by Herron and colleagues introduces a theoretical framework for looking at the causal patterns of family violence. Starting with the premise that any violence (child, spousal, sibling, and elderly) can be extremely disruptive for the family sense of cohesiveness, the authors briefly review problems with definition and discuss a number of causal models whose developments were influenced by the sociohistorical-feminist, couple-family system and individual pathology views. They suggest a comprehensive and multi-determined approach that combines personal and sociostructural frameworks for the understanding of the origins and dynamics of violence within families. Only in this way are we in a position to assess the multiplicity of factors that usually operate when violence in the family occurs. The factors suggested by the Social Etiological Model emphasize the inherent inequality in society among the different groups, in which domination of one group upon another defines the basic nature of the interaction. According to Cornell West (1993), this social-structural violence provides the potential for personal violence. From that perspective, the structure of society and the very structure of the family predispose the members to personal violence. But the fact that not all members of the family and society are violent to one another even in the case of exploitation suggests that other factors are operative as causal factors of personal violence. It is in this context that the authors posit a comprehensive approach, or interactive model, which includes a look at the structural constraints in society and behavioral impediments of the individual. According to these authors, "The structural-personal interaction producing family violence is set in motion by family members who are prone to misuse aggression in conflict resolution." Indeed, there is a great deal of distortion of reality and morality that takes place in the case of family violence, such as when violence is used in the name of discipline or as a focal point to establish personal superiority.

The authors suggest in this regard that different categories of violence may be possible depending upon the motivational factors contributing to its occurrence. *Violence seeker* refers to "abusers who repeatedly rely on violence to express themselves and effect solutions, and the family is just one of the many opportunities that they use." *Opportunistic abuser* refers to abusers "who believe that it is acceptable to discharge their hostility within the family, but not outside of it." *Reactive abuser* refers to those who become abusers as a reaction to an experience of abuse. Regardless of the types of abusers possible, personal dynamics, such as sadomasochistic tendencies, also have to be included as important personal factors contributing to the expression of violence.

The chapter by DiGiuseppe and colleagues attempts to address an even more basic question regarding the problem of violence and violent behavior than the one addressed in the previous contribution by Herron and his associates. According to these authors, an area that has been neglected by social and behavioral scientists interested in understanding violent and aggressive behavior is the area of the preceding emotions, specifically, anger and hostility. Although the causal connection of these emotions with violence and aggressive behavior has not been scientifically proven, it is believed that assessing the extent to which they are present in an individual could prove to be essential in the understanding of this phenomenon. Indeed, the authors recognize that anger may have a profound role in domestic violence, where a conservative estimate of two million women are battered by their husbands or mates in the United States and where more aggressive acts tend to occur during arguments. The authors conclude from their extensive review of the literature that unless a clearer definition of anger, hostility, violence, and aggression is forthcoming, the research, assessment, and treatment of these constructs will remain vague at best. The importance of refining the distinction among these constructs is based on the fact that it may be possible to identify instances of anger not necessarily resulting in aggressive and violent acts. It may also be possible, according to these authors, to identify what they call "instrumental aggression," or aggression without anger. Another reason for clarifying these concepts has to do with the increasing body of literature that relates anger and hostility to risk factors in hypertension and coronary heart disease, which is the leading cause of death in the Western world.

DiGiuseppe and colleagues define *anger* as "an internal, mental, subjective feeling state with associated cognitions and physiological arousal patterns." It can only be assessed by inferences from behavioral reactions, measures of physiological reactivity, and subjective self-report. *Aggression*, on the other hand, is defined as "overt behavior enacted with intent to do harm or injury to a person or object." This definition, unlike that of anger, emphasizes the observable, behavioral aspect of aggression, including verbal aggression, and in which a motivational component can be determined. And finally, *hostility* is defined as "a personality trait evidenced by cross-situational patterns of angry affect in combination with verbal or behavioral aggression." The importance of this definition is that it emphasizes a personality style that is not stimulus bound and that explains the individual's general approach to life. Based upon these definitions, these authors propose a series of criteria that may be used as part of a formal diagnostic category to assess the extent to which the anger-hostility dimension is present in an individual. The authors suggest that by following the inclusion or exclusion criteria clearly delineated in the chapter, it may be possible to distinguish between anger disorder with or without aggression. This distinction is considered essential if an effective intervention to address the phenomenon of violence, and domestic violence specifically, is to be established.

The problem with finding effective treatment for this phenomenon may be related not only to the confusion around definition but to the pervasiveness of certain "beliefs" as well, in which anger and aggression may not be found to be deviant. According to these authors, this is the case when an individual may find anger to be justified and appropriate; or may find ways to blame some external forces for the occurrence of anger and aggression (such as when an individual explains his/her aggressive behavior by saying "s/he provoked me"); or may perceive the target of his anger as a worthless and condemnable individual who deserves the outburst of anger or at least of contempt. An important approach in treating this condition will be to help the patient find alternative scripts to anger-expression where these beliefs are not part of the behavioral equation.

The contributions by Brice-Baker and by Chan and Leong are meant to offer examples of the violence phenomenon in specific cultures as a point of discussion. It would be important to discuss the issue of violence in other cultural groups as we continue to explore this issue further. For the purpose of this book, the chapters by Brice-Baker on African-American and African-Caribbean and by Chan and Leong on Chinese families could provide a guideline as to the issues to be included when discussing other ethnic groups.

The main theme of the chapter by Brice-Baker is that the issue of domestic violence in African-American and African-Caribbean families has to be viewed in its sociopolitical and sociocultural context. After cautioning the reader as to the accuracy of statistics on domestic violence in the black community, she critically examines the different models that have been used to explain the presence of violence in black families. It is her contention that stress is a central factor in explaining the presence of violence. Of the four models discussed (the feminist-political, sociocultural, social-psychological, and the psychiatric), she suggests that only a social-political one incorporates in a substantial way the impact of stress that emerges from socioeconomic and sociopolitical factors, and the stress triggered by the impact of the immigration process. Similarly, she examines the impact of a series of stereotypes or assumptions often made about black women and men that are assumed to eventually contribute to triggering violence. Her treatment recommendations are, in fact, based upon an exploration of these assumptions on the part of the therapist so as to allow for an intervention based upon an accurate assessment of the nature of violence in the family. She sees complications in the kinds of interventions possible in terms of the socioeconomic impact for family members. In the case of the African-Caribbean families, fear of deportation could be a significant barrier.

Chan and Leong's chapter deals with the socioeconomic, sociopolitical, cultural, and linguistic stressors that Chinese immigrant families frequently face and the kinds of adjustment problems they experience. According to the authors, these stressors create the condition necessary for violence in the family to occur as well as for other types of family and individual psychopathology to emerge. After providing a rich discussion of the historical background and cultural influences that are expected to guide and impact on the behavior of Chinese individuals, the authors look at how the resulting cultural scripts come into clash with the expectations of the new culture in America. This is particularly the case with regard to the gender role, in which women are expected to take on a role subservient to the male regardless of their financial contribution to the family's economic condition. The influence of Confucius' teachings in this regard, as well as the influence of Buddhism and Taoism with regard to the individual relationship with one another and the world in general, are also discussed.

The description of the individual emerging from these cultural and religious influences is one that is guided by the rules and expectations of the extended family unit rather than by individual needs; and for whom education, harmony with nature, self-control, and self-actualization are all central values, as is the importance of protecting the family from the experience of "shame," loss of face or dignity. The authors show that these guiding principles of behavior are at the core of the problem facing social and mental health agencies involved in providing services for this population. For it is more likely that incidence of child abuse and family violence will remain unreported in order to save the family from an experience of *shame* and *loss of face*—where the victim, if a report is made, could be further victimized with accusations of having violated critical cultural scripts.

Next, you will find a group of chapters that discuss assessment and treatment issues in relation to violence. Again, our intention is to provide some examples of assessment and treatment interventions regarding violence and aggressive behavior. The series of programs offered by the Victim Services (Aponte, 1993) are meant to handle the emergency aspects of the domestic violence situation and should be considered when appropriate, but will not be included here. Our focus has a more preventive nature than offered by these programs and hence we have only included contributions that address the issue of treatment of violence from this perspective.

For instance, the integrated family systems approach model proposed by Mones and Panitz provides an excellent framework to address the complex nature of domestic violence and the issues discussed by Wyatt and Brice-Baker in the earlier contributions. Their model is based on the fact that many families experiencing domestic violence remain together and that there is an intergenerational history of violence. The perpetuation of such a phenomenon is explained by Mones and Panitz in terms of the developmental needs of the victim–abuser paradigm and of the marital system. As stated by these authors, "spouses in such relationships typically come from families-of-origin where violence was a means of dealing with conflict between spouses and coercion was the dominant mode of childrearing." Strongly recognizing the importance of aggressive interventions to insure the safety of the family members, the authors propose a model that provides treatment for the victim, the batterer, the couple as a unit, and the children. This treatment model attempts to prevent or defuse triangulation and enmeshment of the children in the parental conflict.

However, the problem of violence does not only affect the home, but is pervasive among our youth as well. In fact, according to FBI statistics, juvenile arrests accounted for 17% of all violence-crime arrests in 1991 and 3 of every 10 juvenile murderer arrests involved a victim under the age of 18 (Office of Juvenile Justice and Delinquency Prevention, Justice Department, FBI; *Newsweek*, August 2, 1993). The chapter by Brondolo and colleagues is particularly relevant in this regard. It provides a comprehensive behavioral school-based program to deal with aggression among minority students and the general student population where aggressive behavior is a factor. The authors suggest that the nature of the aggressive behavior cannot be properly assessed unless the physical and mental health of the individuals are considered. They provide ample data to support their contention regarding the role of physical (e.g., brain injury), mental (e.g., childhood depression and untreated ADHD), psychological (e.g., specific cognitive deficits), and social (e.g., low socioeconomic status) variables, which are likely to increase the risk of aggressive behavior. The proposed comprehensive approach, which includes an extensive evaluation of these factors and intensive case management interventions, is based on observations and actual application of a program designed by the authors guided by the token economy and social skill training methods. The students referred to the program had been assigned to a highly restrictive placement because they were unable to function in a regular classroom. Their behavior was described as too aggressive or withdrawn and the goal of the program was to enable the students to move to a less restrictive educational environment. The intervention included programs aimed at the child, the classroom, and the community. Judging from the results, it is clear that although the program was not found to be beneficial in the same manner to all the students involved in the project, it was found to be of great relevance in providing a structure for intervention to encourage prosocial behavior in a difficult student population.

Greene and Pilowsky's chapter addresses another important issue with regard to family violence. We are referring to the impact of family deterioration on a child, which results in a foster care situation. The children they describe are children who have been removed from their parents following abuse, neglect, and/or abandonment by the natural parents. Now they have to develop a sense of themselves in the context of a foster family while the extent of contact with the natural family still remains unresolved. The authors speak about the intrapsychic dilemma in these children related to loyalty conflict, which expresses itself in oppositional behavior against the foster parents. These are traumatized children who have been asked to assume parental roles themselves and to renounce their own dependency needs in the process. This problem becomes even more compounded by a foster care system that is ill-prepared to handle the challenges of an oppositional and angry child, which frequently results in the child's removal from the foster home. In these authors' experience, the issue is not just that these children have been placed in an unnatural family environment but that they may continue to be affected by the unpredictability and inconsistency of the natural parents. These parents are frequently unable to keep scheduled appointments as part of their visitation requests and seriously undermine the child's adjustment to his or her new family. Thus the children remain traumatized and confused as to what to do with their feelings of loyalty and deep resentment.

The final contribution is by Holzman. Her chapter is relevant to the issues discussed here because of the connection of rape with violence and assault as well as the cultural, socioeconomic, sociocultural, and sociopolitical factors inherently present in any act of violence against an individual. In this poignant chapter, she reviews the sociocultural factors that contribute to the phenomenon of rape in our culture and describes the complications related to treatment interventions. According to this author, rape is a tool and a consequence of an interlocking system of oppression based on race, ethnicity, class, and sexual orientation. Even our response to rape seems to be determined by these factors. In this context, she discusses a number of sociohistorical factors, including the reluctance of many victims to trust a system that they experience as more racist, punitive, and judgmental than supportive and helpful. This feeling—conveyed by many of the previous contributors herein with regard to domestic violence—tends to characterize the lives of the disenfranchised in our society. It is clear that a successful treatment of these individuals will have to include an appreciation of the factors discussed by the author.

In summary, the main purpose of this book is to introduce theoretical contributions that can help us understand an issue of great importance for our society, the phenomenon of domestic violence. Issues pertaining to treatment considerations for specific cultural groups are also discussed. It is not our intention to exhaust all possible explanations for such a complex phenomenon or to provide a final pronouncement in this regard; the contributions included are only meant as an invitation for further dialogue. If the reader finds the issues advanced by the contributors intellectually provocative and unsettling, our goal is accomplished. The matter certainly warrants further discussion.

REFERENCES

Alpert, J. L., & Green, D. (1992). Child abuse and neglect: Perspectives on a national emergency. *Journal of Social Distress and the Homeless*, 1 (3/4), 223–236.

Aponte, J. (May, 1993). *Multicultural factors in domestic violence: A program for spouse abusers.* Presented at the Third Annual Conference on Multicultural View on Domestic Violence, St. John's University.

Rubin, G. B. (1992). Multicultural considerations in the application of child protective laws. *Journal of Social Distress and the Homeless*, 1 (3/4), 249–272.

Tseng, O. C. S. (1992). Social distress and theorizations of child victimization. *Journal of Social Distress and the Homeless*, 1, 37–66.

West, C. (1993). *Race matters*. Boston: Beacon Press.

PART I

CONCEPTUAL ISSUES

1

Sociocultural and Epidemiological Issues in the Assessment of Domestic Violence

Gail Elizabeth Wyatt

This paper presents alternative models for the integration of multicultural issues in research on domestic violence. Issues are discussed that illustrate ethnic specific strengths, concerns, and weaknesses of ethnic families and communities. These issues need to be incorporated in future research that more thoroughly examines ethnic and cultural issues in violence research. Alternative strategies for future research are also suggested which call for the incorporation of ethnic and cultural issues on an ongoing basis, so that commonalities across studies can emerge and we can begin to understand the cultural context of domestic violence.

INTRODUCTION

As our society is increasingly confronted with violence in almost every aspect of our lives, we are challenged to develop strategies that will both clarify and enhance the manner in which we study the phenomena and understand its effects.

This paper focuses on the relationship between multiculturalism and violence, an area that has yet to receive enough attention, due to a considerable mount of resistance to accepting that there are sociocultural issues related to violence in our society. Our failure to acknowledge these phenomena and the manner in which they interact has not only influenced the research that defines culture and violence, but has certainly influenced our society's response to them as well. Definitions of these phenomena are as follows:

Multiculturalism. This involves diversity in belief systems and practices that are based on more than one culture. These cultures interact to form a composite of beliefs that reflect the richness of a pluralistic society. Although there is some resistance, we are increasingly becoming accustomed to the notion that America is not a melting pot, nor do differing groups stand in contrast to each other on every issue. We have, however, been slow to accept the fact that one of our strengths is not in homogeneity across issues, nor is the use of one set of norms appropriate to understand diverse behaviors and attitudes. Our strength as a nation is in our heterogeneity and diversity, with the central uniting theme being love of country, family, freedom, and respect for individual rights and differences. The same philosophy is true in research. The more likely research incorporates a variety of issues that represent the complexity of life, the more it reflects the life experience of the populations being studied.

Violence. This society was born in violence and one of the most difficult realities that we must face is that violence has always been a part of life in America (National Academy of Science, 1993). It is important to review how violence has historically been used: The majority of this country was taken by use of force; acts of terrorism began with the treatment of American Indians and Mexicans for land acquisition; Africans were abducted and enslaved to help build this country's economy and then, along with American Indians, were subjected to physical, sexual, emotional abuse and neglect for hundreds of years. Other ethnic groups including the Chinese and Japanese, were similarly maltreated. Women, the physically and mentally challenged and homosexuals, to name a few groups, have their own stories of oppression, abuse, and neglect to tell. Acts of violence, in their more covert and overt forms, persist today. With that reality, we are attempting to develop a strategy to better understand how violence occurs and within that context, identify how groups and individuals are at risk. A multiethnic and multicultural approach to prevention strategies will help us to understand how people perceive violence in their lives and relationships and what facilitates or serves as barriers for change.

HOW VIOLENCE HAS BEEN STUDIED

Most of the research has adopted a cross-sectional, broken chain approach to studying domestic violence. As illustrated in Fig. 1, one or two people, the victim and the perpetrator, are usually identified as the focus of research.

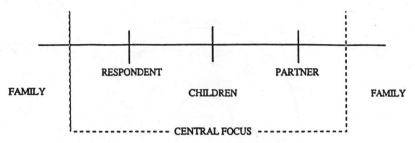

Fig. 1. Traditional approach to violence.

This approach is cross-sectional because it examines one incident or one point in time. It is similar to a broken chain because it selects one aspect of a series of events that may, and usually do occur over extended periods of time. In some cases, two persons may perpetrate violence on another person, usually a partner, an older person or a child, or persons such as children may observe the domestic violence between adults.

However, the history of abuse or patterns of conflict resolution in the unit under study are often missing from this research approach. There are other characteristics of research that limit our understanding of the antecedents and consequence of domestic violence:

1. Research examines only one type of violence (e.g., physical or sexual), and not a variety of types that may occur in a pattern, and which are often antecedents to other forms of violence.

2. The antecedents of events that precede violent acts are not assessed.

3. The resolution of violence is not examined. For example, sometimes sexual intimacy, peace and tranquility, and general tension reduction follows acts of violence and gives family members a temporary sense of well being. During this period, victim(s) develop false hope that the violence will not occur again, only to experience increasing conflict and tension that again results in violence.

4. Research methodologies often assume that there is only one victim and do not assess the effects on those who witness violence along with those on whom violence is perpetrated. The effects of violence on a victim are sometimes exacerbated when the victim observes that others, such as their children are observing the violence.

5. Research usually does not examine the reactions of the people who observe violence or live in high crime areas and are traumatized indirectly.

6. Research has yet to identify individuals who live in violent families, communities, or cultures and who are not violent. We may learn other

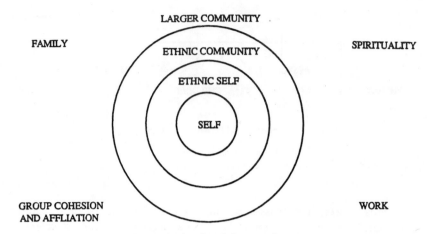

Fig. 2. Sociocultural framework.

methods of coping with being exposed to aggression by examining non violence that should be used in violence prevention programs.

7. While some culturally based practices such as coining among Cam-
bodians are defined as acts of abuse by U.S. standards, they need to be
identified and understood. In order to prevent the reoccurrence of an act
thought by the perpetrator to be a culturally sanctioned practice and to
teach more acceptable methods of behavior, we need to identify the cultural
belief systems that motivate these practices. Behavior change is best ef-
fected when the intervention is based on a variety of belief systems used
to explain behaviors.

In an effort to broaden our understanding of how to incorporate multicultural issues in research on domestic violence, other considerations
should be discussed.

A SOCIOCULTURAL ASSESSMENT

There are dimensions in the lives of ethnic minority group people
that are rarely included in research, as illustrated in Fig. 2.

Indeed, most of the standardized measures used to assess individual
functioning in areas such as achievement, cognition (IQ), personality development, self-esteem, differing levels of mental status and psychopathology do not include the following dimensions:

1. *The Ethnic Self*—the individual identifies as an ethnic person, with
feelings, attitudes, belief systems and knowledge about heritage, the mean-

ing of their cultural affiliation and how it affects them. The ethnic self interacts with and enhances a sense of self, in general, but many times perceptions and attributions to the causes of events are ethnic specific and distinct from attributions to the self. For example, if a Black woman calls the police because of concern that she will be harmed by her spouse and they do not respond or do not seem to be willing to ensure her safety, she may assume that the police reaction is due to stereotypes that the police have about Blacks being violent. She may feel that the police are discriminating against her because she is Black. These perceptions can lower a positive sense of being as an ethnic person.

2. *The Ethnic Community*—bolsters the ethnic self. The community has a life, a political reality, social strata and economic base that is sometimes separate from the larger community and is a critical part of one's life. The ethnic community is where the concerns and cultural values thrive for ethnic persons. For example, employment that is not sanctioned or legal, exists in the ethnic community and co-exists with legal, upstanding professions. Employment, however, does not necessarily define the status that an individual holds in the community. For example, an individual can hold a unskilled job, or have no employment, but attain status in the church by their service to others. In a community, homeless persons can watch a neighbor's house and alert residents to suspicious individuals who loiter or commit crimes when residents are away from home. In return, community residents might feed or temporarily house these persons in inclement weather. In essence, service to and involvement in the ethnic community has its own rewards and obligations which are based more on what you do for others rather then what you do for yourself.

The ethnic community fosters a sense of "healthy paranoia" about political and other figures who express an interest in ongoing concerns, but do not actively work for improvement of the community on a regular basis. Those concerns include disproportionate rates of unemployment, incarceration and crime, high drop-out rates among school age youth, the need for community centers, libraries and parks, the response and treatment of police and other city services, the proliferation of liquor stores and barriers to owning community businesses that are more easily obtained by ethnic groups who do not reside in target areas. Some politicians who do express and demonstrate concern for the ethnic community can garner votes from it's residents for decades, even if they are involved in other more unsavory activities. They are rewarded for their continued link to their ethnic community. Most people realize that persons of color are treated differently in the larger society and sometimes do not condemn community members for unsanctioned practices if their community involvement is above reproach.

3. *Attitudes About and Interactions with the Larger Community*—Rarely does research incorporate issues of isolation in ethnic communities because of high crime rates or the lack of acculturation to the larger community, especially among populations that are monolingual, newly immigrated, or who may have illegal residents. Not all people travel about in large cities and interact with the larger community to the extent that we may assume. This restriction in travel, however, occurs not simply because of being un-acculturated, monolingual, or newly immigrated. Travel can be restricted because of public transportation that limits access to certain areas or communities. Concern about one's safety or literacy can be self-limiting, but transportation restrictions have historically been and continue to be sources of *de facto* segregation.

Dimensions of self are influenced by:

Family and Extended Family. Regardless of whether individuals are related, if they serve the function of family members, their presence in a target person's life can range from being a support to being burdensome. They can widen or reduce one's access to the larger community, by the economic and emotional stress that they bring to the target person's life. Their personal safety or involvement in violence can compromise the target person's feelings of vulnerability in their effort to protect family members.

Spirituality. An individual's relationship to God and their attributions of power—to God or from God through themselves as an instrument of God's will, is an important contributor to perceptions of one's ability to take direct action in life. Such statements as "placing problems in God's hands" imply that an attribution to a more powerful source is outside of oneself, and may appear to be a passive approach to problem solving. However, professionals who work with individuals and communities concerned with the level of violence in their lives need to work with religious persons who can help to reframe spiritual beliefs to activate individuals directly. Spirituality can be a more critical indicator of attributions of power than church attendance and affiliation. One's spirituality involves an individual relationship with God, and can serve as a buffer to stress and trauma. Unfortunately, however, spirituality can also be used to promote passivity in persons who may need to mobilize themselves and the people around them.

Work. One's work can reflect their life purpose or simply a means to acquire financial security in order to achieve their life's purpose. Far too often, researchers assume the former and fail to assess the importance of work or employment in an ethnic minority person's life. Historical restrictions on employment have created different perceptions of the meaning of work. Many people with limited financial resources are still attempting to survive and engage in activities which promote existence, rather than a quality of life. However, to be productive can enhance the quality of one's work, however menial. It is important to assess the meaning of work and the effects of unemployment or productivity, given the high numbers of ethnic minority youth and adults who are chronically unemployed and who do not have opportunities to observe family members who have success in the traditional work world. We also need to better determine if alienation from the work community and increased involvement in illegal forms of work will change perceptions of the meaning of work and productivity in our youth.

Group Cohesion and Affiliation. Belonging to a group, regardless of age or gender, can be an important dimension in life, especially among certain ethnic and cultural groups. Affiliation with a group addresses the question, "To what or whom do you belong?" and is important in cultures that value group affiliation over individual actualization (Akbar, 1985). In other words, the concept of "we" is more essential than "I or me." Group cohesion can foster self-esteem, and enhance feelings about the ethnic self along with feelings about the ethnic and larger community. Group cohesion can also limit one's interaction with persons who do not affiliate with the group. To a person of color, group affiliation is important because, while the larger community often does not value group identification, support and affirmation can and often does come from other group members. This is of increasing value to individuals who encounter high levels of institutional racism in the larger community.

Taken together, these ethnic specific dimensions and the issues that influence them should be incorporated into violence research. They may help to explain why some individuals and communities either succumb to or resist violence. Alternative approaches to studying violence may also help us to understand the context in which violence occurs.

ALTERNATIVE APPROACHES TO VIOLENCE

The study of violence should be multifaced. There are many factors in an individual's (R's) life that can influence violent behaviors. Figure 3 illustrates a "pinwheel" or multifaceted approach to studying violence.

These connections provide a different context in which to examine sociocultural issues related to violence. Research should assess the following that directly impact the target individual:

1. *The Relationship to a Partner and the Power Balance Between Them.* When issues that create conflict between two persons, or a family are explained by perceptions of institutional racism against an ethnic or cultural group, efforts to prevent domestic violence become more complicated. The issues of assessing how power and violence are used to coerce, intimidate,

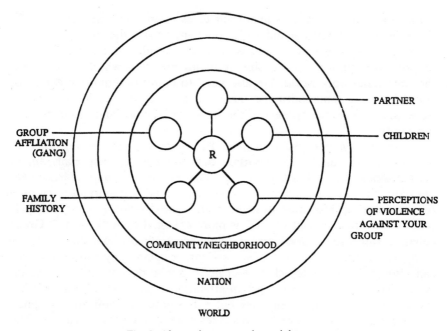

Fig. 3. Alternative approach to violence.

or threaten others into compliance are often mediated by realization that domestic violence is simply a mirror image of the violence that occurs in the larger community. When a relationship is being examined, it is important to determine how violence is perceived on several levels. For example, the terms "violent or violence" are sometimes not used to describe actions perpetrated on a victim. Instead, descriptions often minimize the violent behavior, such as, "He gets angry and gets out of control." In another example, the specifics of exactly what occurred are often vague, "He drinks too much and becomes suspicious of my behavior." These are typical examples of the victim's denial that violence is occurring. However, among ethnic and cultural groups with histories of oppression, a related issue is the use of culturally relevant explanations for violence. For example, if the perpetrator is a family member, keeping the family together may be important to the family's survival in the larger community and world. Given this reality, statements such as: "The children need to see a strong Black (or any other ethnic group identifier) man in our home," or "Everyone thinks that Black families don't have fathers," may have some element of truth, but are a part of the denial that violence is effecting the family.

Victims of domestic violence may make statements about their inability to leave the house that devalue their power or choices in life, such as: "I can't get another man, no one would want me, especially with these kids." Or similarly, "The chances of my remarrying or finding someone who will be able to take care of me and my kids are almost nil. I'd better stay with the father of these children." Given the realities of marriage and remarriage in certain ethnic groups, there is also considerable unreality in these statements (Tucker & Mitchell-Kernan, in press).

Rationalizations for battering sometimes reflect awareness of institutional racism toward ethnic minorities. For example: "Black men are an endangered species. If I report him, he will be more mistreated by the system than other men," or "This racist society does not understand the pressures on a Black man. I don't want to destroy whatever self-esteem that he has left by reporting or leaving him." Other statements reflect some of the realities of being an ethnic minority, such as: "He doesn't have a job and can't be a man. He needs us (his family). I can't leave," or "He treats us the way that he is treated in the world. It would be no different for him if we left. Just more abuse from everyone else in his life."

In order to understand the cultural context of these types of statements, it is important to identify the truth and reality of the statement and separate it from the attribution of power that reinforces domestic violence.

Another culture bound attitude that women who have been oppressed often express involves withstanding abuse perpetrated on others as a demonstration that as a victim they are as equally as tough, such as, "Nobody thinks I'm really hurting or scared. I can take it. My mother did." This statement suggests that perceptions of violence are also associated with expectations of both gender role and ethnic group affiliation. All of the dimensions of these statements need to be understood and incorporated into programs to prevent the reoccurrence of violence in the home.

2. *Children.* How do children interpret the violence that they may witness in their homes and in their communities? The direct and more subtle effects of violence on children's psychological well being deserves more attention, and particularly for children at most risk for observing or being targets of violence. There are some effects of being traumatized by sexual violence that are similar to being a victim of racial discrimination. Researchers need to assess both the effects of violence and the effects of being a child of color (Wyatt, 1990) and conduct analyses that help to determine which of these experiences best predicts different types of psychological sequelae for children. It is also important to identify mediators to the effects of trauma, such as involvement in after school activities, sports, and other special interest groups, church and family activities, that lessen the negative impact of violence on children of color.

3. *Family History of Violence.* Family patterns of violence are important to assess in any person who is a victim or a perpetrator. However, while research traditionally focuses on violence that is reported, there are some acts of violence, such as participating in gang activities or civil unrest for which individuals may not be prosecuted, but may be perceived as a response to unequal justice for oppressed or ethnic minority peoples. These are incidents that may never be reported and would not be in any circumstance, unless respondents are assured that no criminal action will be taken against them if they disclose unreported activities of this nature. Researchers need to obtain a confidentiality certificate and include in consent forms mention of procedures developed in a research project for the handling of unreported criminal activity. This information is important to obtain because these unreported activities can be family or community secrets that convey to children a dual message about committing violent acts: Some violence committed in the larger community may occur to make a statement about economic and political oppression. It would be interesting to know if children understand the difference between acceptable politically motivated crimes and other acts that are deemed by the family as unacceptable.

4. *Group Affiliation.* The meaning and importance of affiliating with groups, often as a substitute for family cohesion, to satisfy the need to be valued and to be autonomous from the family, to establish oneself as an adult or to be characterized with qualities such as fearless, powerful and strong need to be assessed for individuals who are victims of or who perpetrate violent acts. It is critical to recognize that not all aspects of gang activity are associated with criminal activity or are pathological. The need to affiliate oneself must be retained even when gang activity is controlled.

5. *Environment in Which an Individual Lives.* This provides a larger context for understanding violence and its effects. In assessing the *neighborhood and community,* it is important to not only examine the level of violence perpetrated both within and upon the community, but how violence is avoided. What are the strategies or who are the persons that help to minimize or prevent violence from occurring? Far too often, police and other political figures fail to identify and align themselves with neighborhood and community leaders who can inform them of how individuals respond to or avoid violence. Likewise, researchers rarely assess healthy coping strategies in areas with higher rates of violence. Incidents that result in violence are often not new to some communities, but it is the degree to which it occurs today that has overwhelmed the community's response. It is also important to remember that some areas do not have high crime rates and the reasons are not related to the police response in these areas. The means by which those areas or their residents are perceived by others

in the community needs to be assessed. Perceptions of certain neighborhoods and their residents may be related to why less violence occurs in
certain areas.

6 and 7. *The Nation and World.* There are patterns of violence which
target ethnic and cultural groups, as well as countries. For example, some
people of color feel that it is no coincidence that the United States has
been most likely to use armed force in developing countries where people
of color reside. The U.S. is perceived as aggressive towards certain cultural
groups and helpful to others. In the community, persons of color discuss
what appears to be the priority that our political leaders place on the safety
and well being of ethnic and cultural groups, along with the terrorist activities that are tolerated from and upon certain countries. Likewise, the
response to community problems with aggression and a show of force often
illustrates the limitations of leaders to develop alternative strategies to solve
problems. At the same time, however, community residents who fail to develop alternative strategies other than violence to resolve conflict are
severely punished. Our national and international image is called into question when we judge other countries for their lack of recognition of human
rights and fail to observe human rights in our own communities. The Rod-
ney King and Reginald Denny trials were watched all over the world and
discussed as examples of the inequities between law enforcement and the
communities response to what many perceived was the uneven application
of law and order. The national and world view about which groups perpetrate violence, by whom and for what purpose can fuel attitudes that
communities should maintain an aggressive resistance to attempts to control ethnic groups of color through force.

AN ALTERNATIVE ASSESSMENT OF VIOLENCE

As Fig. 4 illustrates, research on violence should incorporate ethnic
and cultural dimensions in a routine fashion, across research studies so
that information can be obtained about culture-bound issues regarding violence and common themes can emerge.

Future research should incorporate an assessment of the ethnic self
with the self, overall. Questions about the extended family and their history
of being both victimized by and perpetrators of violence should also include
their methods of coping with trauma, the level of support generated to
family members when threats or acts of violence occur both within and
outside of the extended family and how they avoid or minimize violence
in their families and communities. The importance of the ethnic community
and its perceptions of and experiences with violence along with efforts to

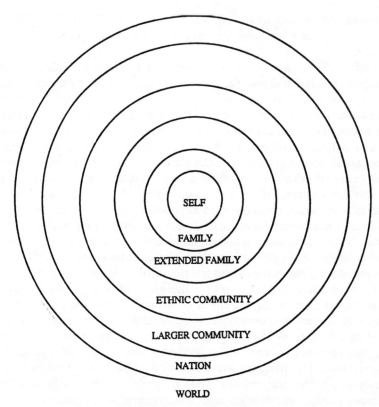

Fig. 4. Sociocultural assessment of the impact of violence.

minimize it deserves more attention in research. Qualitative methods of data collection, with focus groups including diverse segments of target communities held in community locations, are an optimal approach to understanding both problems and coping strategies. The ethnic community's perceptions of neglect by the larger community can isolate its members and increase suspiciousness about outsiders who do not understand the issues and yet wish to study the community.

A sociocultural assessment not only identifies effects of violence on an individual, but seeks to examine its context by examining the effects of domestic violence on ethnic and cultural groups, as well as communities. The nation's neglect of certain problems such as chronic poverty, escalating crime rates and unemployment have created structural changes in families and communities that can no long be ignored. If we are to understand how to minimize violence in our homes, we must understand its connection with other structural and economic problems that have existed for far too long and are breaking down the fiber of the family. We also need to understand that violence is escalating at any given time and location around the world. Issues that affect families are also being addressed on the international front. We can learn much from observing how other countries resolve and support family harmony by examining cross-cultural research for solutions to domestic violence, as well.

DISCUSSION

This paper has discussed a multicultural approach to research on domestic violence and has presented a broader perspective that is useful in understanding both the antecedents and consequences of violence. Violence has become an everyday occurrence and it will require a comprehensive approach to prevent domestic violence in a community, society, and world where violence proliferates. At best, we can only hope to begin by improving the research that documents the effects of violence on individuals, the family and children and understand how violence in the larger community impacts the family.

Violence that occurs at home is prescriptive of our society's tolerance for victimizing weaker or more vulnerable people. Our role models continue to typify characters of the wild west: Anger is confronted with more anger and aggression. How often do we observe people who express their vulnerable feelings being rewarded with power? How often do we see people giving power away to those with less power? Unless we develop a national strategy for violence prevention and portray the value of being in power balanced relationships, with regard for the well being of each citizen, efforts to stem the escalating tide of violence in America will not be realized.

In the effort to improve the research that will, hopefully capture the effects of violence in a more culturally relevant context, the models for examining violence need to change. We need to develop measures that reflect the cultural values and practices as well as life experiences of diverse populations. The samples that are selected for study also require inclusion of underrepresented groups, as well as populations that have yet to be included in research on domestic violence. The antecedents of acts of violence need to be studied, as well as behaviors that develop in a sequence and culminate in violence. We also need to evaluate the best approach to a research question and who is most likely to address that question (Urquiza & Wyatt, in press). For example, funds from a federal agency were recently awarded to a research group to examine the civil unrest that

occurred in Los Angeles, California. However, the research group was located outside of Los Angeles (and California), had no knowledge of the
communities or ethnic groups involved and used telephone interviews as a
method of data collection. This is a very distant approach to understanding
events that occurred in areas with long established histories of social, economic, ethnically related and political problems. The relevant issues could
not be captured by a research group who did not have intimate knowledge
of the seeds of civil unrest in Los Angeles. While efforts are often well
intended, researchers have to be aware of their own limitations. The rigor
of the research design, the sampling methods, selection of appropriate
methods of data collection and relevant research questions notwithstanding,
the most qualified persons to collect highly sensitive and potentially illegal
information from a sample are persons who are familiar with the issues in
that community. This is an example of where a collaboration between community members and a research group could have resulted in a better
designed and more relevant study of a very troublesome issue regarding
violence in the community.

Violence, *per se,* is not viewed as bad by everyone in our society, especially now that it has become such a common method of conflict
resolution. We are reminded of the rates of violence with every television
or radio newscast on a daily basis and our tolerance for it has increased.
Consequently, some national policy on violence prevention is needed and
it must begin not only with violence toward the most vulnerable, but the
marketing of violence as entertainment.

Research needs to examine the relationship between the changes in
the structure and the economic stability of the family and increased rates
of domestic violence. In so doing, we will better understand the context of
violence and who will be most at risk. This is a challenging agenda for
future research and the socialization of new researchers who will, hopefully,
go beyond recording the prevalence of acts of violence and attempt to understand why it is occurring before attempting to prevent it. There has
never been a better time to strengthen the research agenda for studying
domestic violence and there are few problems that are as critical to the
quality of family life as the harmony within it.

ACKNOWLEDGEMENTS

This paper is supported by a Research Scientist Award KO1
MH00269. The author wishes to thank Sarah Lowery for manuscript
preparation.

REFERENCES

Akbar, N. (1985). *The community of self.* Florida: Mind Productions & Association.

LeFranc, E., Wyatt, G. E., Chambers, C. Bain, B., & Ricketts, H. HIV Risks: Focus Groups with Jamaican Women (under review).

National Academy of Sciences (1993). Understanding Child Abuse and Neglect. Panel on Child Abuse and Neglect, Washington, D.C.

Tucker, M. B., & Mitchell-Kernan, C. *The decline of marriage in Black families.* Russell Sage Foundation Press (in press).

Urquiza, A., & Wyatt, G. E. Clinical interviewing with trauma victims: Managing interviewer risk. *Journal of Interpersonal Violence* (in press).

Wyatt, G. E. (1990). Sexual abuse of ethnic minority children: Identifying dimensions of victimization. *Professional Psychology: Research and Practice, 21,* 338-343.

2

Sources of Family Violence

William G. Herron, Rafael Art. Javier, Maura McDonald-Gomez, and Lydia K. Adlerstein

This paper suggests a direction for the exploration of the causes of family violence. Explanatory models of family violence were considered in this regard, with the recommendation that a multidetermined model should be considered to ensure the most accurate explanation. We suggest that family violence will be best understood and prevented or alleviated, if a model is used that considers the interaction of structural violence and the personality features of all the family members.

INTRODUCTION

The historical presence of various forms of violence within families, and the current existence of such violence, are well documented as a severe problem for most societies (Ammerman & Hersen, 1992). However, the focus on this problem is of relatively recent origin, beginning with concerns about child abuse. Family violence as such began to be extensively explored in the 1970s, with some aspects of it, as elder abuse and violence between siblings, now starting to get detailed attention. As a result, there is a limited amount of information available and most theorizing has not yet been subject to empirical validation.

This paper is concerned with causal patterns of family violence. The possible etiologies of a major portion of such violence, namely child abuse, has been explored in a previous paper (Herron, Javier, & Cicone, 1992).

Thus, this paper will emphasize other areas of family violence, such as spousal, sibling, and elder abuse. Although the estimated degree of child abuse in the United States is disturbingly high (Haugaard, 1992), the incidence of adult violence is even higher (Straus, Gelles, & Steinmetz, 1980).

"The data...paint a rather discouraging portrait of violence in U.S. family life. Although laws have been passed...to criminalize acts of violence that occur in families, the family remains an extremely violent group" (Bachman & Pillomer, 1992, p. 118).

The presence of family violence is set within the context of a society that has over time always endorsed violence, yet has also moved to restrict it, and continues to do so. There is considerable agreement on the need for peaceful resolutions, yet both difficulty and ambivalence in acting accordingly seem to be more the norm. The family is a paradoxical setting for violence in that its mission is the opposite, namely to nurture, love, and facilitate its inhabitants. As we examine the possible explanations for family violence, we recognize that too often family life and the world outside the family are askew, with damaging actual and potential effects on all concerned.

The ultimate aim is the development of effective families that are positive social forces, in keeping with the original mission of the family system. Family violence is clearly an obstacle to doing this, and so far effective solutions have not been forthcoming. Although concern about the issue has led to social policies and actions, the understanding of these issues has remained sketchy at best. Newberger (1983) notes in this regard the risk in operating on limited information. Furthermore, this is often a political, emotional issue that can strain objectivity. The purpose here is to use existing theoretical conceptions as data for the development of a more effective, multi-factor causal model that, in turn, would facilitate an increase in harmonious family structures. The proposed model combines personal and social-structural frameworks for the understanding of the origins and dynamics of violence within families.

PROBLEMS

The incidence of family violence is difficult to determine accurately. One major reason for this is that the event is usually private and becomes exposed only under special circumstances. Then, there are numerous methodological problems in data gathering (Herrenkohl, 1990; Wyatt, 1994; Brice-Baker, 1994). A further difficulty is defining violence (Javier, Herron, & Bergman, 1994).

For example, Steinmetz defines violence as, "an act carried out with the intention of, or perceived as having the intention of, physically hurting another person" (1986, p. 52). This definition stresses *intention*, and *physical* violence. The former is difficult to ascertain, and the latter excludes psychological abuse, which could also be considered violence. Similarly, the fact that "unintentional abuse" is not considered in the definition makes Steinmetz' definition of violence somewhat limited.

Gil (1986) offers another perspective, a dialectic definition aimed at the relationship between violence and historical-social contexts. However, such a definition is so broad that it is difficult to operationalize without overestimating the phenomena. More detailed discussion of the problems of assessing violence are available in Ammerman and Hersen (1992) and Lystad (1986).

An exploration of causal patterns is to be understood within the context of difficulties in defining and assessing violence. This is particularly important in understanding the significance of the reported incidence of domestic violence among different ethnic and socioeconomic groups. The public disclosure of violence is dependent on the circumstances surrounding the violence. The family is usually a private place, which often contributes to the secret and continued prevalence of domestic difficulties. However, there is a differential probability of public notice that has tended to foster stereotypes of violent cultures and subcultures of poverty. Also, regardless of the demographics of the families involved, the reality is often elusive. Unfortunately, as Walker notes, "In family violence the truth is almost always worse than either party's version" (1986, p. 80). The author was referring to the version offered by the victim and perpetrator in the abusive situation.

PROBABILITIES

There are a number of types of family violence that bear investigation, namely child, spousal, sibling, and elderly. In fact, any combination of family members can turn the family into a chaotic disruptive place. Most empirical research has focused on child and spousal abuse, so those areas are the primary sources that can be used to illustrate etiological possibilities for the totality of family violence. Also, most of the explorations have emphasized physical violence, recently including marital rape, but psychological/verbal abuse is also involved, sometimes accompanying physical, sometimes by itself. There is an increasing awareness of the importance and interaction of psychological and physical abuse, as well as of the need for more empirical research on all types of family violence. This is particularly the case with regard to the Black and multicultural families, as suggested by Wyatt (1994) and Brice-Baker (1994).

A number of causal models have been proposed that, although not designed as comprehensive, are applicable to one or more forms of family violence. For example, O'Leary and Murphy (1992) suggest a framework of the sociohistorical-feminist, couple-family system, and individual pathology views. Walker (1986) also proposes three possibilities, namely feminist-political, sociocultural, and psychological.

The feminist view explains spousal violence as a function of a male ideology that dominates the family so that the wife and children are vulnerable to abuse by the husband. The systems view sees violence as a product of systemic failure, and is part of both psychological and sociocultural explanations. The latter also addresses the possibilities of cultures and subcultures of violence. The pathological view is primarily psychological, stressing the personality characteristics of those involved in the violence.

McCall and Shields (1986) provide the most comprehensive view, with the possibilities of feminist, cultural, subcultural, family organization, systems, resource/exchange, interactionist, sex role, intergenerational transmission, victim precipitation, and stress/isolation. These are elaborations of the triad, and all tend to overlap, being theories of emphasis rather than universality or exclusivity. Basically the possibilities can be divided into those that stress the role of social factors and those that stress the personalities of the people involved.

The most likely explanation for family violence is a multi-determined one. However, the building blocks for such a model originate from a primary theoretical emphasis, namely social or personal. In viewing each, certain features stand out as probable contributors to a more comprehensive model, and in turn can be incorporated into a interactive social-personal theory of family violence.

Feminist theory illustrates the coupling of societal norms that favor male dominance with the ability to use force against weaker members of the family (Holzman, 1994). This view has applicability only to the abuse of wives, siblings, children, and elders; in its pure form, it is limited when the violent person is not socially empowered, as, for example, the battering wife. Then, there is a need to use psychological explanations, such as violence being learned social behavior. It is seen as an exaggeration of the male sex role, which in turn is imitated by women who are violent.

To speak about cultures of violence as explanatory paradigm in its totality is also problematic because most cultures are selective about their support of violence, such as the endorsement of spanking of children as a disciplinary method. In the United States, for instance, there seems to be often a fascination with violence but the cultural norms in this regard are inconsistent. Indeed, violence against family members is not something that is condoned by most people (Greenblatt, 1983).

Subcultural explanations are more promising (Glaser, 1986), showing variations in the use of violence related to ethnicity and social class. It is probable that certain ethnic norms, such as male dominance, could reinforce the use of violence, but it is also probable that those norms could be tempered by the norms of the larger society. The presence of violence in the lower classes relative to the middle and upper classes could also be a reflection of reporting methods or a differential exposure and/or reaction to psychological and social stressors (Brice-Baker, 1994; Javier, Herron & Bergman, 1994).

The family can be viewed as a system in which there are intense emotions, set roles, and strong vulnerabilities. Family organization can create an environment that is conducive to the expression of violence (Straus & Hotaling, 1980), which tends to be the final alternative in influencing other family members. In any interaction that may lead to violence, consideration can be given to the roles of each person, the meaning of the interaction, and the rules that are in place regarding the use of violence.

Walker (1984) has described a typical pattern for battering. It begins with a tension building phase involving a series of separate abusive incidents which are quickly resolved. However, such incidents continue to occur, with the tension increasing until there is *acute battering*. The violence tends to be severe and is likely to be noticed. Even if the incident is not made public, it usually frightens all involved and results in a *repentance* period with relative tranquility. However, this tends to be temporary, with the cycle restarting. Generally it ceases only when the parties involved are separated, although temporary survival measures are employed before that. These include environmental manipulation, passive-aggressive behavior, splitting, denial, and continued dependency. In understanding the interaction of abused and abuser, as well as the personalities of each, consideration should be given to the reactive nature of what is observed relative to the permanence and generalizability of the behaviors.

Although roles in the family are important, the origination of power in the roles appears to be complex. Childhood sex-role socialization that demarcates roles to the point that boys are consistently aggressors and girls consistently victims have not received empirical support (McCall & Shields, 1986). However, Walker (1986) is critical of the research methodology, and points to the fact that women are most often the ones who are physically abused. At issue is whether men and women have the same propensity for violence, but different means and opportunities.

The intergenerational transmission of patterns of violence has been very popular as a theoretical construct. Sometimes it is viewed as the abused becoming the abuser, particularly in regard to children and elders, and other times as modeling an observed role, either aggressor or victim. Although this behavior can certainly be learned from exposure to it within a family, the inevitability of its repetition has not been established (Herron *et al.,* 1992). Instead it appears as one of many possible contributing factors, along with stress and social isolation.

Tolman (1992) has supplied some guidelines for assessing psychological abuse. Because there is likely to be some conflict within most families, it needs to be at least a pattern of maltreatment, and it generally is not completely distinct from physical abuse. Although there is usually an exchange of unpleasantries and provocations in a relationship, and women have the capability of being abusive, the edge is given to men because they usually have more status, economic power, and the ability to threaten and/or use physical force. The possible psychological abuses include physical and nonphysical threats, isolating to limit contact with the outside world along with domination and behaviors that exhaust the spouse, economic restriction, degrading, and exacting sex-role expectations. Other possibilities are withholding physical and emotional support, insensitivity, contingent giving, and creating doubt as to the spouse's psychological equilibrium.

Thus far the discussion has stressed social factors that are likely to contribute to family violence, but the illustrations of psychological abuse provide a transition into the psychology of the family members participating in violence. Societal norms have played a role in the research as well. Men are most often the abusers of record, and the historical trend was to essentially overlook their personality and focus on the personality of their victims, particularly women. The implication was that personality flaws of the victims, as masochism or provocativeness, caused the problem. Men were viewed as understandably reacting out of frustration because their wives were impossible to deal with in nonviolent ways. As the feminist position has gained power and credibility, in turn debunking the justification of male violence, there has been a continued tendency to avoid the individual psychologies of the parties involved, but now because of a concern that this would refuel blaming the victim.

For example, certain women have been found to have a high rate of sexual victimization. However, Walker (1986) prefers to attribute that frequency to societal factors, namely that because women are the oppressed group they are more likely to be abused, as opposed to the presence of personality profiles in men and women that were not gender-role induced.

The existing research does indicate that the spouse abuser is not represented by a single, distinctive personality style (Hamberger & Hastings, 1986, 1988). However, there is a greater likelihood of alcohol and substance abuse, as well as personality problems, and there is a notable distortion in the degree of emphasis on different forms of aggression (O'Leary & Murphy, 1992). For example, typical aggressive patterns include avoidance and negativism, as well as overt aggression. There is also some information regarding other abusers. Pillomer (1986) suggests that abuser psychopathology is a major factor in elder abuse, and Green (1988) has made a similar observation in regard to sibling incest. In both of these types of abuse the abusers appear to have had models of family violence in their own families. Thus, although the evidence is limited overall, and especially in abusers other than spousal, it does implicate the personality traits of the abuser. In addition, personality characteristics are also of interest in a systemic approach where the focus is on the interaction of the couple or the family. There is evidence supporting the similarity of marital partners, rather than complementarily, so understanding the dynamics of spousal interaction appears relevant (O'Leary & Smith, 1991).

MODELS

Explaining the presence of violence in any form is a rather complex endeavor because there are a number of possible and interrelated explanations for this phenomenon. It is our contention that a multidimensional model may provide the most appropriate explanatory paradigm although it may be the most difficult to implement. Thus, we will be discussing the different models in the context of this multidimensional model approach.

A Social Etiological Model

This model explains family violence by looking at the institutionalization of violence in the society (Gelles,1980; Walker, 1986). According to this model, violence evolves from inequalities that establish and support exploitation and domination of one group by another. Thus, inequalities are not the result of the choices of all the people involved, but of one group taking advantage of another. Once in place, they are justified by social institutions and operate as oppressive norms that foster violence in both the oppressors and the oppressed. The recent South Africa apartheid situation as well as the Haitian and the Ethiopian situations could be viewed as examples of this phenomenon. In some way, the condition for many minority groups in the United States may also fall under this category.

A distinction can be made between social-structural violence, which is part of the social structure such as law enforcement, and personal violence, which conflicts with the social structure. The source of personal violence, according to this model, is the discriminatory aspects of the social system which cause individuals to react in a violent way. Thus the structure of the family would be viewed as the stimulus for the family members to react negatively to each other.

Gil (1986) has noted in this regard that although the American society is a political democracy, it is not an economic one, and although everyone is entitled theoretically to equal social and civil rights, such rights are realized in a differential manner. The fact of the matter is that the reality of the society supports inequality, selfishness, competition, and domination, all essentially endorsing social-structural violence and providing the potential for personal violence (West, 1993). Endorsement of this view is frequently found in the lives of delinquents and other individuals convicted of violent crimes. There is a strong search from these individuals for meaning and for social and economic recognition in an environment where they feel deprived, socially marginal and alienated.

Because of the presence of structural violence outside of the home, or the institutionalization of violence in the society, the family could serve a number of adaptive functions. One is restorative, with the family providing a place to express feelings that have been engendered outside the family and are due to societal stresses. Hostility is often a major element in this pattern, and can bring violence into the family. The ability of the family to deal with the angry feelings of any one of its members is limited by changes in the family structure that are interactive with societal changes. The traditional family structure provided a direction for identifying both probable stresses and the roles of family members in coping with such stresses. That structure has changed and, as a result, the family profile and dynamics has also been altered. In particular, increasingly both husband and wife are employed, with many families considering this a necessity. In addition, there has been an increase in the number of single parent families due to separation or divorce resulting in the division of one household into two households and the creation of extended families. Also, birth patterns have shifted, with delays in childbearing for a substantial number of women, while at the same time there is an increase in the proportion of children being born to young mothers. It would be important to examine in this regard the dilemma faced by individuals who have made single-parenthood more a matter of choice than being a result of separation or divorce (Kirshenbaum, Iasensa, Johnson, & Keren, 1994).

These stresses as well as other stresses, such as women's employment, marital dissolution, and altered birth patterns, all contribute as potential family stressors (Lein, 1986). As the family is altered as functions and responsibilities shift within it, as for example the division of labor for family chores when both parents work, then its adaptive function for external stressors is strained. One of the adaptive functions of the family that become affected is its preparatory function, particularly for children. The family may now focus on developing in their children a readiness for living with violence as it is found in both childrearing and educational practices.

Despite demographic alterations of family profiles, hierarchical family structures and arbitrary controls are still frequently attempted and can result in family violence. The following aspects of family organization have been suggested as contributors (Hotaling & Straus, 1980):

- Amount of time the family spends together;
- Intensity of involvement among the family members;
- The extent to which the members are involved in competing activities;
- Issues related to rights to influence;
- Age and sex discrepancies among the family members;
- Designated roles;
- Privacy;
- Knowledge of social biographies;
- Involuntary membership, and stress.

Thus from a social perspective, the structure of society, and its units, such as the family, predispose the members to personal violence. Because the existing members of the society are living in a system that was in the main fashioned by others who lived before them, these individuals are viewed as having little personal responsibility for the system as well as strong reasons to be reactive to it. If it favors them, then they are likely to perpetuate it, using violence in the process, like in the case of dominant groups in the United States, South Africa, Haiti, and other parts of the world. If it discriminates against them, they will feel resentment and be prone to reactive personal violence.

Personal Psychology Model

Although the social etiological model gives acknowledgment to personal motivations that were involved in the development of the social structures originally, these personal motivations are discounted as a strong etiological factor. The fact that aggression is viewed primarily as a reaction rather than an innate drive or predisposition leaves a number of questions unanswered. For instance, this view neglects the consistent exploitative trends that have persisted in cultures and societies over centuries, and that continue even when there are shifts in power structures. This is continually reflected in the existence of poverty throughout the world (Herron &

Javier, in press). Ultimately, we have to postulate the involvement of a personal dynamic with regard to the etiology of family violence.

There is an understandable concern in the societal view that attention paid to individual dimensions and psychopathology as an etiological force for personal violence will distract from an awareness of the role of social-structural violence, and by so doing, increase the social imbalances that indeed are contributors to violence (West, 1993) and to family violence in particular. However, this concern does not justify the neglect of personal motivations, nor is it accurate to posit social-structural violence as the sole, or even primary, cause of personal violence.

Interactive Model

Cornell West's (1993) analysis of the etiological factors contributing to racial tension strongly suggests the importance of adapting a comprehensive approach, which includes a look at structural constraints in the society and behavioral impediments of the individual. Although in the same vein, we are proposing a paradigm which includes an individual dimension of a more psychological and psychodynamic nature than the one suggested by West's analysis, in addition to the factors proposed by the social etiological model. Thus, an interactive model is proposed which begins with the view suggested by Melanie Klein (1957) that the central conflict for all people throughout their life is between love and hate. These feelings, and their expressions are connected to people and social reality, so that there is continuing interaction. People create social institutions out of personal motivations for structure that provide organization of basic drives and avenues for their expression. In this manner different forms of love and hate become socialized, and can be used to facilitate or inhibit human development.

The family is one of these structures which is supposed to function primarily as a positive developmental force for all its members. However, it also has the potential for becoming a violent place due to both the individual personality characteristics of its members and their systematic interaction, as well as the impact of social-structural violence on the family. The family members need the personal resources to cope with the potential for violence that surrounds them and exists within them. When these resources are lacking, then violence is likely to occur.

Although structural factors such as the distribution of power in the society and the organizational aspects of a family provide a contributory setting for violence, it is the misuse of aggression by individuals within the family that provides the enactment. The structural-personal interaction producing family violence is set in motion by family members who are prone to misuse aggression in conflict resolution. Such is the case when one partner in the relationship opts for the use of physical force to establish or re-establish his/her sense of control over the other partner.

REALITY AND MORALITY DISTORTION IN THE CYCLE OF VIOLENCE

The amount of attention devoted to understanding the personality structures of violent family members has been limited, but clinical impressions are available. Two features stand out, namely distortions in reality and morality. In the first instance, the abuser sees the targets in the family, such as spouse, child, sibling, parent, as being consistently available. There is a confusion of proximity and propensity, so that an assumption is made that the targets' availability is assured. Repeated cycles of violence often reinforce this, until the feelings of the abused surface in a sufficiently resistive way that the violence is seriously called into question. This also challenges the assumption that the feelings of the abused are perfectly attuned to the feelings of the abuser in somehow deserving or provoking the violence. Although provocation may occur, and adaptations may take place that create an illusion of continuity of opportunity, there is a lack of recognition by the abuser of the totality of the feelings of the abused. That lack of recognition was present in the case of a 10-year-old girl from one of the Caribbean islands who found herself most afternoons as the primary target of physical abuse by her alcoholic father. Her mother, also an alcoholic, would either actively participate by also hitting her or by quietly allowing the father to do so in the name of discipline. She was the oldest of four siblings who would also witness the recurrent physical and verbal abuses. The other siblings were often threatened by the father that the same would happen to them if they got out of line. When the parents were asked as to the reason for the continuous wailing by the child, the parents would quickly respond that they were trying to discipline a child who has been disrespectful and irresponsible. They were referring to the child having failed to complete some household chores that had been assigned to her. The frequency of the abuse was such that it was no longer clear to the child or the abuser as to the reason for it and the child began to expect it as part of the afternoon routine when the family was drinking.

It could be said that these kinds of situations are only maintained in a condition where reality is distorted by the abuser as when the abuser finds justification to the act in the name of discipline. The abused's reality is also affected in the same way. An accurate judgment of reality would reflect a much greater awareness of the damage that is being inflicted on the physical and emotional well-being of the child, as well as the probability that there are much better ways to accomplish the goal. Furthermore, from the perspective that there is a good possibility of reactive aggression on the part of the abused, even if it takes a long time to occur, it shows questionable judgment on the part of the abuser. Thus there is an ego deficiency in regard to the use of aggression.

There is also a moral distortion, based on the belief that the abuser actually has the right to be abusive as in the case related above. In the abusive patterns observed, apparent remorse often occurs, with reaction formation to violence, but they do not endure. Instead a pathologically narcissistic view of relationships persists in which the abuser feels justified in using the family as a focal point for violently establishing personal superiority. This is also illusory, because although fear may reign and cause other family members to appear docile, their contempt and resentment are very much alive. In addition, once the violence is exposed, the public disapproval emphasizes the delusion of moral justification.

CLASSIFICATION

A typology of personal violence in the family can now be considered as general organizing categories rather than as a rigid classification.

Violence Seeker. These are a group of abusers who repeatedly rely on violence to express themselves and effect solutions, and the family is just one of many opportunities that they use. They are endorsers of violence whose propensity may be a combination of constitutional endowment and developmental experiences, such as being raised in a violent family. Violence is the only way of life they really understand, and their patterns are very difficult to alter. Individuals prone to psychopathic and sadomasochistic behaviors are likely to fall under this category.

Opportunistic Abuser. A larger group of abusers restrict themselves to family situations. These are opportunistic abusers who believe that it is acceptable to discharge their hostility within the family, but not outside of it. Whatever the roles they play in the external world, they feel restricted and frustrated by the expectations and demands inherent in their interactions with the external world; the family is then used as a convenient outlet for their aggression. This may be a pattern that they observed or endured during their own childhood, or it may be that they discovered that a dominant role can be played out in the family, with structural reinforcement, when the external world is restrictive. Alterations of family patterns are more possible here, in combination with making needed changes in the personality styles and behaviors of the abusers who express aggression through violence. Examples of destructive patterns that are reactive to developmental experiences include abusing an elderly parent because that parent previously had been the abuser; attacking a spouse because of negative feelings about the opposite sex; and picking on a younger sibling because of feelings of personal inadequacy. The personal motivations seek an apparently realistic outlet, in terms of availability, and use the justification of previous negative experiences, narcissistically misusing aggression, demonstrating poor judgment and insensitivity to the rights and feelings of others.

Reactive Abuser. This third group consists of those who react violently to their abusers. For example, women who are treated violently by their husbands could interpret that male violence as an extension of a socialized male role that is appropriate to imitate. Another possibility is that women who become violent are focused on their survival and use violence as the necessary solution. This may occur because they are in a situation that would support the view, or they have a desire to be aggressive that now has apparent justification, or because the atmosphere of the society suggests that violence will be the most adaptive for women if the aversive factors are ever to be changed.

To fully understand violence in the family it is necessary to look at the personality structures of all the family members. Although society reinforces violence in men more than women, family violence is not an acceptable social solution to family problems. Thus, the personal factors that result in crossing the line of appropriate behavior have to be considered. The potential for violence, and the ability to act upon the potential, appear as drives that require control rather than being solely reactions to structural violence, which is, after all, the creation of individuals.

Also, people place themselves in potentially violent situations for a variety of personal motivations that can be broadly grouped as masochistic and sadistic desires. Although it is clearly inaccurate to blame the victim and absolve the victimizer, family violence will not be understood by focusing solely on the abuser, or on the dominant forces of the society. Family violence is a result of interactive processes, namely structural and personal forces as well as the personalities and behavioral styles of all the members of the family. Disentangling all of these, and understanding them, provides the avenues for remedying violent solutions to family conflicts.

CONCLUSIONS

The purpose of this paper has been to suggest a direction for the exploration of the causes of family violence. The history of the study of family violence has been summarized, followed by consideration of the problems in studying family violence. Models of family violence were considered, and broadly categorized into social and personal, with the probability that a multi-determined model will be required to ensure the most accurate explanation. Theories with a specific focus included feminist, cultures and subcultures of violence, family organization, intergenerational transmission, and personal psychopathology. The models in the social category were investigated in terms of their explanations for structural violence and reactive personal violence, with particular emphasis on the organization of the family with its adaptive functions of restoration and preparation. Then the personal misuse of aggression was considered as reflected in distortions of reality and morality, and typologies of family violence were suggested. Finally, it was suggested that family violence will be best understood and prevented or alleviated, if a model is used that considers the interaction of structural violence and the personality features of all the family members.

Our emphasis was on discussing general explanatory principles for the etiology and maintenance of violence in the family. These principles are assumed to be applicable to understanding violence in the minority population as well. Thus, the factors described by Brice-Baker (1994) and by Wyatt (1994) with regard to the minority individual could be subsumed under the categories discussed in this paper. Their emphasis was, in the main, on a discussion of the factors affecting the assessment and intervention of domestic violence in individuals coming from diverse cultural backgrounds. According to these authors one of the major obstacles has to do with the severe stereotyping of minority individuals with regard to the prevalence of domestic violence. The recommendations made by these authors are crucial to allow for a more objective paradigm to take place with regard to assessment and intervention in this population. Once this is accomplished, the categories and concepts referred to in this paper are applicable.

REFERENCES

Ammerman, R. T. & Hersen, M. (1992a). *Assessment of family violence. A clinical and legal source book.* New York: Wiley.

Ammerman, R. T., & Hersen, M. (1992b). Current issues in the assessment of family violence. In R. T. Ammerman & M. Hersen (Eds.), *Assessment of family violence. A clinical and legal source book* (pp. 3-10). New York: Wiley.

Bachman, R., & Pillomer, K. A. (1992). Epidemiology and family violence involving adults. In R. T. Ammerman & M. Hersen (Eds.), *Assessment of family violence. A clinical and legal source book* (pp. 108-120). New York: Wiley.

Brice-Baker, J. R. (1994) Domestic violence African-Caribbean families. *Journal of Social Distress and the Homeless, 3,* 23-38.

Gil, D. G. (1986). Sociocultural aspects of domestic violence. In M. Lystad (Ed.), *Violence in the home: Interdisciplinary perspectives* (pp. 124-149). New York: Brunner/Mazel.

Glaser, D. (1986). Violence in the society. In M. Lystad (Ed.), *Violence in the home: Interdisciplinary perspectives* (pp. 5-31). New York: Brunner/Mazel.

Green, A. H. (1988). Special issues in child sexual abuse. In D. H. Schetky & A. H. Green (Eds.), *Child sexual abuse* (pp. 125-136). New York: Brunner/Mazel.

Greenblatt, C. S. (1983). A hit is a hit...or is it? Approval and tolerance of the use of physical force by spouses. In D. Finkelhor, R. J. Geller, G. T. Hotaling, & M. A. Straus (Eds.), *The dark side of families: Current family violence research* (pp. 235-260). Beverly Hills, CA: Sage.

Hamberger, L. K., & Hastings, J. E. (1986). Personality correlates of men who abuse their partners: A cross-validation study. *Journal of Family Violence, 1,* 323-341.

Hamberger, L. K., & Hastings, J. E. (1988). Characteristics of male spouse abusers consistent with personality disorders. *Hospital and Community Psychiatry, 39,* 763-770.

Haugaard, J. J. (1992). Epidemiology and family violence involving children. In R. T. Ammerman & M. Hersen (Eds.), *Assessment of family violence. A clinical and legal sourcebook* (pp. 89-107). New York: Wiley.

Herrenkohl, R. C. (1990). Research directions related to child abuse and neglect. In R. T. Ammerman & M. Hersen (Eds.), *Children at risk: An evaluation of factors contributing to child abuse and neglect* (pp. 85-108). New York: Plenum Press.

Herron, W. G., & Javier, R. A. (in press). The psychogenesis of poverty: Some psychoanalytic conceptualizations. *Psychoanalytic Review.*

Herron, W. G., Javier, R. A., & Cicone, J. (1992). Etiological patterns of child abuse and neglect. *Journal of Social Distress and the Homeless, 1,* 273-290.

Holzman, C. (1994). Multicultural perspectives on counseling survivors of rape. *Journal of Social Distress and the Homeless, 3,* 81-97.

Hotaling, G. T., & Straus, M. A. (1980). Culture, social organization and irony in the study of family violence. In M. A. Straus & G. T. Hotaling (Eds.), *The social causes of husband-wife violence* (pp. 3-22). Minneapolis: University of Minnesota Press.

Javier, R. A., Herron, W., & Bergman, A. (1994). Introduction to the special issue on a multicultural view of domestic violence. *Journal of Social Distress and the Homeless, 3,* 1-6.

Kirshenbaum, S., Iasensa, S., Johnnson, T., Keren, M. (July 1994). *Gay and lesbian family networks.* Paper presented at the 52nd Annual Conference of the International Council of Psychologists, Lisbon, Portugal.

Klein, M. (1957). *Envy and gratitude.* New York: Delacorte.

Lein, L. (1986). The changing role of the family. In M. Lystad (Ed.), *Violence in the home: Interdisciplinary perspectives* (pp. 32-50). New York: Brunner/Mazel.

Lystad, M. (Ed.) (1986). *Violence in the home: Interdisciplinary Perspectives.* New York: Brunner/Mazel.

McCall, G. J., & Shields, N. M. (1986). Social and structural factors in family violence. In M. Lystad (Ed.), *Violence in the home: Interdisciplinary perspectives* (pp. 98-123). New York: Brunner/Mazel.

Newberger, E. H. (1983). The helping hand strikes again: Unintended consequences of child abuse reporting. *Journal of Clinical Child Psychology, 12,* 307-311.

O'Leary, K. D., & Murphy, C. (1992). Clinical issues in the assessment of spouse abuse. In R. T. Ammerman & M. Hersen (Eds.), *Assessment of family violence. A clinical and legal sourcebook* (pp. 26-46). New York: Wiley.

O'Leary, K. D., & Smith, D. A. (1991). Marital interactions. *Psychological Review, 42,* 191-212.

Pillomer, K. A. (1986). Risk factors in elder abuse: Results from a case-control study. In K. A. Pillomer & R. Wolf (Eds.), *Elder abuse: Conflict in the family* (pp. 239-263). Dover: Auburn House.

Steinmetz, S. K. (1986). The violent family. In M. Lystad (Ed.), *Violence in the home: Interdisciplinary perspectives* (pp. 51-67). New York: Brunner/Mazel.

Straus, M. A., & Hotaling, G. T. (Eds.) (1980). *The social causes of husband-wife violence.* Minneapolis: University of Minnesota Press.

Straus, M. A., Gelles, R. J., & Steinmetz, S. K. (1980). *Behind closed doors. Violence in the American family.* New York: Anchor/Doubleday.

Tolman, R. M. (1992). Psychological abuse of women. In R. T. Ammerman & M. Hersen (Eds.), *Assessment of family violence. A clinical and legal source book* (pp. 291-310). New York: Wiley.

Walker, L. E. (1984). *The battered woman syndrome.* New York: Springer.

Walker, L. E. (1986). Psychological causes of family violence. In M. Lystad (Ed.), *Violence in the home: Interdisciplinary perspectives* (pp. 71-97). New York: Brunner/Mazel.

West, C. (1993). *Race matters.* Boston: Beacon Press.

Wyatt, G. E. (1994). Sociocultural and epidemiological issues in the assessment of domestic violence. *Journal of Social Distress and the Homeless, 3,* 7-22.

3

The Diagnosis and Treatment of Anger in a Cross-Cultural Context

Raymond DiGiuseppe, Christopher Eckhardt, Raymond Tafrate, and Mitchell Robin

This article proposes that while violent behavior has received much attention, the emotion of anger that may underlay violence has relatively been ignored in the psychological literature. The status of anger in the psychological and medical literatures is reviewed. A criteria for a proposal of anger disorder for inclusion in DSM are presented. Psychotherapy outcome studies of anger are briefly reviewed. It is proposed that the primary problem in psychotherapy of anger is a failure to reach a therapeutic alliance with clients in order to change their anger. Suggestions for reaching a therapeutic alliance with angry clients and attaining agreement on the explicit goal of changing their anger are presented. Script theories of emotions are presented as an important tool for understanding the therapeutic alliance in different cultural groups. The creation of new scripts that are acceptable to the patients cultural group is presented as one strategy to formulate the therapeutic alliance.

INTRODUCTION

There seems to be agreement among mental health professionals that America is a violent culture. Wounds inflicted by violence are a leading cause of death and a critical health problem among certain ethnic and age groups. While many social policymakers, practitioners and researchers have focused on violent behavior, we have chosen to reflect on the emotion that usually precedes such behavior, anger. Psychology and psychiatry appear to have overlooked anger as a clinical problem. Throughout the history of medicine and psychology, some scholars and practitioners have recognized the negative physical, interpersonal, and social consequences associated with intense and frequent anger. Despite this awareness, little progress has occurred in defining, understanding, diagnosing, and treating dysfunctional anger. Rothenberg (1971) noted over 20 years ago that, "almost invariably, anger has not been considered an

independent topic worthy of investigation ... [which] has not only deprived anger of its rightful importance in the understanding of human behavior, but has also led to a morass of confused definitions, misconceptions, and simplistic theories" (p. 86). It is our belief that chronic anger can be a debilitating emotional excess to the same extent as clinical depression or anxiety and deserves increased attention in research, clinical practice, and within official diagnostic documents.

As the American population becomes more culturally diverse, the problems of studying anger become more difficult. Mental health practitioners are frequently faced with helping clients from different cultural backgrounds cope with frustration posed by emigration, poverty, and prejudice. This frustration often leads to anger and sometimes to domestic violence. Anger is expressed differently in various cultures. Different stimuli are viewed as insulting by different cultures. Cultures may even differ in the degree of angry emotions that are sanctioned and condemned. Recent immigrants live in two cultures and may have difficulties understanding the social cues and contexts of anger in mainstream American cultural. Without a clear understanding of anger, how can practitioners hope to help clients from different cultures of origin cope with the frustrations and anger which may occur as they live in an alien culture?

In this paper we hope to explore some issues in the definition, diagnosis, and treatment of anger problems which we hope will be applicable to numerous cultural groups.

OVERLOOKING ANGER

We are here to encounter the most outrageous, brutal, dangerous, and intractable of all passions; the most loathsome and unmannerly; nay, the most ridiculous too; and the subduing of this monster will do a great deal toward the establishment of human peace. (Seneca, 40–50 A.D.).

In his essay "On Anger," the stoic philosopher Seneca (L'Estrange, 1817/1917) chronicled the negative effects of anger on a social and individual level. He encouraged abstinence from any experience of anger. To

Seneca, a truly wise individual could form the correct opinions about events so that under any circumstance, anger would not follow. Seneca fervently believed that anger clouded judgment, impaired interpersonal effectiveness, and could collectively imbalance an entire society.

Seneca's position, while extreme, represented the first work on anger. Obviously, humans have experienced extreme suffering as a function of anger and aggression. Given the historical importance afforded anger by philosophers (see Averill, 1981 for a complete review), the lack of attention by psychology and psychiatry in targeting anger as an emotion worthy of scientific study is surprising.

We agree with other theorists that the reason underlying the scarcity of work on anger has been a lack of consensus for a definition of the construct (see Tavris, 1989). Anger has not been regarded as a viable emotional construct on its own and has repeatedly been subsumed under the general rubric of "aggression" (Rothenberg, 1971). Historically, the views proposed by Darwin (1872), Freud (1920), and ethologists such as Eibl-Eibesfeldt (1976) and Lorenz (1966) presupposed a relationship between anger and aggression. Aggression, to these theorists, was either a biological reflex or an instinctive drive, of which anger was but a weaker expression. The message delivered by these authors was that aggression and its "relatives" (i.e., anger, hostility, rage, etc.) are natural drives that resist autonomous control (Lazarus, 1991).

Because of the legacy of the above views of anger and aggression, no agreed upon definition of the constructs of anger, aggression, and hostility has emerged. This lack of definitional clarity has been the most significant factor thwarting research on anger.

ANGER IN CONTEMPORARY PSYCHOLOGY AND MEDICINE

While research appears to attest to the negative influences of anger on ones' health and propensity to aggression, anger is rarely regarded as a debilitating emotion to the same extent as anxiety and depression. These latter two emotions have been the central targets of psychological and psychiatric interventions across the last century, with the National Institutes of Health funding many large-scale anxiety and depression treatment-outcome projects (e.g., Barlowe, Rapee, & Brown, 1992; Imber, Pilkonis, Sotsky, Elkin, Watkins, Collins, Shea, Leber, & Glass, 1989). Research on anger, on the other hand, has been negligible, with notable exceptions being the work of Novaco (1975, 1985), Deffenbacher (1988), and Feindler (1989).

An example of the diminished attention can be found by examining the psychological and medical research literatures. A computer search of Psychological Abstracts between 1985 and March 1993 showed that 7355 articles referenced anxiety, 15,369 referenced depression, yet only 704 referenced anger. A computer search of Index Medicus for the same period revealed a similar trend, with 8850 articles referencing anxiety, 8352 referencing depression, and only 744 referencing anger. In addition to the relative lack of attention given to anger, some conceptual confusion also exists. In the psychological and medical literature, terms such as anger, hostility, and aggression are often used interchangeably; often anger is subsumed under one of these other categories. As a result, the relationship and distinction between anger and aggression remains unclear.

Another indication of the scientific and professional communities' avoidance of anger is the paucity of assessment devices used to measure the construct. The more "mainstream" emotions such as depression and anxiety have experienced substantial advancements in assessment, while similar efforts have been missing in the anger literature. A variety of self-report anger assessment devices have appeared in the last several decades. Biaggio and colleagues (Biaggio, 1980; Biaggio, Supplee, & Curtis, 1981) systematically reviewed four scales: the Buss Durkee Hostility inventory (Buss & Durkee, 1957), the Reaction Inventory (Evans & Strangeland, 1971), the Novaco Anger Inventory (Novaco, 1975), and the Anger Self-Report (Zelin, Adler, & Morrison, 1972). They concluded that all the scales reviewed had only limited evidence of validity and questionable research utility. The poor quality of anger assessment instruments, according to Biaggio, stems from the lack of a firm anger research base and represents the most challenging obstacle toward advancement in theory, research, and treatment.

Since Biaggio's critique, several measures of anger and hostility have appeared such as the Spielberger State-Trait Anger Expression Inventory (STAXI; Spielberger, 1988) and the Multidimensional Anger Inventory (Siegel, 1985). Both are significant advancements in anger measurement, but are in need of further research.

ANGER, VIOLENCE, AND ILLNESS

The consequences of intense and frequent anger have only recently been explored. Research has primarily focused on two areas: the relationship between anger and aggression, and the relationship between anger and physical health.

Anger and Aggression. Aggression and violence are significant and growing problems in the United States. A report compiled by the Federal Bureau of Investigation and the U.S. Department of Justice (Uniform Crime Reports, 1991) estimate that one violent crime occurs in the United States every 17 seconds. On average, 733 shootings take place each day (Cotton, 1992), and approximately one murder is committed every 22 minutes (Schmoke, 1992). Homicide is the second leading cause of death among 15-to-24-year-olds, and the leading cause of death among 15-to-34-year-old Black males (Novello, Shosky, & Froehlke, 1992). The United States has the highest homicide rate of any Western industrialized country (Novello *et al.,* 1992).

The medical community has recently called violence to be a public health issue (Cotton, 1992; Koop & Lundberg, 1992; Schmoke, 1992). According to Rosenberg, O'Carroll, and Powell (1992), "fatal and nonfatal injuries resulting from interpersonal violence have become one of the most important public health problems facing our country." The public health approach consists of epidemiological analysis, careful design of intervention strategies, and implementation and evaluation of outcome. The Centers for Disease Control have made the prevention of violence one of their highest priorities (Rosenberg *et al.,* 1992).

Statistics on violent crime in the United States tell us little about the relationship between anger and violence. Data on the context in which aggression occurs are slightly more revealing. Most aggressive acts occur between people who know one another, and occur during arguments. FBI statistics (Uniform Crime Reports, 1991) confirm that over half of all murder victims were acquainted with their assailants; only 14% of the victims were murdered by strangers. In addition, arguments preceded 34% of the murders documented in 1990.

Anger may have a profound role in domestic violence. Particularly alarming is the prevalence of wife abuse. It is estimated that 2 million women are battered by their husbands or mates each year in the U.S. (Straus & Gelles, 1986); this figure probably underrepresents reality (O'Leary, Barling, Arias, Rosenbaum, Malone, & Tyree, 1989). More than twice as many women were shot and killed by their husbands or intimate acquaintances than were murdered by strangers (Kellermann & Mercy, 1992). Twelve to 18% of all murders are spousal assaults. Forty percent of women murdered each year die at the hands of their husbands (Sigler, 1989). Although women do appear to engage in physical violence (O'Leary *et al.,* 1989), men are more likely than women to commit acts of extreme violence and/or murder their spouses (Berk, Berk, Loseke, & Rauma, 1983). The severity of domestic violence and the lack of clear understanding concerning who is likely to abuse, requires research.

"Although a great deal has been written about men who batter, much of the data has come from women victims, rather than from the men themselves" (Sigler, 1989, p. 19). What little data exist are inconclusive. Early studies focused on the distinguishing characteristics of maritally violent men, and investigated the effects of alcoholism, low self-esteem (Goldstein & Rosenbaum, 1985), poor assertiveness skills (O'Leary & Curley, 1986), and, ironically, the aggressors' wives (Gellen, Hoffman, Jones, & Stone, 1984). Researchers have begun to focus on the role of affect, especially anger, in marital violence.

We know little about the relationship between Domestic violence and the emotion of anger. In the only epidemiological study of the everyday experience of anger, Averill (1982) found that in the majority of anger episodes the target of the anger was either a loved one or someone well-liked. In 13% of the incidents reported was the target a stranger. The data on violent crime seem consistent with Averill's data on anger; both anger and aggression most frequently occur between people who know one another.

The context of the aggressive acts reported in the above statistics are suggestive that anger may indeed be a precursor to many acts of aggression. Some researchers have proposed that anger is a precursor to aggressive and violent behavior (Bandura, 1973; Lazarus, 1991; Novaco, 1975), while others have suggested a direct causal link (Konecni, 1975; Rokeach, 1987). However, only a handful of empirical studies have documented the relationship between anger and aggression. Wife abusers have significantly higher levels of self-reported anger, hostility, and depression than controls (Maiuro, Cahn, Vitaliano, Wagner, & Zegree, 1988; Maiuro, Vitaliano, & Cahn, 1987). Similarly, Margolin and colleagues (Burman, Margolm, & John, 1993; Margolin & Wampold, 1981) have found that in structured laboratory husband–wife conflicts, frequent expressions of anger and hostility differentiated physically abusive men from non-abusive controls. Selby (1984) found that high levels of self-reported anger and hostility successfully discriminated between prison inmates with violent and nonviolent histories. These findings support the idea that anger occurs in the psychological profiles of individuals who engage in assaults. However, given the importance of this issue, more research is needed to clearly establish the role of anger in acts of violence. Since the majority of anger episodes do not lead to violence (Averil, 1982), we need to know what distinguish the anger episodes that lead to aggression from those that do not.

Anger and Illness. The relationship between anger and illness has been studied by medical and social researchers since the 1950s. Anger and hostility have consistently been identified as risk factors in hypertension (Spielberger, 1992) and coronary heart disease (Matthews, Glass, Rosenman, & Bortner, 1977). Heart related illness remains the leading cause of death in

America (U.S. Bureau of the Census, 1991), and the leading cause of death in the Western world (Diamond, 1982).

Research on the relationship between anger and heart disease began with the observation that many individuals who suffered from heart disease shared characteristics such as self-controlled, time conscious, competitive, aggressive, impatient, and hostile. This cluster of characteristics was termed the type A behavior pattern (Friedman & Rosenman, 1959). However, the relationship between type A behavior pattern and heart disease was not replicated in all studies (Dembroski, MacDougall, Costa, & Grandits, 1989; Diamond, 1982; Haynes, Feinleib, & Kannel, 1980). Focus shifted to the variables of anger and hostility, as numerous studies (Suarez & Williams, 1989; Dembroski & MacDougall, 1985; Matthews & Haynes, 1986) showed a link between anger and hostility and coronary artery disease. Anger and hostility were implicated as risk factors in the development of hypertension (Diamond, 1982). Essential hypertension afflicts approximately 10–20% of adult Americans (Diamond, 1982). Hypertension is also considered an independent risk factor for coronary heart disease (Kannel, Schwartz, & McNamara, 1969).

Although anger is implicated as a risk factor in the development of hypertension it should be noted that there are some inconsistent findings in the research literature. Some studies show that "holding anger in" results in greater cardiovascular reactivity (Holroyd & Gorkin, 1983; MacDougall, Dembroski, & Krantz, 1981), while others show that the outward expression of anger is associated with greater reactivity (Dembroski, MacDougall, Shields, Petitto, & Lushane, 1978; Diamond et al., 1984). In an attempt to reconcile these inconsistent findings, Engebretson, Matthews, and Scheier (1989), found that the cardiovascular reactivity quickly declined in those subjects who were permitted to use their preferred mode of anger expression. The reactivity of those subjects asked to engage in their non-preferred mode of anger expression persisted . Many studies have failed account for the subject' s preferred mode of anger expression, and that the timing of the reactivity measurements varied across studies making comparisons problematic.

In addition, while anger and hostility have been proposed as emotional risk factors for both coronary heart disease and essential hypertension, there appear to be different patterns among individuals who suffer from the two disorders. According to Diamond (1982), hypertensives seem to be chronically hostile, resentful, and anxious when provoked to anger. In contrast, coronary patients appear to be more aggressive, more likely to act on their emotional arousal, and are characteristically less ambivalent about expressing anger.

Despite the potential importance of these studies on anger, hostility, and physical illness, we believe that a major weakness has been the quality of the assessment instruments employed. Few investigators have explicitly provided definitions of anger, hostility, and aggressive behavior. In fact, Siegel (1985) included a footnote to her study on anger and illness by noting that anger and hostility were interchangeable terms. This has had the effect of hampering efforts at demonstrating the construct validity of these instruments and has created "the potential for miscommunication and confusion if it is incorrectly assumed that all hostility measures reflect the same psychological construct" (Barefoot, 1992, p. 13).

CULTURAL, LANGUAGE, AND ANGER

Ekman (1974) listed anger as one of the six basic prototype human emotions, along with sadness, happiness, fear, surprise and disgust, that all humans experience regardless of culture. Although there has been substantial debate on the universality of basic emotions, Soloman (1984), and Izard (1977) stated that if any emotion is universal to the human condition, it is anger. However, Wierzbicka (1992) has identified several cultures that have no word for anger. She demonstrated how the words initial translated as "anger" actually represented emotions which have no translation in English. Wierzbicka concludes that, "there is no reason to think that the English word anger represents a 'pan-human prototype'. . . ."

If anger is not an innate emotion, perhaps anger and other emotions are more influenced by culture. A substantial literature exists in the sociology of emotions that psychologists rarely reference (see Kemper, 1991 for a review). We have found the script theory of emotions (Abelson, 1981; deSousa, 1980; Fehr, & Russell, 1984; Sabini & Silver, 1982; Tomkins, 1979) helpful in understanding anger. According to these positions, an emotional experience results from a socially derived scheme concerning a group of sub-events. Accordingly, emotional scripts consist of a scheme that includes the eliciting stimuli, the evaluations and beliefs about those events, culturally sanctioned emotional experiences, and the social expression and behavioral reactions to the emotions. Hochschild (1983) presents the most involved theory. She posited that people chose, often unconsciously, from the culturally appropriate and available options according to five categories of perceptions. These include the perception of: motivation, agency, value, and the relationship between the self and the agent. The emotions that are experienced match a proscribed combination of perceptions. For example, in a culture anger could be the emotional experience tied to these five perceptions: I want to be treated with respect; I do not have X's respect; It is terrible not to have X's respect; X is wrong for not respecting me; X is less worthwhile a person than I. Kemper points out that such theories can be useful to psychologists because the mechanisms by which the culture has its effect are the five categories of perceptions (or cognitions) that are hypothesized to match the emotional experience. The five categories of perceptions Hochschild mentions are similar to constructs in cognitive behavior therapy such as automatic thoughts (Beck, 1976), attributions (Seligman, 1975), and irrational beliefs (Ellis, 1969).

The sociological theories of emotions also provide some clues to indicate when people are motivated to change their emotions. Hochschild (1979) proposed a concept called emotional deviance, which represents the person's perception that the emotion experienced differs from one of the socially prescribed, appropriate emotions. Thoits (1985, 1990) proposed that people are motivated to change their behavior, physiological reactions, situation or emotions when they experience emotional deviance. The recognition that one's emotional reactions are inappropriate or socially unacceptable becomes a primary motivation for emotional change.

Several hypothesis relevant to the diagnosis and treatment of anger follows from these sociological perspectives on emotion. Emigrants to a new culture live in two cultures. First, they may have failed to recognize that their own emotions are regarded as deviant in the new culture. As a result they may not change reactions which bring disdain from others in the mainstream culture. Second, emigrants may not have acculturated the scripts which guide the emotional reactions proscribed by the mainstream culture and they may be perplexed and frustrated by their inability to perceive others emotional reactions. Such individuals may experience confusion because they do not know what to feel. Third, they may be surprised when they respond emotionally with a script from their culture of origin and this emotional experience is perceived as deviant by the new adopted culture. As a result they may believe their emotional reactions are "invalidated" by members of the mainstream culture.

Another implication of script theory concerns individuals learning the scripts of their culture. Individuals may have learned culturally unacceptable scripts and failed to learn accepted ones because of deviant socialization though their family, clan, or subgroup.

Since emotional scripts evolve in a culture across time, cultures may contain numerous or few scripts of each prototype emotion. That is, few or many variations of anger guilt, sadness, etc. Cultures could fail to contain a script or schema for an adaptive form of anger. We believe that the emotional script concept is helpful in understanding maladaptive anger reactions and in treatment of anger disorders. We would hypothesize that American culture possesses too few scripts concerning the prototype of anger and as a result people respond with an anger script which is inappropriate.

Kemper (1978, 1991; Kemper & Collins, 1990) suggests emotions need to be understood in context of the social structure in which the individual resides. Kemper and Collins believe that the factors of power and status are an important influence on emotional scripts. Scripts that include the suppression of anger in relations to superiors or those in power may be most problematic since suppressed anger is strongly related to illness. This group must suppress any annoyance, anger or irritation to passengers' obnoxious behaviors to ensure their future business. Flight attendants report feeling emotionally "numb" and experience considerable emotional problems. Hochschild generalizes from these results to suggests that any individuals in an occupational or social role that includes strong rules to suppress anger will experience similar difficulties as flight attendants. Emigrant and minority groups may often have such rules to suppress emotional expression when they interact with members of the majority group and as a result experience much detrimental suppressed anger.

Little data exists on different base rates of anger or differences on anger scale scores between ethnic minorities and whites or between populations from different countries. Several researchers have reported that American Blacks experience higher anger and are more likely to suppress anger expression (Clark, 1965; Grier & Cobb, 1969; Durel et al., 1989). Other have supported the finding that Blacks suppress anger (Gentry, 1972; Johnson, 1984). Hypertension and cardiovascular disease are related to suppressed anger. Therefore, one would expect Blacks to experience more of these illnesses. Dimsdale (1986) and Durel et al. (1989) reported that Blacks were more likely to have elevated blood pressure. The suppressed anger by American Blacks fits Hochschild (1983) notion social groups who believe that they must suppress their emotional expression or suffer reprisals will experience emotional disorders. The diagnostic problem presented by these data center around diagnosing Blacks for having higher anger, not having an appropriate mechanism for expression of anger, not seeing the problem as a result to an environmental stress or not having a script for an adaptive response to real environmental stress.

ANGER, AGGRESSION, AND THE PROBLEM OF DIAGNOSIS

Perhaps the most significant indication that contemporary psychology, psychiatry, and medicine do not view anger as a significant problem is the lack of a diagnosis category in the Diagnostic and Statistical Manual either the Third Edition Revised (DSM III-R; American Psychiatric Association,

1987) or the Fourth Edition (American Psychiatric Association, 1993). Although the experimental psychology literature abounds with analogue studies involving aggression, few studies that investigated the onset, maintenance, and mediating factors of aggression have *clinical* relevance. Novaco (1985) theorized that a major reason for this problem is the lack of a diagnostic criteria to identify appropriate subject populations.

> While there are multiple clinical categories for depression and anxiety, anger and aggression are not formally identified by a diagnostic category. Anger and aggression are extrinsic to "explosive disorder," but this is an extreme condition. Although associated with various pathological conditions, anger and aggression have no disorder category. (Novaco, 1985, p. 206).

O'Leary and Murphy (1992) and Tavris (1989) have lamented the lack of a diagnostic category addressing chronic anger and aggression problems. There are currently nine potential Axis I diagnoses for adults with anxiety problems, and nine for depression and related mood disorders (APA, 1987). One could argue that anger has received less research attention because it is excluded from the DSM. However, one could also argue that anger's absence from the DSM reflects professionals and researchers avoidance of the topic.

Anger and aggression are addressed by DSM III R and a draft of DSM IV in several ways. The first category of concern is the Axis I diagnosis of "Intermittent Explosive Disorder." This disorder is characterized by "discrete episodes of loss of control of aggressive impulses resulting in serious assaultive attacks or destruction of property" (p. 321). This definition implies that such anger impulses naturally exist in everyone, and that humans cannot stifle such "drives." The disorder results only when "control" is lost. This category appears under "Impulse Control Disorders not Elsewhere Classified," and was reluctantly retained in DSM III R, "despite the fact that many doubt the existence of a clinical syndrome characterized by episodic loss of control that is not symptomatic of ... [another] disorder" (p. 321).

Since this disorder is characterized by loss of control over aggressive impulses and requires some kind of motor behavior, it fails to define anger as an emotional problem or to mention the relationship between anger and aggressive behavior. It has been our experience that many angry clients will not meet the criteria for this disorder because their "explosive" behavior occurs too regularly. Also, anger in the absence of aggressive behavior would not result in an affirmative diagnosis. We have not found this diagnostic category helpful in understanding our angry patients. It is clearly biased toward a psychodynamic point of view by maintaining that all people have aggressive drives and impulses, and that most of us have sufficient "ego functioning" to keep our hidden aggression at bay. Such a notion runs counter to empirical data from cross-cultural research demonstrating a profoundly lower base rate of anger and aggressive behavior in many tribal cultures (see Monatagu, 1976; Tavris, 1989). This notion is also inconsistent with Weirsbecka's (1990) conclusion that there is no evidence for the universality of any emotion.

The second inclusion of anger in the DSM III R is as a symptom of an Axis II personality disorder. Three personality disorders include the subjective experience of anger: paranoid, borderline, and narcissistic. Symptoms of aggressive behavior also appear on Axis II in antisocial, and the provisional category of aggressive-sadistic personality disorders. Aggressive behavior is remarkably stable across time (Olweus, 1979), therefore, it is understandable that aggression may be part of a personality disorder. Perhaps, anger and aggression would not be an Axis I disorder if the personality structure results in the chronic, continuous expression of aggression. However, this is an empirical issue. While aggression is stable, those who are aggressive may not always behave aggressively. The personality predisposition may only emerge when they experience stress. Such a notion would require both Axis I and Axis II categories to complete the diagnostic picture. We have not found the above Axis II disorders helpful in getting a clear diagnostic picture of our angry clients because they only consider anger as a secondary feature of some other overriding personality pattern.

Due to the lack of other diagnostic categories to address anger, it has been our experience that women exhibiting anger and hostility are more likely to receive the diagnosis of borderline personality disorder. Anger is generally considered more socially acceptable for males in our culture, although data indicate that both sexes experience anger at an equal rate (Averill, 1982). Women who express anger may receive a diagnosis of a severe personality disorder because of an implicit gender bias among clinicians, and because of a lack of other diagnostic categories that attend to anger and hostility. Conversely, men may not receive an appropriate diagnosis that focuses on anger and hostility because such behavior is viewed as acceptable and natural.

DSM III, III R, and IV were designed to provide information across five axes. Including aggressive characteristics only on Axis II of DSM subverts the primary reasons for the five axes. Personality characteristic may predispose one to certain behavioral and emotional excesses. But the Axis II diagnosis need not imply that one is in a perpetual state of a clinical syndrome. Those Axis II disorders which include aggression may include individuals predisposed to the emotional excess of anger rather than depression or anxiety. However, it would be best for a diagnostic system to include this emotion on Axis I to differentiate a person with a personality predisposition and presently display an Axis I disorder from those with the same disposition who are presently experience a clinical problem.

DEFINING THE CONSTRUCTS

Elsewhere we have proposed that a primary reason why research in anger has been thwarted and no adequate diagnostic category exists is the lack of agreement on definitions of terms (DiGiuseppe, Eckhardt, & Tafrate, 1993). The terms anger, hostility, and aggression are used interchangeably and may have different meaning for members of different ethnic and cultural groups. The first step in the study of clinical constructs is consensus on working definitions of those constructs. Without accepted definitions or hypotheses, the ability to measure the anger is obviously hampered as is the ability to demonstrate adequate construct validity of assessment instruments. This then impedes efforts at integrating the anger data into a viable theoretical framework (Chesney, 1985). Averill (1981), Tavris (1989), and Spielberger *et al.* (1983) have reviewed the evolution of attempts to define anger, hostility, and aggression and concluded that providing adequate definitions for these constructs remains an elusive task. Chesney (1985) concluded that our confusion about the anger construct and how it is unique both in its characteristics and its relationships with other variables continues to thwart efforts in assessment, treatment, and prevention. Our definitions were devised to be as culture free as possible and have served as the foundation for our research and clinical work with anger. These definitions are empirical questions; they are to be regarded as hypotheses open for empirical scrutiny in the cross-cultural study of these constructs.

Anger. Anger is *an internal, mental, subjective feeling state with associated cognitions and physiological arousal patterns.* This definition posits anger as a covert phenomenon that can only be assessed by observer inferences from behavioral reactions, measures of physiological reactivity, subject self-report. While several other authors have attempted to define anger, they have defined it almost entirely in terms of cognition (i.e., Ellis, 1977, Lazarus, 1991), or have not emphasized cognition enough (i.e., Novaco, 1975), or have over-emphasized anger's link to aggression (e.g., Rubin, 1986). This definition is closely aligned to the definition offered by Spielberger (Spielberger, 1988; Spielberger, Jacobs, Russell, & Crane, 1983), who also view anger as a phenomenological construct. We believe that it is important to separate anger from the behavioral acts of aggression. In a series of surveys, college students and community residents were asked to describe in detail their most recent episodes of anger. It was found that the most frequent responses to anger were nonaggressive. Physical aggression occurred in 10% of the anger responses. Linking the definition of anger to aggressive acts would result in a great underestimation of the occurrence of angry episodes.

We have also attempted to define anger independent of any eliciting stimuli. Cultures may differ considerably in the eliciting stimuli for an anger episode in their respective scripts. Older theories, such as the frustration-aggression hypothesis (Dollard, Doob, Miller, Mowrer, & Sears, 1939) defined aggression and anger as resulting when an organism's goal-directed behaviors are blocked. Including such causative elements in the definition of a construct begs the question of research to verify that cause. Also, Averill found that over 85% of the angry episodes recorded in his study involved a perceived voluntary injustice or a potentially avoidable accident. Instead of anger being the result of a frustrating stimulus event, "anger is a response to some perceived misdeed" (Averill, 1983, p. 1150). Averill's emphasis on the perception of environmental events rather than on the events themselves is more consistent with a cognitive etiology of anger. Theoretically, all stimuli have the ability to elicit anger, through conditioning, modeling, instruction, or operant control. However, it is obvious that different people have different and highly individual stimuli that evoke anger that need not be present to elicit the emotion. Such a cognitive view would allow for the diversity of eliciting stimuli by different cultures. Research is needed to verify this cognitive causation.

Berkowitz (1989, 1990) recently reformulated the frustration-aggression hypothesis into a clearer and theoretically strong framework. According to his cognitive-neoassociationistic theory of anger, an aversive event automatically gives rise to general negative affect or discomfort, primarily in the absence of cognition. Shortly after this initial "frustration," thoughts, attitudes, and memories enter the picture as thought is given to what has occurred, why it has happened, and what possible consequences might follow. The purpose of this second stage is to more fully define and elaborate the emotion. In our view, Berkowitz's conception of anger as a largely internal process involving stimulus events, physiological arousal, and cognitive processes adequately fills in the gaps left by Spielberger's work and may be consistent with the sociological theory of Hochschild (1983).

Aggression. Aggression is defined as overt behavior enacted with the intent to do harm or injury to a person or object. This definition emphasizes the observable, behavioral aspect of aggression, and includes a motivational component ("intent") to separate aggression that is accidental (e.g., running into someone while turning a corner) from more intentional and deliberate aggression (e.g., approaching, confronting, and knocking an enemy to the ground).

In a review of the literature on aggression, Geen (1990) offered a tridimensional definition of aggression. The first component is the widely used definition of aggression given by Buss (1961, p. 1): Aggression is "a response that delivers noxious stimuli to another organism. " Second, the noxious stimuli are delivered with the intent to harm the victim. Third, the aggressor expects that the noxious stimuli will have their desired effects. This definition takes into account the distinction originally made by Feshbach (1964) between "hostile" aggression, where aggressive behavior is enacted to do harm, and "instrumental" aggression, where the purpose is to obtain some object or goal in the absence of anger. Since Geen's second and third components of aggression are largely similar, we combined these latter two aspects into our clause on intent.

The relationship between anger and aggression is unclear. However, many therapists and researchers assume the two are inextricably linked (Tavris, 1989). One way to reduce this confusion is avoid definitional overlap between anger and aggression. One can be angry and not be aggressive, and one could be aggressive and not angry. Patients who seek treatment for beating their spouse because they "just lost it," or "couldn't take it any more" are angry and aggressive. The court-referred sociopath is an example of the "instrumental aggression" without anger. The individual who comes to treatment because of pent up, unexpressed anger would be an example of the anger without aggression.

We find it useful to distinguish *behavioral* from *verbal* aggression. According to our definition, behavioral aggression is an observable, overt action designed to harm someone or something. Although this is straightforward, the issue of verbal aggression is another matter. We define verbal aggression in terms of the content of the statement and the intent of the speaker, rather than the emotional or behavioral consequences of the receiver of the remark. For example, a man who angrily yells at his wife shouting curses, threats, and personal attacks in the absence of behavioral aggression is exhibiting verbal aggression regardless of his wife's perception of these comments. Certainly, many women would respond with fear, anxiety, and confusion after receiving these comments, but it is by no means a linear relationship between the sender's verbal aggression and the receiver's emotional consequences. Other women may respond with apathy or disgust in the absence of fear or anxiety, or may respond with an even more heated verbal volley.

The importance of this definition is highlighted when a statement intended by the sender to be non-valuative is constructed by the target as being aggressive. Thus, *any* statement has the ability to be labeled as aggressive if the receiver deems it so, which limits precision and adds unnecessary confusion. Because of this possibility, we regard the consequences of the statement to be irrelevant. Thus, in accordance with cognitive theories of emotion (e.g., Ellis, 1962, Beck, 1976; Lazarus, 1991), our definition of verbal aggression focuses on the intent of the statement instead of the effects of the statement.

Hostility. Hostility is defined as a personality trait evidenced by cross-situational patterns of angry affect in combination with verbal or behavioral aggression. The term hostility is often considered interchangeable with aggression or anger, and is rarely explicitly defined. Our definition emphasizes a personality style evidenced in a number of situations that is not stimulus bound. This is consistent with research that examined the relationship between hostility and physical health. While different researchers have varying views on hostility, the common theme is a pervasive, chronic display of angry affect and aggressive behaviors. Our definition is similar to Spielberger's (1988) notion of trait anger, defined as "the disposition to perceive a wide range of situations as annoying or frustrating, and the tendency to respond to such situations with more frequent elevations in state anger" (p. 1). Last, we would note that the concept of hostility also refers to some action in addition to the angry affect. For this reason we have included a behavioral or verbal aggression requirement.

The vagueness of the term "hostility" as well as its association with other phenomena (i.e., anger, aggression, disgust, cynicism, type A behavior, etc.), have led to many definitions. Spielberger and his colleagues (Spielberger, 1988; Spielberger, Jacobs, Russell, and Crane, 1983) emphasized the multifarious nature of hostility, defining it as a "complex set of feelings and attitudes that motivate aggressive and often vindictive behavior" (Spielberger, 1988, p. 6). A similar theme is Barefoot's (1992), who organized the facets of hostility into cognitive (negative attributions about others' actions), affective (ANS activation), and behavioral (physical aggression) components. Although these definitions differ in specificity, both highlight research data demonstrating the complex multivariate nature of hostility.

Research investigating the relationship between hostility and health typically assess hostility using structured interview (SI) methods rather than self-report. An example of this assessment method that sheds light on current conceptions of hostility is the Interpersonal Hostility Assessment Technique (IHAT; Barefoot, 1992), which assesses stylistic variables associated with type A behavior patterns. As the investigator can only assess hostility in the clinical interview, the assumption is made that "hostile" individuals are just as hostile in the interview as they are in other domains of their life. Thus, the IHAT measures subject's response styles such as Hostile withhold/evade (failing to answer interviewer question due to uncooperative manner), Direct challenge (openly confronting and contradicting the interviewer), Indirect challenge (interviewee answers the question in a manner suggesting the question was trivial), and Irritation (evidence of arousal in subject's voice). The total score of this SI significantly correlated with the severity of heart disease, although the subscale for Indirect Challenge had the highest correlation with disease severity (Barefoot, 1992). Again, the implication is that hostility is more than just angry affect, and more than a discrete aggressive episode. It is cross-situational and multivariate, including an affective, attitudinal, and behavioral dimension.

By explicitly defining these three constructs and their variations, we hope to provide a guideline for future clinical research in this long-neglected area. The question nevertheless remains as to what makes the occurrence of anger, aggression, hostility, or any combination thereof clinically significant? Ethnic groups may differ in the extent to which they experience these reactions and such research is important. By setting such definitions we are also in a position to see when cultural groups present emotional experience that diverge from these definitions. With these definitions we have nothing to contrast the emotions of other cultural and linguistic groups.

A MODEST PROPOSAL

Given these definitions, and the demonstrated ill-effects of anger, aggression, and hostility, we proposed a formal diagnostic category for chronic and debilitating anger and hostility.

CRITERIA FOR A GENERAL ANGER/HOSTILITY DISORDER

A. Excessive and intense feelings of anger for a period of 6 months or longer, during which the person experiences angry episodes more days than not in response to any of the following perceived or actual:

(1) insult, rejection, criticism or threat
(2) stressful life events
(3) minor daily hassles
(4) frustration in attempt to achieve one's goals
(5) physical discomfort

B. The degree of anger expressed is out of proportion to the cultural norm for the precipitating stressor(s).

C. The disturbance does not occur only during the course of a psychotic disorder or intoxication.

D. It cannot be established that an organic factor initiated or maintains the disturbance.

E. The disturbance in A and B significantly interferes with work, social activities or relationships with others (e.g., individuals may avoid contact with the patient or avoid actions that may elicit an angry response; the patient may later express confusion or regret about the consequences of an angry outburst).

F. At least two of the following symptoms are present when angry.

G. *Awareness of physiological arousal:*
    (1) accelerated heart rate
    (2) flushes (hot flashes)
    (3) muscle tension
    (4) trembling in the hands
    (5) rapid breathing
    (6) stomach pains or nausea

H. *Cognitions:*
    (7) demands that ones desires be met
    (8) belief that ones angry outbursts are an effective means of controlling others
    (9) the belief that an angry response is justified due to others behavior
    (10) racing thoughts
    (11) difficulties concentrating on things other than the target of anger
    (12) beliefs that one is being treated unfairly
    (13) blaming of others or putting down of others

I. *Behaviors:*
    (14) yelling or screaming
    (15) verbal threats or insults
    (16) assaultive gestures
    (17) seeking out confrontation
    (18) assaultive acts
    (19) destruction of property
    (20) passively blocks the path of the target of the anger

If the person meets all the criteria they receive the diagnosis. If they meet all the criteria but I, they are diagnosed as *ANGER DISORDER WITHOUT AGGRESSION.*

The frequency of days with anger episodes was chosen as a result of a limited sample of our patients. It was not unusual to have patients who reported feeling angry every day in our sample. Research is needed to assess how frequently disturbed individuals experience anger so that a cut off can be set based on empirical data.

It is important to note that one can not receive the diagnosis of anger disorder if the anger occurs while under the influence of alcohol or others drugs, for then substance abuse or dependence would be the primary diagnosis. Also, one would not receive the diagnosis if the anger outburst were the result ᵓf neurological impairment.

Professioɾáɪs also need to be sensitive to cultural issues in assigning this diagnosis. For this reason we do not wish to include any criteria of the disorder that represent atypical eliciting stimuli of nondisturbed angry reactions. A person that has a nondisturbed, limited angry reaction to stimuli that few people in the main stream society consider as an appropriate stimulus for anger would not meet the criteria.

The criteria specifically state that the anger is an overreaction and excessive as defined by the patient's cultural group. We have struggled with two cross-cultural issues in proposing these criteria. Should anger and aggression be considered a nondisturbed reaction if the individual's cultural referent group defines the emotion or behavior as normal, but the behavior harms another or the emotion of anger harms the individual. For example, if a man uses aggression to coerce his wife to comply with his commands and the cultural group considers this acceptable, is the behavior disturbed? We would answer yes. Although the behavior may not be considered disturbed by the mainstream culture, it my be considered disturbed by the wives who fail to speak up because they fear reprisals. We propose that the continued use of aggression to coerce others into an imbalanced social contract is disturbed. The continued anger and aggression necessary to enforce imbalanced contracts are dysfunctional and will eventually deplete the aggressor of resources and energy. We recognize that this may be a controversial position. Such controversy is necessary in a muticultural environment to foster debate on when anger and aggression should be treated by mental health professional.

Another question concerns the sustained anger, hostility and suppressed anger directed towards a truly oppressive social system or individual. Are there situations where an individual or group has been wronged where sustained anger is functional and not being angry is to accept and condone the transgressions against oneself or one's group? We believe that it is precisely the belief by therapist and political activists that anger is the appropriate reaction to real institutionalized or individual oppression that has clouded the definition of anger. We believe that sustained, high anger can be a disturbed. Because the anger usually does not lead to adaptive responses to end the oppression. In the words of Don Corleone in the film "The Godfather" never be angry at your enemies, it clouds your judgment. However, to have a neutral or positive emotion in such situations is also disturbed. The problem here is one of too few scripts for the prototype angry emotions. There are appropriate nondisturbed negative emotions which involve sustained dedication to end the oppression without excessive physiological arousal, impulsive retaliation, and functional behavior to end the oppression. The dedicated resolve and indignation of Martin Luther King, Jr. to end racial prejudice is a model of such a script.

Research is needed to assess the inter-clinician reliability as well as the construct and discriminative validity of this proposed diagnostic category. However, we believe that such a diagnosis requires tremendous treatment utility. We have already devised self-report and structured interview assessment devises based on these criteria (DiGiuseppe, Eckhardt, Tafrate, & Robin, 1993). Careful assessment of all the areas mentioned in the criteria has led to uncovering many more specific incidence of violent behavior and anger emotional arousal than we had before with our angry patients. It appears to us that angry patients are often less forthcoming in revealing their emotions and behaviors. Structured comprehensive assessment of anger, hostility, and aggression appears necessary for adequate treatment planning.

INTERVENTIONS WITH ANGER

Another indication of the avoidance of anger by the mental health community is the small amount of psychotherapy outcome research on anger. Compared to depression and anxiety there is less research to guide clinical services. The research which does exist suggests that anger can be treated successfully.

We recently completed a meta-analytic review of anger outcome studies (DiGiuseppe, Eckhardt, & Tafrate, 1993). What is most notable besides the small number of outcome studies on anger, was the lack of representation of many popular psychotherapies. There were no studies assessing the efficacy of rational emotive therapy, cognitive therapy, family therapy, psychoanalytic therapy, experiential therapy, or client centered therapy for treating anger problems. Thus we know little or nothing about the effectiveness of many of the most frequently used orientations employed by practitioners to treat anger.

Most of the studies employed college students and there was no indication that the subjects experienced anger that was sufficient enough to be considered a clinical problem. The representativeness of the research samples to actual patients with clinically significant anger problems is questioned.

The Problem of the Therapeutic Alliance

The volunteer subjects in the existing studies on anger are unrepresentative of clients who actually present for treatment with anger. Angry people often do not seek treatment, they seek supervision. Most angry clients want help changing the target of their anger. They are sometimes forced into treatment. Such clients do not generally seek treatment with the goal of changing their angry response to a healthier one. Spouses, courts, or employee assistance programs usually instigate the referral. As a result we have experienced difficulty formulating a therapeutic alliance with angry clients (DiGiuseppe, 1991; Ellis, 1977). Our conversations with other therapists who treat angry patients lead us to believe that failure to obtain a therapeutic alliance with such patients is common.

Research and theory needs to explore the nature of the therapeutic alliance with angry clients and proposes why the problem of formulating a therapeutic alliance might exist for this emotional disorder more than for others. Bordin (1976) proposed that a successful therapeutic alliance includes three elements: (1) agreement between the therapist and client on the goals of therapy; (2) agreement on the tasks of therapy; and (3) the bond — a warm, accepting, trusting relationship. We propose that clients who come to therapy for anger are less likely to reach agreement on the goals of therapy than clients with other emotional problems.

DiGiuseppe (1991) and Ellis (1977) have suggested that the cognitions associated with anger may be instrumental in preventing the development of the therapeutic alliance. Specifically these beliefs may interfere with reaching an agreement on the goal to change one's anger. These factors include:

1. *Anger is Justified and appropriate* — Angry clients may not experience their emotions as deviant because they cling to emotional scripts that sanction the emotion. This may occur because they have not been socialized to alternative scripts, their subculture does not have sufficient scripts or they fail to evaluate their scripts as deviant.

2. *Emotional responsibility and other blame* — Angry people often fail to take responsibility for their emotions and assign responsibility for emotions to external events. It is common to hear angry clients report, "He (She or It) made me angry." As long as the cause of anger lies outside of themselves they are unlikely to act to change it. Since someone else is responsible by behaving badly, that other person needs to change. Even if they perceive their emotion as deviant they will not take steps to manage the emotions if they believe emotions are externally controlled.

3. *Other condemnation* — Anger usually involves the cognition that the target of one's anger is a totally worthless human being. Since the target

of their anger is such a worthless condemnable individual they deserve the
wrath and must pay for their transgression. The worthless individual is perceived as deserving of the anger outburst or at least of contempt.

4. *Self-righteousness* — Angry patients usually report believing that
they have been treated unfairly. The transgressor is portrayed as morally
wrong while the patient sees him/her self as the aggrieved party. Self-righteousness leads one to believe that justice and God are on his or her side.

5. *Cathartic expression* — Most angry clients maintain the belief that
one must let out their anger. Our American culture seems to promote a
hydraulic model of anger along with the notion that it must be dissipated
or it will build up and explode. Clients believe that holding it their anger
will eventually lead to greater anger outbursts and that anger expression
is healthy and necessary.

6. *Short-term reinforcement* — Patients are often temporarily reinforced for their temper tantrums by the compliance of significant others
with their requests. These rewards appear to be offset by the negative consequences of using coercive processes in a relationship. While significant
others often comply, they remain resentful, bitter, and distant. The angry
party seems unaware of the negative effect the anger has on their interpersonal relationships. The attention to the short-term reinforcement of
one's behavior and the ignoring of long-term consequences of the same
behavior is a common human foible and is referred to as a social trap.

In our experience angry individuals seek mental health consultation
desiring help in changing others. In therapy supervision, we often have
found therapists working to change their clients' anger, while the clients
are working to change the person at whom they are angry. The clients fail
to agree to change their anger because they do not recognize that it is
problematic to them. They may believe that they are justified and it is appropriate to feel anger, or they may not believe that any other emotional
reaction would be appropriate to the event. Therapists and clients clash
because they disagree on the goal of intervention. The therapist desires to
change the emotion while the patient desires revenge, condemnation or
change in the transgressor.

Therapists' attempts to change the patient's anger may be perceived
by the patient as indicating that the therapist does believe that the transgressor is responsible for the problem, or that the therapist does not agree
that the patient was aggrieved, or that the therapist does not believe the
transgressor was wrong (Walen, DiGiuseppe, & Dryden, 1992). Patients
may experience attempts to change their anger as invalidating their moral
outrage against the offender or as disagreement by the therapist with their
moral standard.

Prochaska and DiClemete (1988) have investigated the process of change both inside and outside psychotherapy. They recently identified five stages of attitudes people have about change: the pre-contemplative stage; the contemplative stage; the readiness stage; the action stage and the maintenance stage (Prochaska, DiClemente, & Norcross, 1992). Most consumers of psychotherapy arrive for treatment in the contemplative stage or the action stage. That is they are thinking that they should change and wish to explore the possibility, or they have decided to change. Using Prochaska and DiClemente's scheme, it appears that most angry clients arrive for therapy in the pre-contemplative stage. They want to change others who make them angry. I would predict that research using Prochaska and DiClemente's stages of change measure would provide evidence for our hypothesis that most angry clients have not reached the decision to change when they arrive for therapy. Prochaska and DiClemete suggest that clients in the precontemplative stage of change, may not respond to active directive therapeutic procedures. They suggest one utilize strategies that focus on self-awareness instead.

To help the client focus on the goal of changing their destructive anger it may be first necessary to acknowledge and validate their frustration and disappointment at the hands of their enemy. Even then, however, changing the anger may not become a goal for patients until they gain self-awareness and reach two insights. First, they understand that their present emotion, i.e., anger, is dysfunctional. Second, they can conceptualize an alternative emotion reaction that is socially and personally acceptable to them. I believe that these two insights are prerequisites to formulating a therapeutic alliance for any problem. However, such insights are usually reached quite readily by anxious or depressed clients, often before they arrive at therapy. In such instances these insights may even be the motivator to seek treatment.

Distinguishing Types of Anger. Ellis' rational emotive theory posits (Ellis, 1989; Ellis & DiGiuseppe, in press; Walen, DiGiuseppe, Dryden, 1992) that people may fail to target any emotion for change because of the common lack of semantic precision in affective expression. Anger is a particular problem in this regard. Colloquial American use of the word anger includes a wide range of affective states with numerous behavioral responses. The English language makes the distinction between the distressed emotion of depression and the experience of sadness. Also, anxiety, which is a response to imagined threat, is differentiated from fear, which is a reaction to real threat. While other standard English words may fall in the same arena as anger, such as annoyance and irritated, they are not commonly used. I propose that the lack of common usage of a nondisturbed affect word in the anger arena prevents people from distinguishing between disturbed and nondisturbed experiences. Clients initial reactions to the suggestion that they change their anger is often shock or disbelief. One recent client responded to the suggestion that he target his anger for change with surprise. He readily admitted that he never considered not feeling angry because he did not know what other emotional reaction he might experience instead.

Most patients and therapists would consider anger as varying along one quantitative continuum. Rational emotive theory maintains that emotions differ not only on a quantitative continuum. It posits that adaptive and maladaptive variants of each emotion exist that differ qualitatively as well. As Izard (1989) has pointed out emotions differ in phenomenological experience, social expression, behavioral predisposition, and physiologic arousal. Of these only physiological arousal is a quantitative continuum.

To accept one's anger as a target for mental health intervention requires that one recognize at least two different anger related emotional alternatives. The first, adaptive nondisturbed anger (or what Ellis, 1977 refers to as annoyance), would have several components. Cognitively, it would acknowledge that the person was aggrieved and that the transgressor's action was wrong. It would include an experiential negative affect along a continuum in the anger arena. It could lead to clear assertive communications by the aggrieved party communicating his/her feelings and desires. It would lead to any other adaptive behavior that would avoid victimization in the future. If no adaptive behavior was readily available in the persons repertoire, this emotion might initiate problem solving activities to consider and evaluate new responses. Also, this state would not lead to the unnecessary disruption of the person's functioning. Such an emotion may have moderate but not excessive affective arousal.

The second type of anger, dysfunctional, or clinical anger, would lead to a more painful phenomenlogical experience. It would include a more intense hostile and attacking form of social expression, which might cause more long-term problems. It may interfere with problem solving and restrict consideration of more adaptive behavior that would avoid victimization in the future. Finally, it would lead to disturbed affect and rumination which greatly interferes with the individual's functioning. In regards to Hochschild (1983) sociological model presented above, these two scripts for anger differ in several perceptual or cognitive aspects.

Some support for the view that people can distinguish between disturbed clinical anger and nonclinical, functional annoyance types of anger comes from Averill (1983). His data suggests that people view anger as a more intense emotional experience than annoyance and they also view anger as a more serious or inappropriate emotional reaction.

The rational emotive theory of emotions is similar to the script theories of emotions mentioned above. Discussions of the script concept with angry clients usually results in several themes. First, they usually defend their angry script and report that it is necessary to attack all transgressors or they will be overwhelmed by them. Second, they often insist that it is important to express anger to avoid the negative health consequences that accompany anger suppression. It seems to us that our culture has limited scripts for anger. These common American cultural scripts usually incorporate an instinctual link between anger and aggression and they stress the importance of cathartic release of anger. We propose anger and its treatment will be better understood if researchers investigate the common scripts people hold concerning anger, how these scripts relate to adaptive behavior, and how scripts relate to labeling anger as a problem.

CULTURE, FAMILIES, AND EMOTIONAL SCRIPTS

Cross-cultural considerations appear most important in helping build such a therapeutic alliance when working with clients with anger problems. Different cultural groups may have quite different scripts concerning whether or not anger is acceptable or socially sanctioned. The development of a nondisturbed, functional alternative emotion such as annoyance may depend on the availability of such a script in the culture and its having been modeled in the family. Over the years two of us (RD & MR) have had considerable experience training therapists in RET throughout the world. From this experience it has become clear that therapists from different cultural groups have varying difficulty accepting Ellis' notion of both disturbed and nondisturbed versions of emotions. Those from English speaking countries have difficulty understanding the difference between disturbed anger and nondisturbed annoyance. It is not that the English language does not have alternative words for anger type emotions. Rather it appears the term anger is used very indiscriminately. One can use the word anger to reflect a range of emotions form the mildest irritation to homicidal rage. Therapists from Spanish speaking countries on the other hand seem to grasp the distinction easily. They report that their language commonly uses words similar to English to express disturbed variations of anger such as "rabio" and "furioso." These words are used much more precisely in Spanish. Israeli therapists seemed to have the greatest difficulty attempting to apply Ellis' distinction in their language. They claimed that there was only one commonly used word for what we call anger which literally translates as, "I am nervous at you." Not surprisingly, they reported difficulty helping clients to accept the goal of changing their anger and had few culturally accepted scripts to replace dysfunctional anger.

The existence of vocabulary words to make distinctions between emotional scripts does not appear to be sufficient to determine the availability of scripts. Instead, it would appear to be the frequency with which such distinctions are made in the language, and the fact that different words actually represent different scripts rather than represent a synonym for the same script, that influence the availability of alternative emotional scripts. The more that different words are used to describe emotional alternatives to similar events the more these alternative words would be accessed in the culture.

It follows that cultures, subcultures, or linguistic groups whose language does not often access different emotional words for the same situation will have fewer emotional scripts. The fewer alternative emotional scripts that can be accessed by a vocabulary word, the more difficulty people in that group will have with that emotion. Simply stated, the lack of acceptable, socially sanctioned emotional scripts leads to inflexibility of responses. This hypothesis can be tested by cross-cultural research which attends to the emotional scripts and the vocabulary used to express them in various cultures.

Cultural scripts for anger are likely to differ by gender. Many propose gender-specific patterns of anger expression and inhibition (see Tavris, 1989, 1991). Biological arguments suggest that since infra-human males tend to be more aggressive so too are human males. Another view suggests that men and women are equally capable of anger expression, but our male-dominated society inhibits female anger expression. Averill's (1983) data showed that men and women experience and express anger at a similar frequency, with similar intensity, and for similar reasons. The only gender difference was that when angry, women reported crying significantly more than did men.

Cultures and their languages may vary greatly on the distinctions they make between affective states. Therapists need to be aware of how the emotional script for anger (or any other emotional state) is valued in a patient's culture or subculture and what alternative scripts are available from that culture. If the patient's cultural, subculture, or family group has no alternative script for a functional emotional response the therapists will have to attempt to build a scheme for them.

In our experience families may have idiosyncratic scripts that may differ from their culture. Most often we find that families with anger problems have too few emotional scripts. Family members fail to make distinctions between various reactions they can have to events. Perhaps because only one emotional script has been modeled clients will behave rigidly with the same emotional reaction. This lack of flexibility will result in dysfunctional family interactions.

Building an Alliance

To help deal with these problems the following strategies are suggested:

1. *Assess the clients goals* — The therapist needs to clearly assess whether angry clients have as their goal a change in their anger. Failure to closely attend to the issue of agreement on the therapeutic goals will clearly lead to an alliance rupture.

2. *Agree on a goal to explore* — If the client does not wish to change their anger and the therapist believes that anger is a problem the therapist may seek an agreement that they spend some time reviewing the functionality and adaptiveness of the client's anger.

3. *Explore the consequences on the anger* — The therapists can lead clients, by Socratic dialogue, through an analysis of the consequences of their anger. Clients are likely to focus on the immediate consequences of their anger rather than the longer term social consequences. Thus a client might focus on the consequence that s/he ventilated their feeling or succeeded in getting someone to comply with his/her rules, but avoid the fact that they seriously damaged the relationship. Frequently, clients lack empathy on how their anger effects others. It is helpful for them to recount how they feel when others are angry at them and use this to imagine how significant others feel when the client gets angry. This stage of therapy may take a while. However, we suggest that the therapist continue for as long as the client agrees or until the client appears to have some insight into the dysfunctional nature of his/ her anger.

4. *Explore alternative scripts* — Once the client agrees that it is in his/her best interest to change their anger, they still can be thwarted because they may not know what to replace it with. They may have a limited scheme or scripts to apply to the situation or alternative scripts may be considered socially inappropriate to the individual's status in their group. Helping the client generate alternative scripts is similar to generating alternative solutions in the problem solving model of adjustment (Spivack, Platt, & Shure, 1976). This can often be achieved by having the client recall the successful reactions of others whom they respect. This helps to generate a model for an alternative script. Clients from very dysfunctional families may have few such models. The therapist may have to suggest models from the general culture or from the literature, folklore, or film of the clients culture. After a model is chosen for an alternative script, it is important to review the consequences of the model's behavior following the script. Next, the client is asked to imagine that they react in the same manner as the script and imagine that the consequences happen to them. In this way the client can provide information on how they believe the script may not

be socially or personally acceptable to a person in their situation. This process is repeated until the client accepts the alternative emotional script.

Once the therapist and client have successfully accomplished these steps the therapist can continue with the treatment of the client's anger. The therapist is free to implement any strategy s/he and the client mutually agree upon. The strategy suggested above helps motivate the client to continue with therapy. We often find it helpful to quickly review the steps at the beginning of each session or the initiation of a discussion on a new anger arousing event. After a client reports a new situation which they felt angry about, the therapist might respond:

> OK, Jack you said that your typical angry reaction usually backfires on you and causes more problems in the long run. Do you think you can respond with the new alternative emotional response you thought would be more helpful in this situation.

By reviewing these steps it is hoped that the client is motivated to keep working at anger control. The review can also be considered a restatement of the therapeutic alliance.

REFERENCES

Abelson, R. (1981). The psychological status of script concepts. *American Psychologist, 36*, 715-729.
Achenbach, T., McCanaughy, S., & Howell, C. (1987). Child/adolescent behavioral and emotional problems: Implications of cross informant correlates for situation specificity. *Psychological Bulletin, 101*, 192-212.
American Psychiatric Association (1987). *Diagnostic and Statistical Manual* (3rd ed.), Washington, D.C.: Author.
Averill, J. A. (1982). *Anger and aggression: An essay on emotion.* New York: Springer/Verlag.
Averill, J. A. (1983). Studies on anger and Aggression: Implications for theories on emotion. *American Psychologist, 38*, 1145-1160.
Bandura, A. (1973). *Aggression: A social learning analysis.* Englewood Cliffs, NJ: Prentice Hall.
Barefoot, J. C. (1992). Developments in the measure of hostility. In H. S. Friedman (Ed.), *Hostility, coping, and health.* Washington, D.C.: American Psychological Association.
Barlow, D., Rapee, R. M., & Brown, T. A. (1992). Behavioral treatment of generalized anxiety disorder. *Behavior Therapy, 23*, 551-570.
Beck, A. T. (1976). *Cognitive therapy and the emotional disorders.* New York: International Universities Press.
Berk, R. A., Berk, S. F., Loseke, D. R., & Rauma, D. (1983). *Mutual combat and other family violence myths, in the dark side of families: Current family violence research.* In D. Finkelhor, R. J. Gelles, G. T. Hotaling, & M. A. Straus (Eds.), Beverly Hills: Sage.
Berkowitz, L. (1989). Frustration-aggression hypothesis. *Psychological Bulletin, 106*, 59-73.
Berkowitz, L. (1990). On the formulation and regulation of anger and aggression: A cognitive-neoassociationistic analysis. *American Psychologist, 45*, 494-503.
Biaggio, M. K. (1980). Assessment of anger arousal. *Journal of Personality Assessment, 44*, 289-298.
Biaggio, M. K., Supplee, K., & Curtis, N. (1981). Reliability and validity of four anger scales. *Journal of Personality Assessment, 45*, 639-648.
Blashfield, R., Sprock, J., & Fuller, K. (1990). Suggested guidelines for including or excluding categories in the DSM IV. *Comprehensive Psychiatry, 31*, 15-19.

Bordin, E. S. (1975). The generalizability of the psychoanalytic concept of the working alliance. *Psychotherapy: Theory, Research, and Practice, 16,* 252-260.

Burman, B., Margolin, G., & John, R. S. (1993). America's angriest home videos: Behavioral contingencies observed in home reenactment of marital conflict. *Journal of Consulting and Clinical Psychology, 61,* 28-39.

Buss, A. H. (1961). *The psychology of aggression.* New York: Wiley.

Buss, A. H., & Durkee, A. (1957). The inventory for assessing different kinds of hostility. *Journal of Consulting Psychology, 21,* 343-349.

Caplan, P. (1991). Delusional dominating personality disorder. *Feminism & Psychology, 1,* 171-174.

Chesney, M. A. (1985). Anger and hostility: Future implications for behavioral medicine. In M. A. Chesney & R. H. Rosenman (Eds.), *Anger and hostility in behavioral disorders.* Washington, D.C. Hemisphere.

Clark, K. B. (1965). *Dark ghetto.* New York: Harper Tourch.

Costa, P. T., & McCrae, R. R. (1992). *Manual for the NEO personality Inventory* (rev. ed.). Odessa, FL: Psychological Assessment Resources.

Cotton, P. (1992). Gun-associated violence increasingly viewed as a public health challenge. *Journal of the American Medical Association, 267,* 1171-1174.

Darwin, C. (1965). *The expression of emotion in man and animals.* Chicago: University of Chicago Press (Original work published 1872).

Deffenbacher, J. L., & Stark, R. S. (1992). Relaxation and cognitive-relaxation treatments of general anger. *Journal of Counseling Psychology, 39,* 158-167.

Dembroski, T. M., & MacDougall J. M. (1985). Beyond global Type A: Relationship of paralinguistic attributes, hostility,. and anger-in to coronary heart disease. In T. Field, P. McAbe & N. Schneiderman (Eds.), *Stress and coping.* Hillside, NJ: Erlbaum.

Dembroski, T. M., MacDougall, J. M., Costa, P. T., & Grandits, G. A. (1989). Components of hostility as predictors of sudden death and myocardial infarction in the Multiple Risk Factor Invention Trial. *Psychosomatic Medicine, 51,* 514-522.

de Sousa, R. (1980). The rationality of emotions. In A. O. Rorty (Ed.), *Explaining emotions* (pp. 127-152). Berkeley, CA: University of California Press.

Diamond, E. (1982). The role of anger and hostility in essential hypertension and coronary heart disease. *Psychological Bulletin, 92,* 410-433.

Diamond, E. L., Schneiderman, N., Schwartz, D., Smith, J. C., Vorp, R., & Pasin, R. D. (1984).

Harassment, hostility, and type A as determinants of cardiovascular reactivity during competition. *Journal of Behavioral Medicine, 7,* 171-189.

DiGiuseppe, R. (1991). (Speaker) *What do I do with my anger.* New York: Institute for Rational Emotive Therapy.

Dimsdale (1986). Suppressed anger and blood pressure. *Psychosomatic Medicine, 48*(6), 430-436.

Dollard, J., Doob, L., Miller, N., Mowrer, O., & Sears, R. (1939). *Frustration and aggression.* New Haven, CT: Yale University Press.

Durel, L., Carver, C., Spitzer, S., Llabre, M., Kumari-Weintraub, J., Saab, P., & Sherwood, A. (1989). Associations of blood pressure with self report measures of anger and hostility among black and white men and women. *Health Psychology, 8*(5), 557-576.

Eibl-Eibesfeldt, I. (1971). *Love and hate: The natural history of behavior patterns.* New York: Holt, Rinehart, & Winston.

Ekman, P. (1974). Universal facial expression of emotions. In R. LeVine (Ed.), *Culture and personality: Contemporary readings* (pp. 38-15). Chicago: Aldine.

Ellis, A. (1962). *Reason and emotion in psychotherapy.* New York: Citadel Press.

Ellis, A. (1977). *How to live with and without anger.* New York: Readers' Digest Press.

Ellis, A. (1989). Comments on my critics. In M. Bernard & R. DiGiuseppe (Eds.) *Inside rational emotive therapy: A critical appraisal of the theory and therapy of Albert Ellis.* Orlando, FL: Academic Press.

Ellis, A., & DiGiuseppe, R. (in press). Are inappropriate or appropriate feelings in RET qualitative or quantitative: A response to Craemerf and Fong. *Cognitive Therapy and Research.*

Endler, N. S., & Hunt, J. M. (1968). S-R inventories of hostility and comparisons of the proportions of variance from persons, responses, and situations for hostility and anxiousness. *Journal of Personality and Social Psychology, 2,* 309-315.

Engebretson, T. O., Matthews, K. A., & Scheier, M. F. (1989). Relations between anger expression and cardiovascular reactivity: Reconciling inconsistent findings through a matching hypothesis. *Journal of Personality and Social Psychology, 57,* 513-521.

Evans, D. R., & Strangaland, M. (1971). Development of the Reaction Inventory to measure anger. *Psychological Reports, 29,* 412-414.

Fava, M., Anderson, K., & Rosenbaum, J. (1990). "Anger attacks": Possible variants of panic and major depressive disorder. *American Journal of Psychiatry, 147,* 867-870.

Fehr, B., & Russell, J. (1984). Concepts of emotions viewed from a prototype perspective. *Journal of Experimental Psychology: General, 113,* 464-486.

Feindler, E. (1991). Cognitive strategies in anger control interventions for children and adolescents. In P. Kendall (Ed.), *Child and adolescent therapy: Cognitive behavioral procedures.* New York: Guilford.

Feshbach, S. (1964). The function aggression and the regulation of aggressive drive. *Psychological Review, 71,* 257-272.

Forehand, R., & McMahon, R. J. (1981). *Helping the noncompliant child: A clinician's guide to parent training.* New York: Guilford.

Freud, S. (1920). *A general introduction to psychoanalysis* (translated by G. S. Hall). New York: Boni and Liveright.

Friedman, M., & Rosenman, R. H. (1959). Association of specific overt behavior pattern with blood and cardiovascular findings. *Journal of the American Medical Association, 162,* 1286-1296.

Geen, T. (1990). *Human aggression.* Pacific Grove, CA: Brooks/Cole.

Gellen, M. I., Hoffman, R. A., Jones, M., & Stone, M. (1984). Abused and non-abused women: MMPI profile differences. *Personnel and Guidance Journal, 62,* 109-119.

Gentry, W. D. (1972). Biracial aggression: I. effects of verbal attack and sex of victim. *Journal of Social Psychology, 88,* 75-82.

Goldstein, D., & Rosenbaum, A. (1985). An evaluation of the self-esteem of maritally violent men. *Family Relations, 34,* 425-428.

Grier, W. H., & Cobb, P. M. (1969). *Black rage.* New York: Bantam.

Haynes, S. G., Feinleib, M., & Kannel, W. B. (1980). The relationship of psychosocial factors to coronary heart disease in the Framingham study. Part III: Eight-year incidence of CHD. *American Journal of Epidemiology, 3,* 37-58.

Hochschild, A. R. (1979). Emotion work, feeling rules and social structure. *American Journal of Sociology, 85,* 551-575.

Hochschild, A. R. (1983). *The managed heart: Commercialization of human feelings.* Berkeley: University of California Press.

Holroyd, K. A., & Gorkin, L. (1983). Young adults at risk for hypertension: Effects of family history and anger management in determining responses to interpersonal conflicts. *Journal of Psychosomatic Research, 27,* 131-138.

Hecker, M., & Lunde, D. (1985). On the diagnosis and treatment of chronically hostile individuals. In M. A. Chesney & R. H. Rosenman (Eds.), *Anger and hostility in cardiovascular and behavioral disorders.* Washington, D.C.: Hemisphere.

Imber, S. D., Pilkonis, P. A., Sotsky, S. M., Elkin, I., Watkins, J. T., Collins, J. F., Shea, M. T., Leber, W. R., & Glass, D. R. (1989). Mode-specific effects among three treatments for depression. *Journal of Consulting and Clinical Psychology, 58,* 352-359.

Izard, C. (1977). *Human emotions.* New York: Plenum.

Johnson, E. H. (1984). *Anger and Anxiety as Determinants of Elevated Blood Pressure in adolescents: The Tampa Study.* Unpublished doctoral dissertation, University of South Florida, Tampa, FL.

Kannel, W. B., Schwartz, M. J., & McNamara, P. M. (1969). Blood pressure and risk of coronary heart disease: The Framingham study. *Diseases of the Chest, 56,* 43-52.

Kazdin, A. (1987). *Conduct disorders in childhood and adolescents.* Beverly Hills, CA: Sage.

Kellerman, A. L., & Mercy, J. A. (1992). Men, women, and murder: Gender-specific differences in rates of fatal violence and victimization. *Journal of Trauma, 33,* 1-5.

Kemper, T. (1991). An introduction to the sociology of emotions. In K. T. Strongman (Ed.), *International review of studies of emotion* (pp. 301-349). New York: Wiley.

Kemper, T. D. (1978). *A social interaction theory of emotions.* New York: Wiley.

Kemper, T. D., & Collins, R. (1990). Dimensions of microinteractions. *American Journal of Sociology, 96,* 32-98.

Kendall, P. C., Kortlander, E., Chansky, T. E., & Brady, E. U. (1992). Comorbidity of anxiety and depression in youth: Treatment implications. *Journal of Consulting and Clinical Psychology, 60,* 869-880.

Konecni, V. J. (1975). Annoyance, type and duration of post-annoyance activity and aggression: "The cathartic effect." *Journal of Experimental Psychology, 104,* 76-102.

Koop, C. E., & Lundberg, G. D. (1992). Violence an America: A public health emergency. *Journal of the American Medical Association, 267,* 3075-3076.

Lazarus, R. S. (1991). *Emotion and adaptation.* New York: Oxford. L'Estrange, R. (1917). *Seneca's morals.* New York: Harper & Brothers (original work published 1817).

Leaf, R., DiGiuseppe, R., Ellis, A., Mass, R., Backex, W., Wolfe, J., & Alington, D. (1990). Healthy correlates of MCMI personality disorder scales 4, 5, 6, and 7. *Journal of Personality Disorders, 4,* 312-328.

Lore, R. K., & Schultz, L. A. (1993). Control of human aggression: A comparative perspective. *American Psychologist, 48,* 16-25.

Lorenz, K. (1966). *On aggression.* New York: Harcourt, Brace & World.

MacDougall, J. M., Dembroski, T. M., & Krantz, D. S. (1981). Effects of types of challenges on pressor and heart rate responses in type A and B women. *Psychophysiology, 18,* 1-9.

Maiuro, R. D., Vitaliano, P. P., & Cahn, T. S. (1987). A brief measure for the assessment of anger and aggression. *Journal of Interpersonal Violence, 2,* 166-178.

Maiuro, R. D., Cahn, T. S., Vitaliano, P. P., Wagner, B. C., & Zegree, J. B. (1988). Anger, hostility, and depression in domestically violent versus generally assaultive men and nonviolent controls. *Journal of Consulting and Clinical Psychology, 56,* 17-23.

Margolin, G., & Wampold, B. E. (1981). Sequential analysis of conflict and accord in distressed and non-distressed marital partners. *Journal of Consulting and Clinical Psychology, 49,* 554-567.

Margolin, G., John, R. S., & Gleberman, L. (1988). Affective responses to conflictual discussions in violent and nonviolent couples. *Journal of Consulting and Clinical Psychology, 56,* 24-33.

Matthews, K., & Haynes, S. G. (1986). Type A behavior pattern and coronary risk: Update and critical evaluation. *American Journal of Epidemiology, 123,* 923-960.

Matthews, K. A., Glass, D. C., Rosenman, R. H., & Bortner, R. W. (1977). Competitive drive, pattern A, and coronary heart disease: A further analysis of some data from the Western Collaborative Group Study. *Journal of Chronic Diseases, 30,* 489-498.

McElroy, S. L., Hudson, J. I., Pope, H. G., Keck, P. E., & Aizley, H. G. (1992). The DSM III-R Impulse Control Disorders not Elsewhere Classified: Clinical characteristics and relationship to other psychiatric disorders. *American Journal of Psychiatry, 149,* 318-327.

Monatagu, A. (1976). *The nature of human aggression.* Oxford: Oxford University Press.

Nolen-Hoeksema, S. (1990). *Sex differences in depression.* Stanford, CA: Stanford University Press.

Novaco, R. W. (1975). *Anger control.* Lexington, MA: Lexington.

Novaco, R. W. (1985). Anger in its therapeutic regulation. In M. A. Chesney & R. H. Rosenman (Eds.), *Anger and hostility in cardiovascular and behavioral disorders.* Washington, D.C.: Hemisphere.

Novello, A., Shosky, S., & Froehlke, R. (1992). From the Surgeon General, U.S. Public Health Service: A medical response to violence. *Journal of the American Medical Association, 267,* 3007.

O'Leary, K. D., & Curley, A. D. (1986). Assertion and family violence: Correlates of spouse abuse. *Journal of Marital and Family Therapy, 12,* 281-289.

O'Leary, K. D., Barling, J., Arias, I., Rosenbaum, A., Malone, J., & Tyree, A. (1989). Prevalence and stability of physical aggression between spouses: A longitudinal analysis. *Journal of Consulting and Clinical Psychology, 57,* 263-268.

O'Leary, K. D., & Murphy, C. (1992). Clinical issues in the assessment of spouse abuse. In R. T. Ammerman & M. Hersen (Eds.), *Assessment of family violence.* New York: Wiley.

Olweus, D. (1979). Stability of aggressive reaction patterns in males: A review. *Psychological Bulletin, 86,* 852-875.

Patterson, G. R. (1986). Performance models for antisocial boys. *American Psychologist,* 432-444.

Patterson, G. R., DeBaryshe, B. D., & Ramsey, E. (1989). A developmental perspective on antisocial behavior. *American Psychologist, 44,* 329-335.

Peele, S. (1989). *Diseasing of America: Addiction treatment out of control.* Lexington, MA: Health.

Pincus, H. A., Frances, A., Davis, W. W., First, M. B., & Widiger, T. A. (1992). DSM-IV and new diagnostic categories: Holding the line on proliferation. *American Journal of Psychiatry, 149,* 112-117.

Prochaska, J., & DiClemente, C. (1988). *The transtheoretical approach to therapy.* Chicago: The Dorsey Press.

Prochaska, J., DiClemente, C., & Norcross, J. (1992). In search of how people change: Application to addictive behaviors. *American Psychologist, 47*(9), 1102-1115.

Rokach, A. (1987). Anger and aggression control training: Replacing attack with interaction. *Psychotherapy, 24,* 353-362.

Rosenberg, M., O'Carroll, P., & Powell, K. (1992). Let's be clear, violence is a public health problem. *Journal of the American Medical Association, 267,* 3071-3072.

Rothenberg, A. (1971). On anger. *American Journal of Psychiatry, 128,* 86-92.

Rubin, J. (1986). The emotion of anger: Some conceptual and theoretical issues. *Professional Psychology: Research and Practice, 17,* 115-124.

Sabini, J., & Silver, M. (1982). *Mortalities of everyday life.* Oxford, England: Oxford University Press.

Schmoke, K. L. (1992). A public health solution to violent crime. *Archives of Otolaryngology and Head and Neck Surgery, 118,* 575-576.

Selby, M. (1984). Assessment of violence potential using measures of anger, hostility and social desirability. *Journal of Personality Assessment, 48,* 531-544.

Seligman, M. (1975). *Helplessness: On depression, development and death.* San Francisco: Freeman and Company.

Siegal, J. M. (1985). The measurement of anger as a multidimensional construct. In M. A. Chesney & R. H. Rosenman (Eds.), *Anger and hostility in cardiovascular and behavioral disorders.* Washington, D.C.: Hemisphere.

Sigler, R. T. (1989). *Domestic violence in context: An assessment of community attitudes.* Lexington, MA: Lexington Books.

Solomon, R. (1984). Getting angry: The Jamesian theory of emotions in anthropology. In R. Shweder & R. LeVine (Ed.), *Culture theory: Essays on mind, self, and emotion* (pp. 238-255). Cambridge: Cambridge University Press.

Spielberger, C. D. (1988). *Manual for the State Trait Anger Expression Inventory.* Odessa, FL: Psychological Assessment Resources.

Spielberger, C. D. (August, 1992), *Anger/Hostility, Heart Disease and Cancer.* Paper presented at the American Psychological Association, Washington, D.C.

Spielberger, C. D., Jacobs, G. A., Russell, S., & Crane, R. S. (1983). Assessment of anger: The state-trait anger scale. In J. N. Butchner & C. D. Spielberger (Eds.), *Advances in personality assessment.* Hillside, NJ: Erlbaum.

Spielberger, C. D., Johnson, E. H., Russell, S., Crane, R. S., Jacobs, G. A., & Worden, T. J. (1985). The experience and expression of anger: Construction and validation of an anger expression scale. In M. A. Chesney & R. H. Rosenman (Eds.), *Anger and hostility in cardiovascular and behavioral disorders.* Washington, D.C.: Hemisphere.

Spivack, G., Platt, J., & Shure, M. (1976). *The problem solving approach to adjustment.* San Francisco, CA: Jossey-Bass.

Straus, M. A., & Gelles, R. J. (1986). Societal change and change in family violence from 1975 to 1985 as revealed by two national surveys. *Journal of Marriage and the Family, 48,* 465-479.

Suarez, E. C., & Williams, R. B. (1989). Situational determinants of cardiovascular and emotional reactivity in high and low hostile men. Psychosomatic Medicine, 51, 404-418.

Task Force on DSM IV (1993). *DSM IV draft criteria.* Washington, D.C.: American Psychiatric Association.

Tavris, C. (1989). Anger the misunderstood emotion (2nd ed.,). New York: Touchstone.

Tavris, C. (1992). *The mismeasure of woman.* New York Simon & Schuster.

Tomkins, S. (1979). Script theory: Differential magnification of affect. In H. E. Howe & R. A. Dienstbier (Eds.), *Nebraska symposium of motivation 1978* (pp. 201-236). Lincoln, Nebraska: University of Nebraska Press.

United States Bureau of the Census (1991). *Statistical abstract of the United States* (11th ed.). Washington, D.C.: U.S. Government Printing Office.

U.S. Department of Justice (1991). *Uniform Crime Reports, 1990.* Washington, D.C., U.S. Government Printing Office.

Walen, S., Giuseppe, R., & Dryden, W. (1992). *The practitioner's guide to rational emotive therapy* (2nd ed.), New York: Oxford University Press.

Watson, D., & Clark, L. A. (1984). Negative affectivity: The disposition to experience aversive emotional states. *Psychological Bulletin, 96,* 465-490.

Wierzbicka, A. (1992). *Semantics, culture. and cognition: Universal human concepts in culture specific configurations.* New York: Oxford University Press.

Zelin, M. L., Adler, G., & Myerson, P. G. (1972). Anger self-report: An objective questionnaire for the measurement of aggression. *Journal of Consulting and Clinical Psychology, 39,* 340.

4

Domestic Violence in African-American and African-Caribbean Families

Janet R. Brice-Baker

This article explores domestic violence, specifically spouse abuse, in African-American and African-Caribbean families in the United States. Its purpose is to review the existing literature on Black couples and violence, examine the applicability of current theories of violence to Blacks, and outline the barriers to the treatment of domestic violence in this population. The variables of institutionalized racism and internalized racism, as factors in lowering self-esteem, are examined as contributors to Black women's acceptance of mistreatment. Suggestions are made for empirical research to close the gaps in the literature.

INTRODUCTION

The prevention, assessment, and treatment of domestic violence is an overwhelming task. While the problem is an old and very widespread one it has taken years for people in the helping professions to recognize it and want to do something about it. Our ambivalence toward the subject is multifaceted. Violence of any kind is frightening and the violence between one family member and another is perhaps the most frightening. However, despite these intense feelings, over the past three decades social scientists have attempted to explain the phenomenon of domestic abuse.

In order to consolidate and expand our present knowledge base, we need to examine the lenses that we have been using to view this problem.

One very important lens is culture. Culture has not so much been ignored as limited to a reflection of the White middle class. As America continues to "brown," it becomes increasingly important to consider other cultures.

> "The programming of service delivery, the structuring of services for people, the engagement of patients and clients in the help-giving process, the degree to which people use services, the assessment and treatment of problems, and the evaluation of outcomes are all in some way influenced by cultural values and traditions" (Pinderhughes, 1989, p. 13).

This article will focus on domestic violence, specifically spouse abuse, in the African-American and African-Caribbean or West Indian cultures. Emphasis will be placed on examining the "goodness-of-fit" between existing research conclusions and theories and the reality of Black family life.

PREVALENCE

It is quite difficult to estimate the rates of spouse abuse in the African-American and African-Caribbean populations. Gelles (1980) indicates that in the majority of studies on the subject "abuse was typically defined in an operational sense as those instances in which the victim became publicly known and labeled by an official or professional" (p. 875). Economic inequity between the races results in biased statistics. Whites are more likely than Blacks to have access to private physicians who are less likely to label a woman's battered condition as abuse and, even if identified as such, to report that abuse. (It should be noted that reporting abuse only applies to children.) Several explanations may be posited for the private practitioners reluctance to intervene in cases of spouse abuse. The physician may perceive a racial and socioeconomic similarity between him/herself and the couple and therefore find it inconceivable that "someone like me" would be in this situation. He/she might fear losing patients with whom he/she has had a long relationship. The physician might also have a misguided sense that he/she can counsel the couple to improve their marriage.

Blacks are likely to use public facilities such as clinics and hospital emergency rooms for their medical care. Abuse is more likely to be suspected and noted in these places where there is less perceived similarity between the caregiver and the patient, no long-term history of association between the doctor and patient and little concern about financial loss if the patient does not return.

The prevalence of abuse in the White population is really unknown and makes comparisons between the races difficult. Abusers do not step forward unless made to by the criminal justice system. Battered women do not tell for fear of further and worse reprisals. Women do not always seek medical treatment for their injuries and that cuts down on contacts with professional who may he able to help and keep some type of record of the event. Finally, there is the pervasive belief that what goes on in a family between its members should stay within the family. That kind of thinking can inhibit individuals, who might under other circumstances, be very influential with various family members.

The information we do have comes from hospital emergency room statistics, family court records, police reports on domestic violence complaints and battered women's shelters (Gelles, 1980). The substance of the research from the past three decades is limited in its generalizability to the African-American and African-Caribbean populations. Most of the research has been done by Whites on White subjects (Asbury, 1987). In cases where people of color have been included in the studies, no distinctions were made among people of color (e.g., Asians, Blacks, American Indians, etc.). When the distinctions have been made, the numbers of people of color were not proportionate to their representation in the general population of the United States (Gelles, 1980). Black people have been treated as a homogeneous group with no attention paid to regional differences within the United States, differences between African-Americans and African-Caribbeans, differences among African-Caribbeans or differences between African-Americans and Africans. In the future, whatever information researchers collect about African-Caribbeans in this country must be used with caution. Little can be said about the prevalence or meaning of spouse abuse in the culture if only the immigrant population is tapped.

A further limitation of the information gleaned from studies thus far is that it comes from a segment of the abused population. We really don't know about the women who don't file the police reports, who don't get medical care and who don't go to shelters.

THEORIES

Several theories have been proposed and revised over the years to explain family violence. As the research in this area continues it would be useful for investigators to examine the adequacy of each theory as it applies to various people of color.

The feminist-political theory "suggests that men beat women to gain the power to which they feel entitled because of the structure of a patriarchal society which teaches men to expect to be dominant" (Walker, 1986; Dobash & Dobash, 1979). While it is true that this is a patriarchal society we have to be careful about making generalizations to all men. Black men are not taught to expect to be dominant or to expect to be in charge of anything. An examination of the tremendous gap in earning power between Black men and White men and the disproportionate number of White men in decision-making positions in this country's government are just two examples of this.

Another aspect of this theory is the supposition that men end up expecting to be dominant because of the way they have been socialized. Such a thesis assumes that all people are socialized in the same way. Lewis (1975) disagrees and proposes the idea that in African-American families the socialization of male and female children is not so divergent as it is in White families.

The sociocultural theory also examines society as a whole and as a shaper of family violence. However, it differs from the patriarchal or feminist political theory in terms of its foci. This theory gives consideration to the extent to which American society tolerates violence and the extent to which certain cultures within our society condone violence in situations that do not involve self-defense (Gelles, 1980; Walker, 1986). Up until this point, investigators have mainly talked about the tolerance for violence against women and children. An afrocentric and Afro-Caribbean viewpoint must also consider the tolerance for violence against Blacks in this country. Additionally, further studies need to be done to help dispel the myth that violence is an accepted and condoned part of Black culture and therefore Black family life.

Perhaps the theory which is most suitable for analyzing violence in the African-American and African-Caribbean family is the social-psychological one. It posits that

> violence and abuse can best be understood by a careful examination of the external environmental factors which impact on the family. In addition, this model considers which everyday family interactions are precursors to violence. Theoretical approaches which examine stress, the transmission of violence from one generation to another and family interaction patterns fit into the social psychological model" (Gelles, 1980, p. 881).

This model is very useful for the professional who is trying to intervene with the African-Caribbean family because of the consideration given to stress. The process of migration yields substantial concrete as well as psychological sources of stress (Brice, 1982). The immigrant has to negotiate in and adjust to strange surroundings. People from the Caribbean islands are not accustomed to the extreme cold weather found in some of the urban regions of the United States. Familiar foods may not be available at all forcing people to develop a new palate. When foods from home are available they may be difficult to obtain and expensive. In some cases, when the immigrant is from non-English speaking islands language is an additional burden (Brice, 1982).

Employment may be hard to come by, and when jobs are available they may be in positions lower in status than what the individual was educated to do at home. Often, African-Caribbeans have dealt with the low pay and racism in hiring by working multiple jobs and getting paid "under the table." The African-Caribbean who is chosen by the family to come to the United States is carrying a lot of responsibility. There are expectations from the family about this individual's success. Spouses who journey to the States later may not fully understand the spouse who has been here for some time and who may have already done some acculturating. This can lead to marital tension and conflict. A family at particular risk for conflict may be one in which the wife came to this country first and whose husband followed later. Her knowledge of life in the United States places him at a distinct disadvantage.

Of course all immigrant families do not have marital problems and are not violent toward one another. However, if we want to look at some of the risk factors for stress we must consider the ones associated with the process of migration and not assume that everyone's experience in America is identical. While there certainly are commonalities among the experiences of all immigrants, the immigrant of color is unique in his/her inability to ever assimilate.

Before leaving the issue of stress, two more contributing factors bear looking at: double discrimination and intermarriage. "While racism has been part of the history of the Caribbean, and continues today in various forms on the islands, it is perceived and experienced differently by British West Indians than by American Blacks . . ." (Brice, 1982, p. 126). This situation creates the potential for ostracization from the White majority in this country as well as ostracization from other Blacks who are not West Indian. These differences are certainly amplified when there is an intermarriage between Blacks and Whites or between African-American and African-Caribbeans.

Last is the psychiatric model which has been medically driven and focused on individual pathology. In the case of spouse abuse researchers have attempted to come up with a psychological profile of the batterer. The profile includes low self-esteem, a low threshold for frustration, an inability to be self-examining, an inability to take criticism, a failure to take responsibility for his own behavior, a tendency to act without thinking about the consequences, a possible substance abuse history and a history of using assaultive behavior to solve problems (Bell & Chance-Hill, 1987).

An examination of the mental health of Black individuals must include a look at the role of institutionalized racism and internalized racism as factors in low self-esteem. Racism is defined as "the practice of discrimination, segregation, persecution, and domination on the basis of race" (Webster,

1983, p. 1485). Institutionalized racism refers to the extent to which this society has incorporated prejudice on the basis of skin color in our institutions. Internalized racism occurs when Black individuals take these negative stereotypes and incorporate them into their self-image. At its worst it results in divisiveness among Blacks and self-hatred. If the profile of the batterer considers low self-esteem as a contributing factor then finding ways to combat internalized racism must be a part of the treatment process.

IMPACT OF STEREOTYPES

McGoldrick (1982) points out that "ethnicity is a powerful influence in determining identity" (p. 5). She further indicates that there are several factors which shape the degree and the way in which ethnicity manifests itself in a family, and by extension, an individual. These factors include: whether or not there has been an intermarriage, politics, religion, the community where the family lives, race, where the family is in the life cycle, when they migrated and the reasons for that migration and what languages are spoken (McGoldrick, 1982).

It is my contention that an additional factor be considered; namely, the popular and stereotypical images of the ethnic group in American society. The import of these images lie in their ability to mold the self-esteem of their subjects. The domestic violence literature repeatedly points to the issue of self-esteem as a significant and contributing variable in attempts to explain why men batter and why women stay in abusive relationships (Bell & Chance-Hill, 1988). The dictionary defines a stereotype as:

> An unvarying form or pattern; fixed or conventional expression, notion, character, mental pattern, etc., having no individuality, as though cast from a mold; as, the Negro is too often portrayed as a stereotype (Webster, 1983, p. 1785).

While no suggestion is made in this definition about the negative or positive nature of a stereotype one has only to examine the print, television and movie media to conclude that an overwhelming majority of the images of Black people are stereotypes of a negative or derogatory nature.

Black women are considered physically unattractive and therefore undesirable when measured against the White yardstick of attractiveness. Russell, Wilson, and Hall (1992) point out just how much of a concern this is for Black women in their discussion of the use of skin lightening products, hair straightening techniques, dieting, colored contact lenses, (and when affordable) plastic surgery among these women. The phenomenon of the halo effect is well illustrated in the media: women who are perceived as attractive are treated well and are entitled to everything. Asbury (1993) suggests that Black women perceive themselves as unattractive and therefore feel entitled to nothing. Such feelings can extend to a belief that they are deserving of the abuse they encounter at the hands of their battering spouses.

Another stereotype is that Black women are strong and can take care of themselves and everyone around them. A belief in this stereotype can lead many Black women to deny the violence and subjugate their own needs to the needs of others (Asbury, 1993). Of additional concern are the consequences of this kind of thinking by the professionals working with Black domestic violence victims. Professionals can overestimate the Black female's ability to cope, underestimate the impact of the abuse on her and assume that it is less destructive for her than for her White counterparts.

A long held stereotype is that Black women are emasculating matriarchs (Asbury, 1993, Moynihan, 1965) who strip their husbands of their masculine dignity. It is easy to see how this idea could further perpetuate the notion of "blaming the victim" as one envisions the Black woman provoking her poor husband.

The Black woman as exotic love object and sexual temptress is still another image they are burdened with (Asbury, 1993). An acceptance of this notion can erroneously suggest that these Black women bring the abuse on themselves by "getting men all riled up" and/or soliciting the attention of men who are not their husbands and this "understandably" invokes his jealous rage.

The image of the Black woman as the glue that holds her family together is not necessarily a bad image. The negativity stems from the assumptions people make about the necessity for her to be the one who holds the family together (e.g., alleged male irresponsibility). Those considerations aside, any Black woman who believes that the responsibility for the viability and success of the family is hers and hers alone will be far less likely to take steps to get away from her abusive husband.

There are just as many damaging stereotypes about the Black male as there are about the Black female. Many of these images have their roots in slavery when Whites needed a justification for their treatment of Blacks. Men were thought of as strong Black "bucks" or "mandingo warriors" who were animal-like, primitive, and naturally aggressive. The image further suggested that Black male slaves possessed unnaturally high and untamable sexual proclivities. Not only did this justify the violence Whites inflicted on Blacks but it established the sweeping generalization that violence was an innate part of the Black man's nature. Any acceptance of this idea on the part of professionals would influence their beliefs in the Black male abuser's ability to benefit from any kind of treatment.

The Black family has suffered much malignment from the fictional family constellations on television to the more "erudite" literature of academia. These myths include but are not limited to: (1) the idea that all

Blacks are poor, living on public assistance, and residing in high crime areas, (2) Black families are fragmented, disorganized, and lacking in morals, (3) all Blacks believe that violence is a legitimate way to solve problems, and (4) violence is endemic to the Black community and therefore Black individuals have little or no value for human life (Hawkins, 1987).

Because they share the same skin color, African-Caribbeans are the recipients of some of the same attitudes and misconceptions that people have about African-Americans. However, African-Caribbeans have the added distinction of being immigrants. There are myths about immigrants in general and African-Caribbeans in particular.

One myth about immigrants is that they are bad people who led questionable, if not downright criminal, lives in their countries of origin. The assumption is that the nefariousness of their deeds is what prompted their migration or in some cases deportation. Another myth is that when immigrants come to the United States they do so to continue their criminal activity, rejecting legitimate work, and draining this country of its resources in the process. It is easy to see that such a description immediately categorizes them as part of some disenfranchised group whose members are lazy, impulsive, lacking any achievement motivation, and having a low tolerance for frustration. These are some of the same characteristics that have been attributed to the batterer (Bell & Chance-Hill, 1988).

Gopaul-McNicol (1993) enumerates the various misconceptions about West Indians (or African-Caribbeans); among those listed: "West Indian men are abusive to their women because they are so controlling" (p. 158). Shorey-Bryan (1986) suggest that money is a key source of conflict in the West Indian marriage.

The interactions between women and men are dominated by women's constant demand for money. This is one aspect that men resent. Barrow's study on men's attitudes toward women supports the view that many men see women as avaricious and demanding and therefore resent them. Many of these tensions between men and women have their roots in economic issues; but these tensions are also born of social expectation (p. 71).

While the author was not specifically referring to spouse abuse, one can see how a culturally insensitive person could construe that women are money hungry people who nag their spouses, placing tremendous pressure on them resulting in insurmountable stress and retaliation in physical abuse. It should be kept in mind when examining any of these myths that explaining the abusive behavior of Black men by the behavior of Black women suggests that Black women are somehow at fault. This is just another form of "blaming the victim."

The tropics themselves and the Caribbean in particular, are frequently depicted as a lover's paradise. A popular stereotype is that people from warm climates are naturally sensual, carefree and primarily interested in the pursuit of pleasure. Since the majority of people from tropical locales are people of color, one can infer that this stereotype has been applied the African-Caribbeans. Once again, this suggests that the Black woman is an accomplished seductress. And as Asbury (1993) has indicated, sexually alluring women are frequently thought to provoke any attacks made on them. The irony of this all is the very schizophrenic picture of Black women. On the one hand they do not fit society's idea of what is beautiful and attractive, but on the other hand they are thought to possess such powerful sensuality.

WHY WOMEN STAY

In considering the treatment of African-American women and African-Caribbean women in abusive relationships we must consider all of the reasons why they stay with their mates. Economics, while a factor for White women, is even more of an issue for Black women. A larger percentage of the White female population than the Black female population is married to men who earn large salaries. If a divorce settlement were to be reached, they are in a better position to get money that will help them until they get on their feet. Black women are not likely to be the beneficiaries of a whole lot of money in a divorce settlement. Factor into this the fact that Black men and women do not make the equivalent of their White counterparts even when they have equal or better education. For poor women, welfare has always been seen as an option. However, there are many African-American women who are too embarrassed to apply for it. Further, there are African-Caribbean female immigrants who are not yet citizens and therefore are not eligible for public assistance.

The availability of shelters in the African-American and African-Caribbean communities is another issue (Asbury, 1987). How accessible is a hiding place and if one is found will they accept these women? For the African-Caribbean woman the issue is more than a matter of finding shelter in an urban area vs. a suburban area. It is a matter of making your home, albeit temporary, in a place even further removed from her Caribbean culture. As with any immigrant group, people tend to live in small pockets of the city where their fellow countrymen are. It is often stressful enough to have to leave the small confines of that community and venture into foreign areas to work. Imagine the stress for the African-Caribbean woman who has to spend all her waking and sleeping hours in a strange place (Asbury, 1993). Related to this issue is the doubt that Black women have of finding therapists, and other professionals, who are knowledgeable about their experiences as members of a double minority (Asbury, 1993). The isolation of the African-Caribbean woman is further exacerbated by the fact that her support system of extended family and friends may not be in this country. And if she comes from one of the Dutch, Spanish, or French islands, she may not speak English and will therefore be at the mercy of those people who can interpret for her. An immigrant who does not speak English is not a unique situation. However, in those instances one usually relies upon a more acculturated family member to interpret. In the case of spouse abuse that person may very well be the batterer.

Even if women do not leave their partners, every time they are battered they are confronted with the decision of whether or not to file a police complaint. Blacks have not had very favorable experiences with the police. Often, even law abiding individuals will refrain from calling the police in order to keep them out of the community and from a belief that police will be reluctant to see Blacks as victims.

The literature points to a number of factors that are thought to differentiate women who stay in abusive relationships from women who leave. First, there is the belief that leaving does not change anything because abuse occurs in all marriages. Second, the woman can have ambivalent feelings about her abusive partner. Third, the woman believes that the abuse is unacceptable behavior on the part of her spouse but she thinks that she can save him. Fourth, she is paralyzed by fear and believes that any move toward separation will bring an onslaught of violence that will be fatal this time.

Any or all of these factors can exist in the African-American and African-Caribbean female. There is an additional factor which is the burden of being responsible for the perceptions and integrity of the Black man. This is what I call the Anita Hill–Clarence Thomas syndrome. There were some members of the Black community who professed a belief that Clarence Thomas did in fact do what he was accused of doing. However, they took exception with the fact that Anita Hill brought his misconduct to light. The implication being that, in a racist society which already holds and perpetuates so many pejorative stereotypes about Black people, it is the job of all the cultures' members to collude in not besmirching those images any further. Therefore, an African-American woman or an African-Caribbean woman who reveals the abuse she suffers at the hands of her spouse risks being seen as disloyal to the race.

TREATMENT ISSUES

The beginning phase of any treatment protocol has to start with the therapist. Boyd-Franklin (1989) talks about the need for therapists who are working with ethnic minorities to participate in values clarification training workshops. In this particular population, it is necessary to examine your attitudes toward racism and sexism. Also, what are your attitudes about family violence? How aware are you about how your ideas about family relationships were shaped by your own family of origin? Who are the people in your family who had the overt and the covert power? What were the symbols of power in your family? How were people brought in line? How did you know when there was conflict? How was conflict resolved? How was anger expressed by those family members considered powerful and by those family members not considered powerful? Was there ever any physical violence in your family? If so, how, when and by whom was it used? How was the behavior of the abuser explained? What, if anything, was done to help the victim? Therapists who have participated in TOF (Therapist's Own Family) groups during their training have had the experience of tracing family patterns through the generations. However, the specific question of physical abuse may not be raised when we are in such a setting with our colleagues. In cases where the therapist has no personal experience with domestic violence, he/she needs to explore where he/she got his/her information about the subject (television, books, friends, neighbors, etc.). This last point is important because without the personal experience and having only input from selected sources people can get a skewed view of the problem. One starts to conclude that only people from a certain neighborhood, or people from a certain ethnic group or people from a certain socioeconomic class beat their wives. And, as mentioned earlier, such conclusions are erroneous.

Another aspect of values clarification training is exploring one's motivation for working with a given population; in this case, domestic violence perpetrators and their victims. The therapist needs to be knowledgeable about why he/she has chosen to do this work. Does the therapist feel superior to Black people or people from a certain socioeconomic class or people who's lives include domestic violence? If the therapist needs to work with a certain population in order to feel good about who he/she is then that will interfere with treatment (Greene, 1985). Also, treatment will be compromised by a therapist who is using the process and the patient to work through his/her own personal experiences of domestic violence. Once the therapist has a clear sense of his/her cultural identity, attitudes about racism and sexism and motivation for doing this work then he/she can begin intervening.

There are several barriers to the treatment of domestic violence in Black families. A very basic problem exist for African-Caribbean people from non-English speaking islands and that is language. Investigators have warned therapists about the pitfalls of utilizing interpreters. However, in some instances it cannot be avoided and then one should be careful about who he/she chooses to act as interpreters. All too often in agencies non-therapist staff are called upon to act as interpreters. This violates the individual's right to confidentiality and leaves the therapist with data which is suspect because the interpretation was not verbatim but a summarization of what the individual said. The domestic violence situation also presents a unique problem because often when people are non-English speaking they rely on family members to interpret. If a therapist is seeing a couple where the wife speaks little or no English but the husband is fluent, obviously he cannot be used as an interpreter for his spouse. Likewise, a family member, who is not the batterer and who brings the battered woman for treatment, may have his/her own opinions about how the woman should handle her affairs and those opinions could influence the interpretation.

Fear of deportation is a significant barrier to seeking help for African-Caribbeans. Very early on the therapist should outline specifically how he/she or how the agency he/she works for interfaces with immigration and naturalization services. Keep in mind that if this is a concern, the individual is not going to raise the issue because to do so would automatically identify her as a possible illegal alien. The onus will be on the therapist to raise the issue and allay fears. Failure to do so early in a meeting will result in stonewalling. It should also be kept in mind that not all family members may have the same status in this country. A battered woman may be here legally and fear that doing something to stop the abuse will result in her husband's deportation. A "split" agenda is very common among abused women who may want the abuse to stop but not want something "bad" to happen to their spouses.

In a real crisis situation the therapist may be called upon to find alternate housing for a woman and her children. The therapist or other professional needs to research beforehand and become familiar with the shelters operating in the Black communities. In addition to the comfort associated with being surrounded by the familiar, Black women will be very concerned about getting to jobs from the shelter. African-Caribbean women who are sending money home and supporting families here in the States will be very worried about losing their jobs. One of the common myths about the African-Caribbeans is that they are "only interested in making money, therefore, they work several jobs at the expense of their families" (Gopaul-McNicol, 1993, p. 157). While it is true that employment is a high priority, women are socialized to place an extremely strong emphasis on motherhood over all other roles. Therefore, stressing he safety of young children will definitely appeal to the African-Caribbean woman who may initially express ambivalence about going to a shelter.

When the family system has calmed down sufficiently to do couples work, then the assessment phase becomes critical. It is important to know who is in the family here and "at home" because there might be key people who influence the cycle of violence. Constructing a genogram for an African-American or African-Caribbean family can be difficult because of the number of "adoptive" relatives whose adoptive status is not necessarily revealed to the therapist.

The therapist will want to know how each spouse defines the problem. What do they have conflicts about and how are those conflicts solved? Do they think that violence is a problem in their relationship and if so, how? When assessing levels of stress in African-American and African-Caribbean families, it is important to look at sources of stress from a multi-systems perspective. Are there personal goals that the individual feels frustrated about? To what degree does the individual feel that the attainment of certain family goals is his/her responsibility? And what about extended family and community commitments? In working with African-Caribbeans, the therapist must look at problems generated by immigration and whether or not the individual or family plan is to remain in the states.

Before offering solutions to the domestic violence problem it is helpful to find out who the individual would have turned to for help at home. For many Black people, family elders and religious leaders are sources of comfort and advice. In the Caribbean, the institution of witchcraft is very strong and people of all classes turn to the obeah woman for help (Brice, 1982; Gopaul-McNicol, 1993). It would not be unheard of for spiritual possession to be used as an explanation for a man's abusive behavior. A natural outgrowth of that belief could prompt a woman to turn to an obeah practitioner to lift the evil spirits from her husband. On the other hand, the obeah woman could just as easily be sought to weave a spell for the purposes of revenge. In either instance, such talk should not be dismissed as "crazy" or viewed as threatening to therapy. Paying attention to the way in which a woman wishes to use witchcraft is diagnostic. For example, the belief that the "evil" in her husband can be lifted can be indicative of strong rescue fantasies (e.g., If only she could get her husband the help he needs everything would be all right.) These are not uncommon thoughts among battered women. A psychotherapist can reinforce the idea that the batterer needs powerful help while at the same time communicating the message that the woman does not have to be the one to get him that help. If she thinks that the therapist believes in obeah or at the very least is open to her belief in it then the foundation for a therapeutic alliance is present.

In the other instance where a woman wants to utilize obeah for revenge, the therapist can provide an accepting environment for her to express her feelings of anger, frustration, and helplessness. An alliance between the obeah woman and the therapist can take some of the burden off the abused woman and free her to put her energies into taking care of herself.

Another part of the treatment should address key people who may influence the marital dyad. In the African-Caribbean family the mother–son relationship is an extremely strong one. That relationship persists even after marriage and it is not uncommon for men to seek their mother's approval of their choice of wife. Therefore, the triangle of wife, husband and husband's mother cannot be ignored. Very early on the therapist needs to know if the husband's mother is living, where she is and the type and extent of her influence on the couple. In fact, it would be wise to approach her first and get her permission to see the family and use her as a consultant. This illustrates the therapist's respect for elders in general and recognition of the mother in law's position.

An equally crucial triangle is wife, husband and eldest son. In African-Caribbean families much more emphasis is placed on the woman's role as mother than her role as spouse. And mother–son relationships, as mentioned above, are particularly strong. A son will see himself as his mother's protector.

A woman's treatment plan can involve an educational/support group as well as individual or couples' work. Groups provide emotional support and decrease isolation. It is important to have all Black female groups include structured exercises focused on building self-esteem. The way in which these groups would differ from those for White women is that there would be a focus on the racial stereotypes of Black women and how they effect self-esteem. The group leader would need to point out that anything which serves to lower self-esteem contributes to an individual accepting various forms of mistreatment. Phase one of the group would be educational and geared toward increasing the participant's awareness of just what the stereotypes of Black women are, how prevalent are these stereotypes and just what do they say about Black women. Phase two of the group would he devoted to assessment. A formal instrument measuring self-esteem could he administered followed by an exploration by each participant of the extent to which she feels she approximates the negative stereotypes. How disturbing or not disturbing is that to the woman? Also, how is she perceived by significant others in her life regarding these stereotypes. (For example, If the main stream definition of beauty is straight hair and a Black woman wears corn rows, dreadlocks, or an afro does she get messages from her husband, or other family members that she would be prettier if only she straightened her hair?) Another way of looking at this is to ask does the extent to which Black women approximate mainstream standards of success effect the way they think of themselves?

Phase three of the group would focus on the development or reinforcement of already existing coping skills: (1) exploring why Black women need to accept mainstream standards of success, (2) redefining standards of success for themselves based on African-American and African-Caribbean standards, and (3) finding illustrations of this in history and the current mass media.

There are some advantages to this type of group. Because it is not a therapy group there is no stigma attached. In fact, it is probably best if it is run outside of an institution in the community. It can be geared for prevention purposes as well as post-prevention purposes. And finally, any of these discussions can be incorporated into individual therapy with an abused woman.

When we turn our attention to the treatment of abusive Black men, different treatment issues are revealed. Certainly abusive men are difficult to treat regardless of their color. However, additional issues exist in considering the treatment of Black men. The main issue is how to communicate disapproval of his battering behavior without perpetuating racist stereotypes.

FUTURE DIRECTIONS

There continues to be a great many unanswered questions in this area. Empirical research in the following areas could close some of the gaps:

(1) Surveys need to be done in the African-American and African-Caribbean communities to determine what their attitudes are about family violence.

(2) Results from the above survey need to be compared to data collected from White families to see if there are any significant differences.

(3) Studies of African-American and African-Caribbean families where there is no domestic violence would broaden our knowledge of their coping skills.

(4) An investigation of the Black middle class would be useful to determine the prevalence of domestic violence there.

REFERENCES

Asbury, J. (1987). African American women in violent relationships. In R. Hampton (Ed.), *Violence in the Black family: Correlates and consequences* (pp. 89-105). Lexington, Massachusetts: Lexington Books.

Asbury, J. (March 1993). *Domestic violence: A culturally sensitive approach to violence in families of color.* Symposium conducted at the Meeting of the Association of Women in Psychology, Atlanta, Georgia.

Bell, C., & Chance-Hill, G. (1988). Treatment of violent families. *Journal of the National Medical Association, 83*(3), 203-208.

Boyd-Franklin, N. (1989). *Black families in therapy.* New York: Guilford.

Brice, J. (1982). West Indians. In M. McGoldrick, J. Pearce, and J. Giordano (Eds.), *Ethnicity and family therapy* (pp. 123-133). New York: Guilford.

Dobash, R., & Dobash, R. (1979). *Violence against wives.* New York: The Free Press.

Gelles, R. (1980). Violence in the family: A review of research in the seventies. *Journal of Marriage and the Family,* 873-885.

Gopaul-McNicol, S. (1993). *Working with West Indian families.* New York: Guilford.

Greene, B. (1985). Considerations in the treatment of Black patients by White therapists. *Journal of Psychotherapy, 22*(25), 389-393.

Hawkins, D. (1987). Devalued lives and racial stereotypes: Barriers to the prevention of family violence among Blacks. In R. Hampton (Ed.), *Violence in the Black family: Correlates and consequences* (pp. 189-205). Lexington, Massachusetts: Lexington Books.

Lewis, D. (1975). The Black family: Socialization and sex roles. *Phylon, 36*(3), 221-237.

McGoldrick, M. (1982). Ethnicity and family therapy: An overview. In M. McGoldrick, J. Pearce, and J. Giordano (Eds.), *Ethnicity and family therapy* (pp. 3-30). New York: Guilford.

Moynihan, D. P. (1965). The tangle of pathology. In R. Staples (Ed.), *The Black family: Essays and studies* (pp. 3-13). Belmont, California: Wadsworth.

Pinderhughes, E. (1989). *Understanding race ethnicity and power: The key to efficacy in clinical practice.* New York: The Free Press.

Russell, K., Wilson, M., & Hall, R. (1992). *The color complex: The politics of skin color among African Americans.* New York: Harcourt, Brace and Jovanovitch.

Shorey-Bryan, N. (1986). The making of male–female relationships in the caribbean. In P. Ellis (Ed.), *Women of the Caribbean.* Atlantic Highlands, New Jersey: Zed Books, Ltd.

Walker, L. (1986). Psychological causes of family violence. In M. Lystad (Ed.), *Violence in the home: Interdisciplinary perspectives* (pp. 71-94). New York: Bruner/Mazel.

Webster's new universal unabridged dictionary (2nd ed.) (1983). New York: Simon and Schuster.

5

Chinese Families in Transition: Cultural Conflicts and Adjustment Problems

Susan Chan and Cynthia W. Leong

Challenged to cope with two different cultures, Chinese American immi-grant families face many stressors and conflicts. Such difficulties faced by these individuals usually stem from language, religious, and value differ-ences. Furthermore, family members are faced with role and status changes due to differing rates and levels of acculturation. As a result, there is a great need for mental health services. However, due to cultural barriers, mental health services are not accessible nor acceptable to many Chinese Americans. Effective intervention strategies which integrate the Chinese cultural values and norms with psychotherapy are recommended.

INTRODUCTION

It is difficult to describe the experience and characteristic of Asian families in the context of this culture. Part of the reason for this difficulty relates to the multidimensional and multicultural factors that tend to char-acterize an Asian individual. To begin with, there is a great deal of confu-sion as to the definition because the concept *Asian* is applied to individuals whose history, culture, and language are not necessarily homogeneous. This notwithstanding, there are a number of characteristics that can be applied to individuals coming from the Asian region.

Thus, in the case of the Asian American, the term can only be under-stood by looking at the multiplicity of groups and subgroups which charac-terize this population in America. Indeed, we are dealing with individuals whose reference group may have come from China, India, Japan, Cambodia, Korea, Pakistan, the Philippines, or Vietnam. It is estimated that there are more than 30 different Asian ethnic groups in New York City (U.S. Department of Commerce Economics & Statistics Administration Bureau of the Census, 1992). Although, it would be essential to discuss these Asian ethnic groups in detail, for the purpose of this paper we will only focus on one of these groups, the Chinese, to discuss important issues relevant to many Asian individuals. We recognize, however, that our comments may only have limited applicability with regard to other Asian groups.

CHINESE AMERICAN FAMILIES

The success stories of some Chinese Americans, especially in the fields of business, technology, and academic performance, have made it difficult to assess the true nature of the struggle that many immigrant Asian families have had to face in order to survive in this country. They have had to adapt to a different culture and lifestyle in a new home who's views and life perspective are so different (Sue, 1983). Although it is clear that many of them may have adjusted well and have made a smooth transition, others have been reported to have developed serious adjustment problems in the transition process (Sue, 1983). They experienced cultural change, cultural shock, and cultural conflicts similar to those experienced by the immigrants of the past. Many faced underemployment or unemployment, social isolation and racial tension, and suffered from poor health, mental disorders, and alcoholism (Lee, 1982; Kim, McLeod, & Shantzis, 1992). An increase in domestic violence and youth gang activities have also been observed in the Chinese communities (Sung, 1987). These are indicators that many Chinese American families are indeed not only in transition, but are also in crisis.

Crisis is not necessarily a negative force, rather it is translated in Chinese to mean *danger* and *opportunity*. The problems faced by the Chinese families are dangerous to their well-being, but also give them opportunities to overcome their problems and to lead a fuller life in this country. There are, indeed, a variety of stressors common to the lives of most immigrant individuals; nevertheless, there are specific sociopolitical, cultural, and socioeconomic conditions that are unique to Chinese immigrant families. We will describe these stressors in the ensuing paragraphs as these are assumed to impact on family cohesion and mental health.

STRESSORS

A Historical Overview

Each immigrant group has been subjected to discrimination in this country, but Asian Americans were the first group subjected to a legalized discrimination and rejection (Sue, 1983). Takaki (1989), for instance, described the history of various ethnic groups who migrated from Asia. According to this author, migration varied considerably from group to group, but the goal was the same — looking for a better economic stability and a living condition.

There were basically two major waves of immigrants who came to the United States from Asia. The first was a pre-1920 wave in which Chinese, Japanese, and Filipinos came as contract laborers to work in gold mines and on railroads. According to Fong (1979), the Chinese who came into the United States at this time were mainly from the coastal province of Kwangtung. This area of China was facing serious times of flooding and famine during that period; so when the opportunity for a better life was available in the United States, many flocked to America. With the passing of the Chinese Exclusion Act in 1882, a long period of restrictive entry ensued from 1924 to 1965 during which very few Asian immigrants could come to this country (Sung, 1987).

The Chinese Exclusion laws were finally repealed in 1943 and the immigration laws were amended in 1965 allowing a quota of 20,000 immigrants from each country per year (Takiki, 1989). This gave way to a second wave of immigration from Asia beginning in 1965 until today (Sung, 1987). Chinese individuals coming in these waves were from many areas of Mainland China, Hong Kong, Taiwan, and Southeast Asia. More Asians were allowed to come after the Korean and Vietnam Wars, making the Asian population in this country very noticeable.

The noticeable increase in the Asian population was clearly detailed in the 1990 census (U.S. Department of Commerce Economics & Statistics Administration Bureau of the Census, 1992). According to this Census, the Asian American population in New York City is 512,719, which represents 7% of the city's total population. The data shows that the largest groups were Chinese (47%), followed by Asian Indians (18%), Koreans (14%), Filipinos (8%), Japanese (3%), Vietnamese (2%), and other Asians (8%). This data reflects a population growth of 178.3% since 1980 (U.S. Department of Commerce Economics & Statistics Administration Bureau of the Census, 1988) and a 300% growth from 1965 (U.S. Department of Com-

merce Economics & Statistics Administration Bureau of the Census, 1965).
It is predicted that this population will double by the year 2000.

Problem with Discrimination

This apparently positive movement has serious consequences for the
lives of Asians in the United States. We are referring to the issue of discrimination and the problem of stereotypes that challenged the lives first
for the Chinese, then the Japanese and Filipinos. Discrimination against
these groups became part of a general policy and which resulted in one of
the darkest times in the Asian experience in America. They were not only
excluded from entering this country, but were also prohibited from becoming American citizens, owning property, or testifying in court (Daniels,
1988; Sung, 1987). In 1942, Japanese Americans were sent to "relocation
centers" in isolated areas of the country until the end of World War II
(Daniels, 1988).

Although, such blatant discrimination has long ceased to exist, a subtle form of discrimination is still part of the lives of many Asians. It has
been suggested that the fact that many Asians remain mainly connected
to an Asian community, with limited or no knowledge of English (Chinese
American Planning Council, United Way of Tri-State and Regional Plan
Association, 1988), may have contributed toward giving these individuals a
sense of isolation and rejection (Uba, 1994).

It is clear that as a group, Asians are not doing well socially and
economically. That was also the conclusion reached by Takaki (1989) when
he compared the differences in employment patterns, income levels, and
needs for services among the Asian American groups. Asians work longer
hours than most people, often in restaurants, garment factories, small gro-
ceries, and fish and produce markets.

Underemployment is a serious problem among new immigrants. Asian
immigrants tend to experience a sharp downward mobility in employment
after coming to the United States. They tend to live in an ethnic community
where housing is deteriorated and overcrowded, and community resources
are limited. Many of these people are trapped in dead-end jobs without
much hope for a better living, which may explain the prevalence of depression and low self-esteem among this population (Shon & Ja, 1982). More
serious clinical symptoms are expected to develop if the socioeconomic condition continues.

An example of the kind of clinical deterioration that may appear in
many immigrant families can be seen in the case of Sue Ling. She is a
16-year-old female student who was referred for mental health services by

a local high school because of depression and her difficulty in keeping up with school demands. According to the report, immediately prior to the referral, she had become increasingly socially isolated, missed several classes often and had difficulty completing her assignments. The school counselor's attempt to set up a meeting with Sue's parents was met with a typical reaction of passive refusal, as the need for such a meeting was not found to be necessary.

Sue Ling came to this country with her parents and two younger brothers (ages 11 and 13) 6 years ago from Hong Kong. They settled down in a two bedroom apartment in an old tenement building in Chinatown. Upon their arrival, Sue's father went to work in his uncle's restaurant in a small town in New Jersey and only coming home on his off day. Sue's mother, on the other hand, went to work in a garment factory. Sue and her two brothers attended public school and went to an after school day care program until their mother picked them up at the end of her shift around six o'clock.

Sue was about 10 years old when she first came to this country. Being the older sibling, she had to assume the mother's helper role by handling the household chores. So, it was Sue's responsibility to make sure that the house was orderly and meals were prepared. Regarding discipline, Sue's mother became very strict and protective of the children in the absence of the father, as she feared the street crime in Chinatown. Thus, the children's movements were restricted and they were not allowed to play outside.

Since Sue's parents did not speak English, they often relied on Sue and neighbors to manage the family and social affairs. It was not until Sue turned 14 that conflicts with her mother began. It was at this point that she began to express her resentment for the family obligations she had to assume. She was also unhappy that she could not spend time with her friends and felt guilt for having conflicts with her parents.

As indicated earlier, Sue's experience is not unique as it is characteristic of many Asian families. Her experience is fraught with conflicts related to sociocultural stressors, family relationships, gender roles, and developmental challenges.

SOCIAL-CULTURAL AND PSYCHOLOGICAL ISSUES FOR CHINESE IMMIGRANTS

In our case example, the family had come to the United States in search of better economic and educational opportunities and a better life. However, similar to many other Chinese immigrants, they were immediately forced to take on jobs that were restricted to working-class positions due to limited English language ability. With a work week that is six days, 10–12 hours long, and at a low wage, it is often impossible for parents of growing children to find time to learn English (Shon & Ja, 1982) and Sue's family's case is no exception. Finally, this family's living situation is rather typical. Unable to afford better housing, they had to settle in small quarters in run-down apartment dwellings located in unsafe neighborhoods.

Let us review the basic sociocultural and psychological stressors normally confronted by this and other immigrant Asian families in order to appreciate the nature of their plight.

Language: A Barrier to Full Participation

Chinese may share some similarities from an agricultural background and a spiritual kinship. However, Chinese dialects are very different from each other. For example, among the Chinese in New York City, there may be over 20 different spoken dialects. Thus, it is not surprising that Chinese may not understand one another. Further, the fact that Chinese and English languages are so diverse, it is much more difficult for a Chinese to learn English than in the case of a European whose languages may have strong similarities with the English language.

But language is so crucial for higher education, employment, and utilization of available public services that we can appreciate how immigrants who speak little or no English are, indeed, trapped in their own community. They are often not only unable to speak with members of the community at large but with Asian immigrants coming from different geographical locations than theirs. This limitation also prevents them from participating in civil and political life and hence adding to their sense of alienation. They are left with a strong feeling of frustration,' their children, unable to adjust to the American school system, become members instead of the increasing number of school drop-outs and youth gangs (Sung, 1987).

Religion and Folk Beliefs

Among the many different and distinct cultures and traditions in Asia, religion maintains a very central role in the lives of Asian individuals. The major religions and/or philosophies derive from the teachings of Buddhism, Confucianism, and Taoism. These teachings have a profound influence on the Asians' way of life, their attitudes toward health and treatment of disease, and their concepts of life and death. Buddhism as a religion, in particular, is an integral part of daily life of many people in Asia. Its teachings have led people to accept and tolerate misery, pain, and life stresses as a normal part of existence.

The major difference between Eastern religion and Western religion is that in Western religion (Christianity), God the Omnipotent is the Creator and Father of all humanity and through Him comes salvation to mankind. In Buddhism, the fundamental objective is to attain complete perfect enlightenment through the spiritual cultivation and the eightfold path.

An important component of Buddhism is the teaching of the law of cause and effect — for every consequence there is a cause. According to the Buddhist Theory of Causation, although bad karma may have been sown in the past life, it is possible that by cultivating good deeds diligently, this karma may be deferred and even neutralized. Buddha also teaches that all of life is subject to suffering because we are contaminated by desires and egoistic thoughts (Chan, Ragi al Fauqi, Kitagawa, & Raju, 1969). The way of salvation from suffering is the eightfold path — the right viewpoint, aspiration, speech, behavior, occupation, effort, thinking, and meditation (Ridenour, 1967; Soothill, 1929). Salvation from suffering is not necessarily during this life but in the afterlife.

Confucianism (an ethical system and philosophy taught by Confucius 2500 years ago in China), on the other hand, emphasizes the virtues of filial piety, social order, benevolence, education, justice, and fidelity (Chan *et al.*, 1969; Soothill, 1929). This teaching advances family responsibility, self-control, self-sacrifice, social order, and obedience to authority and has a profound influence in China, Japan, Korea, and Southeast Asia. In sum, Confucius provided a way for regulating "proper" human relationships, which helped maintain social order (Chan, 1992).

Taoism, which also originated in China, was the most important teaching that influenced the development of Chinese medicine as widely practiced throughout Asia. It teaches "naturalism," "fatalism," "noninterference," and the theory of "yin–yang" in the universe (Chan *et al.*, 1969; Soothill, 1929). The theory that health is the balance of the "positive" and "negative" energy in the mind and body is based on "yin–yang." Chinese medicine believes that there is a definite relationship between the external and internal system of a human being. It treats a person as a whole and uses herbs and acupuncture for treatment of physical and psychological problems.

Based on the influence of Buddhism and Taoism, people generally believe that illness has something to do with the imbalance of the "energy" in the body or mind, as a punishment for wrongdoing, or a supernatural phenomenon caused by bad luck or evil spirits.

From this perspective, we can appreciate Sue Ling's parents' strong work ethic and their response to the counselor's request for a meeting.

Many of the virtues of hard work and the acceptance of what life brings them come from these beliefs. These beliefs are the greatest challenges to mental health professionals as the understanding of illness often contradicts the ideas of therapy. It is not unusual for many Chinese, as it was the case with Sue's parents, to refuse to talk with an outsider about their problems since the causes are perceived to come from other external factors.

Basic Cultural Values

As suggested earlier, the development of Chinese culture has been based primarily on its agricultural civilizations over thousands of years. Thus, it is not surprising that Chinese people still maintain the highest respect for nature, and the wisdom and origin of the culture derived from these influences. In this context, the individual is defined in terms of an extended family unit which serves as his/her fundamental social and economic unit. Thus, harmony with nature, the family welfare before the individual, education, self-control, and self-actualization are all central values for Chinese individuals (Lee, 1982; Shon & Ja, 1982; Sue & Morishima, 1982).

These values cannot be easily compared to Western cultural values, although some attempts have been made in this regard. For instance, when comparison between the two cultures are made regarding value orientations, an interesting picture emerges (Kluckholn, 1958). Time orientation of Chinese culture is found to emphasize the past, while American culture focuses on the future. Similarly, the primary relational orientations of the Chinese is toward lineal ties, while American people tend to be individualistic. Chinese culture expectations regarding man–nature orientation and activity orientation stress harmony with nature and emphasize the individual as he is, as being, with emphasis also on his development. The value and activity orientations for the dominant American culture, on the other hand, stress man-master over nature and place greater emphasis on doing, accomplishing, and succeeding rather than harmonious co-existence (Kluckholn, 1958).

We must give credit to Kluckholn for making an effort to compare the different value orientations of very different cultures. However, for individuals whose understanding of the background of Asian culture is limited, the presentation of this study can perpetuate misconceptions, especially in the area of activity orientations and time orientation. By looking at these differences, these individuals may get the impression that Chinese culture values the past and the individual as he is now, and puts little or no emphasis on action or progress. Yet the Chinese are generally thought of as hardworking and their civilization has had an important role in the world. If we look deeper into the activity orientations in Asian and Western cultures, we also see more similarities in both cultures. Both cultures place emphasis on doing, accomplishing, and succeeding and emphasize the development and cultivation of the "self." The only difference is that the "self" in Chinese culture is a "mass person" in which the interests of the family/group take precedent over those of the "self". This is comparable to the concept of "Familial Self" described by Roland (1988) in reference to the Japanese and Indian.

It can be said that conflict with these values was at the very core of Sue Ling's psychological dilemma. She was expected to work hard to bring honor to her family while the Western values of individualism, separation, and individuation required a different set of behaviors from her. At the end, the conflict between Sue and her parents became intensified.

Family Structure and Relationships

As indicated earlier, family interaction and structure are heavily influenced by the teachings of Confucius which emphasize filial piety. It is an extended patriarchal/hierarchal unit where the father/elder has a great deal of authority. This authority gets its strength from the cultural emphasis on the importance of honoring the origin of the family through ancestor worship.

With regard to gender role and status in the family, which we will describe further later in this paper, a woman's position may appear as less desirable or central than that of a man's if viewed from a more traditional perspective. Similarly, interpersonal interactions are determined more by prescribed roles, obligations, and duties than by a person-oriented process. Family members learn to respect their elders and be interdependent upon each other as a matter of course. In fact, childrearing is aimed toward interdependence rather than independence. The role that "shame" and "loss of face" or "dignity" play in childrearing should be mentioned in this regard. They are powerful tools used by the family to discipline a child in which loss of face is seen as affecting the whole family unit, including one's ancestors.

These are the basic principles to understand the different kinship systems, such as husband–wife, parent-child, siblings, and intergenerational systems. Marriage is usually arranged and the woman is expected to leave her original family and become part of the husband's family (Shon & Ja, 1982). The parent–child relationship is vertical where communication is from the top down. This vertical relationship is also shown in the sibling systems in which the elder son has authority over the younger siblings, while the elder daughter becomes the substitute caretaker for the mother (Lee, 1982). In the intergenerational system, the vertical communication is shown in the fact that the oldest generational head gets the most respect and attention.

Further Issues in Gender Roles

In every society throughout history, there are prescribed roles for men and women and Chinese culture is not an exception. A system where the family unit is more important than the individual and roles are more important than the person's feelings or thinking, can only result in a specific gender role definition which may appear controversial. But the cultural influences that guide gender relationships are more complicated and deserve further attention.

Cultural Mythology About Femininity and Masculinity. According to the theory of "yin and yang," the universe is guided by the presence of opposite forces which are also present in everything and action. This theory of "dualism" is prevalent in Chinese philosophy, folklore, divination, religion, and science. In this "dualism" theory, the "yin" is the female — the negative and dark side of the natural force. By contrast, the "yang," the male represents the positive and bright side of the natural force (Chan *et al.,* 1969; Soothill, 1929). It is important to understand that in this theory masculinity and femininity are in an equal power base, complementary to each other in creation. The concept of negative and positive force in this regard has to be seen only in relationship to one another and not as indicating levels of desirability.

The "yin" and the "yang" maintain a reciprocal and complementary role to one another in which the male is compared to heaven and female to earth. The Heaven is taking care of everything on earth, and the Earth is nurturing everything growing in the soil. In this context, "Heaven and Earth" symbolism of male and female carries no power connotation in either sex. The power connotation did not develop until later when the issue of control of family property became important.

That was the case when, in keeping with a patriarchal family system, Chinese families felt the need to insure that their property was left to their sons, and thus giving primacy to "sons" over "daughters." It was felt that the best way to guarantee this was by controlling their women's sexual and social freedom. Virginity and faithfulness to a husband was thus highly valued (Hsu, 1981). The roles for men and women became then clearly defined along those dimensions in which man is the head of the family and the decision maker. As part of this role, he is expected to work outside the home and take care of all the business, while the woman is expected to stay home and take care of the children and the household chores. She is expected to be a devoted helper to her mother-in-law and to bear children.

The view of women derived from these cultural norms can only lead to women taking a subservient role to the male. We can see the impact of this tradition further by reviewing Confucius' teachings in that regard. According to his teachings, women should be brought up and socialized according to the doctrine of *three* obediences and *four* virtues. The three obediences are: to obey her father before marriage, her husband after marriage, and her son after the death of her husband (Shon & Ja, 1982). The four virtues are: good appearance and manner, ability in domestic work, language, and self-respect.

This tradition illustrates rather eloquently the subservient roles Asian women have been asked to take over the centuries. They have been asked to suffer in silence without a voice, a name, and power to determine their own destiny. Their identity was only possible in relationship to significant males in their life (i.e., father, husband, and elder son). Having a good son or becoming a mother-in-law was their only way to power (Shon & Ja, 1982).

The first major change for Asian women was in the 1950s when America was having its civil rights movement. It was at that time that China was also experiencing its peoples' liberation movement. The appeal of Communism to liberate all those being oppressed in China, including peasants, poor laborers, racial minorities, and women, created a new atmosphere for Chinese women. Chairman Mao's declaration that women were holding up half the sky was indeed regarded by many women as a turning point. It resulted in some significant changes for woman in Chinese society.

Another way in which the gender role became apparent was in the way the issue of sexuality was handled. Sex is considered "taboo" even today among many of our Chinese immigrant families. Indeed, sexual attractiveness is downplayed and pre-marital and extra-marital relationships are not socially accepted; virginity is still a highly valued cultural virtue (Hsu, 1981). It is not surprising, then, that dating among adolescents is strongly discouraged and any sexual expression away from the norm (i.e., homosexuality) is not tolerated and found unacceptable.

Close friendships only between men and only between women are generally encouraged and accepted. By contrast, close friendships between married men and married women are frowned upon. Affection, especially with a sexual undertone, is expressed subtly and is expected to be only in private.

Women's Roles in Chinese Immigrant Families. Due to racial oppression and Chinese exclusion, there were very few Chinese women in the

United States before the 1950s. However, many Chinese women were married to immigrant men and were left behind in their own countries. These women could not join their husbands, sometimes for years, sometimes for decades. The prolonged separations among families had a profound impact on their lives. Many women suffered from loneliness and hardship and died during those waiting years; however, many grew stronger because they had to shoulder the family burdens by themselves. They had to take care of their families on their own with money sent back from their husbands. They played key roles in raising their children and managing the family unit. These women, when compared to the traditional Chinese women, were stronger and more independent.

The Chinese women who came to the United States between the 1960's and 1990 were still confronted with many problems and multiple oppression in this new land while they worked side-by-side with their husbands. Additionally, they were still expected to assume most of the household chores and be the primary caretakers for the young and the old. Their spouses also worked very long hours but rarely helped with housework. What is so unbelievable in all this is that education only had a moderate impact of the way women fared in this country (Woo, 1989).

Men's Roles in Chinese Immigrant Families. The traditional role of men are to provide for the family financially, to be the disciplinarian of the children, and to handle whatever happens outside the family (Lee, 1982). He is the leader of the family and when he makes decisions, his authority is not questioned (Shon & Ja, 1982). However, due to long working hours and being away from their families for long periods of time, it is often difficult for the father to maintain his traditional roles (Lee, 1982).

In Sue Ling's family, it is apparent that their family is similar to other immigrant families in this regard. Both of the parents worked just to make ends meet. Since the parents were often away, Sue Ling was given the responsibility to take care of the home and her two younger brothers. It has been suggested that the long working hours by parents and the language barrier between the non-English speaking parents and the more Americanized adolescents result in the parental role becoming diminished in substantial ways in many families (Sung, 1987).

Elder Status

Taking care of the elderly has been a strong tradition common to all Asian cultures. However, after coming to this country, many immigrants have to struggle for survival. At the same time, some of the traditional values also change. Care for this group has been increasingly more difficult. According to the 1980 Census, there were 22,048 Asian elderly (U.S. Department of Commerce Economics & Statistics Administration Bureau of the Census, 1988), and in 1990, the numbers increased to 54,731 (U.S. Department of Commerce Economics & Statistics Administration Bureau of the Census, 1992). Most of these elderly live in poverty. In addition, due to historical immigration patterns, many elder Chinese males live alone without family support. Many of these elderly neither read nor write English and cannot participate in or receive social services other than from programs in their own ethnic community. The problem of caring for the elderly in this country has created additional stress in an already overtaxed family structure.

CHALLENGES FOR MENTAL HEALTH PROVIDERS

Using Sue and Sue's (1971) theory of personality development of Chinese Americans, one can infer from the three characterological categories of Asian American individuals, namely the traditionalist, the marginal man, and the Asian American, that there are three corresponding types of Chinese American families. These are the traditional family, marginal family, and Chinese American bicultural family. These three types of Chinese Americans or Chinese American families bring different problems to social or mental health facilities. The traditional families usually speak no English, reside in Chinatown or with other Chinese families, and generally have more problems with their social systems. Marginal families usually have problems in the areas of generational conflicts, role, and identity. The Chinese American families are expected to have adapted better to this country, may have few social adjustment problems, but psychologically, they may be extremely sensitive and suspicious due to subtle racism. They may also have problems with self-pride and identity if they have not successfully assimilated.

There are a number of obstacles to psychotherapy delivery that can be derived from the cultural issues discussed earlier in this paper. Judging by the underutilization of existing mental health services (Ryan, 1979), it is clear that these services need to be reformulated along cultural dimensions. Only in this way can a more meaningful and functional relationship between cultural and mental health needs be obtained.

Medical Orientation

We suggested earlier that, in general, Chinese Americans do not readily accept psychotherapy as a solution to their problems. We demonstrated in this regard that mental health concepts as they exist in the current practice in this country are rather contradictory to their beliefs. Specifically, the principles in psychotherapy of individualism, self-determination, and self-fulfillment are in conflict with the traditional Asian cultural values which stress collectivism, interdependence, and loyalty to the family. Additionally, Asian immigrants' medical orientation and view of health services are based on the concepts of Chinese medicine. In this context, mental health is viewed as the harmony of the function of body, mind, and spirit, or the balance of "yin and yang." Physical or mental illness are viewed as organic disorders, that is, the imbalance of "yin and yang," or as punishment, or fate.

Mental illness is highly stigmatized and going to see a mental health counselor can bring shame to the family. By looking at the possible reasons normally given to explain mental illness (Shon & Ja, 1982), we can appreciate further the nature of the challenge for the mental health providers. Mental illness has been said to reflect (a) a hereditary trait that runs in the family line; (b) a punishment for past wrongs of the family; and (c) poor guidance and discipline from the family leader. Such attitudes may explain some of the reasons for the underutilization of mental health facilities among the Asian families.

The attitude toward physical and mental illness is one of denial, delay, and finally acceptance and tolerance. It is not unusual to observe patients who have suffered from emotional disorders for many years, and only come seeking help after they have had an acute episode. Chinese culture discourages the display or expression of emotion and hence encourages somatization of psychiatric problems such as anxiety and depression into physical illness (Kleinman, 1981). When the need for treatment emerges, traditional treatments such as spiritual healing, herbs, or acupuncture are more likely to prevail. Only when they exhaust all the traditional treatment methods and the family can no longer take care of the problem, will they come to a mental health clinic. The problem is that the same expectation of instant remedy and relief for their symptoms are brought to the mental health clinician's doorstep (Lee, 1982). As a result, a long treatment approach without a tangible benefit is doomed to failure.

Assessment and Diagnosis

In assessing Chinese American families, special attention must be given to the degree of social and psychological stress on the family due to role/status changes and the degree of acculturation of each family member to the American culture. Many mental health problems among Chinese Americans are caused by social and psychological stress.

Since, as we indicated earlier, Chinese Americans represent many different subgroups, the suggested guideline for clinical assessment must include: (1) language; (2) current and past stressors due to the migration or refugee experience; (3) assessment of family strengths, cultural beliefs, and responses to mental health problems; (4) assessment of the differences between cultural traits vs. clinical pathologies.

Language

With regard to language, it is important to find out what language and dialect the patient speaks. If the therapist has to work with an interpreter, you must make sure that the interpreter is trained and can provide correct language and cultural translation. There are serious consequences with regard to assessment and treatment when untrained interpreters are used (Vazquez & Javier, 1991).

Current and Past Stressors

It is important to find out the history of the patient and his/her family and the stresses due to migration, past migration, and acculturation. The pace and degree of acculturation depends on the immigrant's age, education, and the exposure to Western culture.

Assessment of Family Strengths and Cultural Beliefs

Many Chinese Americans still hold onto their traditional beliefs even after they have lived in the United States for many years. It is important to identify their cultural beliefs and coping mechanisms in dealing with mental health problems. Equally important is the assessment of the family's strengths and having their support in working out a treatment plan. At times, the therapist may have to work in collaboration with other culturally appropriate treatment in the patient's community.

Assessment of the Differences between Cultural Traits Vs Clinical Pathologies

Normality and abnormality must be judged in the context of one's cultural traits. Therefore, a therapist has to know the patient's culture in order to make a correct diagnosis. When assessing a Chinese patient, it is important to realize that certain behaviors, such as lack of eye contact, shyness, and passivity, might be appropriate to their culture and thus should not be viewed as a sign of emotional disturbance. Another cultural specific behavior is the custom of talking to the deceased. Talking to the deceased may be accepted as a grief process and should not be taken as a hallucinatory condition (Uba, 1994).

Clinical Manifestations of Mental Health Problems

Kleinman and Lim's (1981) study indicates that Chinese culture discourages the display of emotions, an observation also supported by our own experience with this population. Indeed, it is more likely that the Chinese would channel the communication of conditions such as anxiety and depression through physical illness. Other prominent problems are personality disorders with passive/aggressive traits and sexual and sexuality problems which are not directly and openly discussed. All these problems have deep roots in cultural repression of feelings, especially sexual feelings. In general, it seems that the Chinese population tends to be relatively introverted and emotionally reserved.

This is the kind of clinical picture that a professional dealing with this population is likely to observe. The first author has also observed this picture at her Mental health Center in which the following patient profiles were found: schizophrenia accounted for 35% of mental illness while major depression/affective disorders and adjustment disorders accounted for only 16% and 10%, respectively. Other nonpsychotic problems found included personality disorders, marital conflicts, parent–child problems, child abuse, alcoholism and gambling. There were more somatizers than nonsomatizers among these patients. Kuo (1988) found in this regard that social support plays an important role in the dynamics and processes of somatization. It appears that social support helps to eliminate physical symptoms in the initial stages of somatization. These findings have an important implication for the treatment of Chinese patients.

TREATMENT APPROACHES

Thus, based on the kind of cultural information discussed in this paper and our own experience with this population, the following treatment approaches are strongly suggested:

1. A psychosocial rather than psychological approach should be considered. Many mental problems among Chinese Americans are more psy-

chosocial in nature due to cultural change. Attention must be given to social service needs while dealing with clinical problems.

2. An autocratic rather than democratic approach should be preferred. The therapist will be more effective if he/she assumes a clear leadership role and provides guidance and direction when requested by the patient.

3. The formulation of treatment goals and plans should be centered around the family rather than the individual. As suggested earlier, the Chinese family relationship is more interdependent than what can be expected in the case of a Western family. Therefore, the entire family has to be engaged as part of the treatment equation. It is important to keep in mind that the traditional concepts of family therapy are not easily workable with the Chinese family. Individual approach guided by the family therapy concept is more appropriate.

4. The individual approach is also preferred to group approach. It is contrary to Chinese tradition to express one's feelings, especially negative feelings, openly. Individual approach may facilitate the expression of these feelings without adding additional sense of shame and guilt.

5. It is important to respect and accept the patient's need for dependency in a therapeutic relationship. Chinese patients tend to depend on the therapist more than the Western patient due to a cultural respect for authority.

6. It is also important to respect and accept culturally relevant alternative treatment modalities. Otherwise, your patients may not share with you what they are doing after they leave your office.

7. And finally, it will be crucial to remove any "social stigmas" by utilizing the patients' cultural values as an incentive for treatment. For instance, since most Chinese individuals value education and work, providing concrete assistance in this regard may encourage them to stay in treatment for emotional and mental problems.

CONCLUDING COMMENTS

In this paper we provided a general overview of the cultural characteristics that tend to guide the behaviors of Chinese individuals and families. It is clear that the lives of chinese individuals are fraught with stressors whose intensity may lead to family violence and other pathological transformations. It is also clear that working with these individuals and families can be very challenging and trying because of cultural norms amply described in this paper. We demonstrated how mental health service delivery is affected by these qualities and made specific recommendations for its improvement.

ACKNOWLEDGMENTS

Portions of this paper were presented by the first author at the Second Annual Multicultural Conference, St. John's University, Jamaica, New York, May 1992.
The authors wish to give special thanks to Mr. Frank T. Modica for his help in editing, Miss Una Shih for her help in researching, and to Mrs. Linnit Lawton and Miss Joan Young for their help in the preparation of this manuscript. Dr. Rafael Art. Javier read and made important contributions in an earlier version of this manuscript.

REFERENCES

American Psychiatric Association. (1987). *Diagnostic and statistical manual of mental disorders* (3rd ed.). Washington, D.C.: Author.

Chan, S. (1992). Families with Asian roots. In E. W. Lynch & M. J. Hanson (Eds.), *Developing cross-cultural competence* (pp. 181-257). Baltimore, MD: Paul H. Brookes.

Chan, W. T., Ragi al Faruqi, I., Kitagawa, J. M., & Raju, P. T. (1969). *The great Asian religions: An anthology.* New York: Macmillan.

Chinese American Planning Council, Inc., United Way of Tri-State, & Regional Plan Associations (1988). *Outlook — The growing Asian Presence in the Tri-State region.* New York: Author.

Daniels, R. (1988). *Asian America: Chinese and Japanese in the United States since 1850.* Seattle, WA: University of Washington Press.

Fong, S. L. M. (1979). Identity conflicts of Chinese adolescents in San Francisco. In E. B. Brody (Ed.), *Minority group adolescents in the United States* (pp. 111-132). Huntington, NY: Robert E. Krieger.

Hsu, F. K. L. (1981). *Americans & Chinese: Passages to differences* (3rd ed.). Honolulu: HI: University of Hawaii Press.

Kim, S., McLeod, J. H., & Shantzis, C. (1992). Cultural competence for evaluators working with Asian–American communities: Some practical considerations. In M. A. Orlandi, R. Weston, & L. G. Epstein (Eds.), *Cultural competence for evaluators: A guide for alcohol and other drug abuse prevention practitioners working with ethnic/racial communities* (pp. 203-260). Rockville, MD: U.S. Department of Health and Human Services.

Kleinman, A. M. (1981). Culture and patient care: Psychiatry among the Chinese. *Drug Therapy, 11,* 134-140.

Kleinman, A. M., & Lim, T. (Eds.) (1981). *Normal and abnormal behavior in Chinese culture.* Holland: D. Reidel.

Kluckholn, F. R. (1958). Family diagnosis. I. Variations in the basic values of family systems. *Social Casework, 39,* 66-69.

Kuo, C. L. (1988). *Somatization, social support, and semantics in Chinatown.* Unpublished manuscript, Chinatown Family Consultation Center, New York.

Lee, E. (1982). A social systems approach to assessment and treatment for Chinese American families. In M. McGoldrick, J. K. Pearce, & J. Giordano (Eds.), *Ethnicity and family therapy* (pp. 527-551). New York: Guilford.

Ridenour, F. (1967). *So what's the difference?* Ventura, CA: Regal Books.

Roland, A. (1988). *In search of self in India and Japan.* Princeton: Princeton University Press.

Ryan, A. S. (1979). *Mental health needs of Asian Americans.* New York: Hunter College.

Shon, S. P., & Ja, D. Y. (1982). Asian families. In M. McGoldrick, J. K. Pearce, & J. Giordano (Eds.), *Ethnicity and family therapy* (pp. 208-228). New York: Guilford.

Soothill, W. E. (1929). *The three religions of China* (3rd ed.). Totowa, NJ: Rowman & Littlefield.

Sue, D. W. (1983). Ethnic identity: The impact of two cultures on the psychological development of Asians in America. In D. R. Atkinson, G. Morten, & D. W. Sue (Eds.), *Counseling American Minorities* (2nd ed.) (pp. 85-96). Dubuque, IA: Wm. C. Brown.

Sue, S., & Morishima, J. K. (1982). *The mental health of Asian Americans.* San Francisco, CA: Jossey-Bass.

Sue, S., & Sue, D. W. (1971). Chinese-American personality and mental health. *Amerasia Journal, 1,* 36-49.

Sung, B. L. (1987). *The adjustment experience of Chinese immigrant children in New York City.* New York: Center for Migration Studies.

Takaki, R. (1989). Strangers from a different shore: *A history of Asian Americans.* Boston: Little Brown.

Uba, L. (1994). *Asian Americans: Personality Patterns, identity, and mental health.* New York: Guilford.

U.S. Department of Commerce Economics & Statistics Administration Bureau of the Census. (1965). *Asian & Pacific Islander Population in the United States: 1965.* Washington, D.C.: U.S. Government Printing Office.

U.S. Department of Commerce Economics & Statistics Administration Bureau of the Census (1988). *Asian & Pacific Islander Population in the United States: 1980.* Washington, D.C.: U.S. Government Printing Office.

U.S. Department of Commerce Economics & Statistics Administration Bureau of the Census (1992). *1990 census of population: General population characteristics metropolitan areas.* Washington, D.C.: U.S. Government Printing Office.

Vazquez, C., & Javier, R. A. (1991). Problems with interpreters: Communicating with Spanish-speaking patients. *Hospital and Community Psychiatry, 42*(2), 163-65.

Woo, D. (1989). The gap between striving and achieving: The case of Asian American Women. In Asian Women United of California (Ed.), *Making waves, an anthology of writings by and about Asian American women,* Boston, MA: Beacon Press.

PART II

TREATMENT ISSUES

6

Marital Violence: An Integrated Systems Approach

Arthur G. Mones and Pamela E. Panitz

A review of current issues and approaches to the problem of marital vio-lence is presented. In order to understand volatile relationships, these attachments are discussed within the context of the normal progression of events in the formation and development of a marriage. A systems model that integrates current conceptual thinking is presented. The article con-cludes with a paradigm for therapeutic decision-making and strategies that flow from the integrated systems model.

INTRODUCTION

Using Thomas Kuhn's (1962/1970) terminology, the literature on domestic violence can be characterized as being in a "pre-paradigmatic" stage. At this stage, there is not one single paradigm that unifies science, research, or clinical practice. Rather, there is a proliferation of theoretical constructions attempting to explain the regularly occurring events, in this case, domestic violence.

At present, however, there seems to be a push toward utilizing this existing multifaceted conception of domestic violence in providing theoret-ical and treatment approaches for this problem (Berliner, 1990; Goldner, 1992; Weidman, 1986). The integrative approach proposed in this paper is designed to utilize the best of what the field has to offer in creating a framework for understanding and treating domestic violence. This integra-tive approach will proceed from focusing on the individual psychologies of the family members through provision of a framework for the integration of treatment modalities and service-providing agencies.

BACKGROUND

Several investigators point to the need to view the etiology of violence in families using a multidimensional framework. Gelles (1980), in a review of the literature, found that there are a number of factors associated with family violence. Weidman (1986) summarized these factors into four categories: the intergenerational cycle of violence, socioeconomic status, social stress, and social isolation.

O'Leary and Vivian (1990) explain the etiology of domestic violence using biological, sociological, and psychological models. Included in the sociological model are resource and exchange theories, and patriarchal conceptualizations. Included in the psychological model are classical conditioning, operant analyses, modeling, a cognitive-affective model, and a social learning perspective.

Goldner, Penn, Sheinberg, and Walker (1990) delineate four levels of description and explanation of volatile attachments. The psychodynamic level proposes inquiry about an individual's ideas, beliefs, and internal representation of oneself and others. According to Goldner *et al.* (1990), these conceptions may be out of awareness, but often when elucidated, seem to constitute the "organizing and unworkable premises underlying these couples' fierce attachments" (p. 346).

The social learning level inquires about men and women's socialization into their gendered positions in the relationship. The sociopolitical level includes the external power differential between men and women. According to Goldner and her colleagues, this power differential gives rise to ". . . men's subjective sense of entitlement, privilege and permission to rule women, and women's subjective belief that they must serve men . . ." (p. 346). At the systemic level, one is interested in analyzing the transactional sequences in a couple's relationship, as positive feedback loops appear to constitute the immediate cause of the escalations that lead to violence. Also included at the systemic level are inquiries about the interaction between the couple, extended families and treatment and social services that constitute the "problem-maintaining system" (p. 346).

This variety of theoretical perspectives has given rise to a multitude of treatment approaches. Scher and Stevens (1987) and Sakai (1991) conclude that group intervention seems to work more effectively than individual counseling in treating domestic abusers. Sakai (1991) asserts that "group work reduces participant's sense of isolation and provides an atmosphere that facilitates sharing of inner secrets with persons who can relate and understand them" (p. 537). She provides a cognitive-behavioral strategy for helping domestic abusers clarify their need for control and power in their relationships.

Jennings' (1990) approach also focuses on the treatment of the male batterer. His approach, however, questions the enormous demands for change that are placed on the abusive man. Jennings promotes looking at domestic violence within a substance abuse treatment paradigm. This approach has, at the least, face validity as the co-occurrence of domestic violence and substance abuse has been well documented (Gorney, 1986; Roberts, 1987).

Jennings' approach focuses on "long-term relapse prevention and supportive maintenance" (p. 50). Releasing the abusive man from the "myth" that relapse is indicative of treatment failure, also allows the clinician to feel less pressure and uses the relapse episode as a learning tool to examine what habits, situations, and beliefs led to the relapse. Jennings (1990) asserts that halting violence, while an important behavioral change, is only a prerequisite to recovery from the "underlying attitudinal disease" (p. 52).

Some theorists and clinicians have chosen to focus psychodynamically on the function of violence with respect to the "victim," or the individual who is aggressed against. Seagull and Seagull (1991) suggest that inner conflict exists over whether to allow the psychic wound resulting from early traumata (physical and/or sexual abuse) to heal. This conflict is based on the victim's ". . . unconscious belief that full recovery from the wound would exonerate the perpetrator . . ." (p. 16). This "accusatory suffering" is a result of trauma and is treated using a post-traumatic therapy paradigm.

Similarly, Young and Gerson (1991) apply psychoanalytic concepts in attempting to understand the difficulties people in abusive relationships have in departing, and the high rate of reunion. In particular, Young and Gerson (1991) suggest that ". . . many chronic battering relationships have their roots in the caretaker–infant relationship . . . and are more often victims and survivors of a traumatic childhood. It is the need for the love of rejecting and hostile love objects that makes a child accept suffering as if it were love" (pp. 32-33). In addition, Young and Gerson (1991) suggest that the cycle of violence can be understood within a psychoanalytic frame from the dynamics of control, defensive operations of denial, identification and projection, and low self-esteem and depressive affect. These investigators suggest that a "contemporary" treatment approach which considers social, economic, as well as pathogenic conditions would be most suitable.

Injected into the debate about etiology and treatment are other issues which have served to further fragment the provision of services to families suffering from domestic violence. McGregor (1990) asserts that domestic violence is a social and political issue. She asserts that therapeutic interventions constitute denial of the need to respond to male violence as a crime and the necessity of law reform. She states that "theories and methods of family therapy which are used for other "problems," are inappropriate in response to the crime of violence" (p. 66).

The focus on swift elimination of violence appears to be partially fueled by the emotionality of the reality that children are often involved. Davies (1991) proposes that until the 1980s, children were unrecognized as secondary victims of spouse abuse in the literature. Davies (1991) suggests that witnessing parental violence may predispose male children to become violent in future relationships. He provides a treatment strategy aimed at very young male children (aged 15 to 36 months) who have witnessed spouse abuse. While it is relatively easy to muster empathy for children, this is not enough. As clinicians, we are also left with the responsibility of providing services to these young clients.

In treating domestic violence, one must be aware of one's audience. Treating a man and/or family who come willingly for treatment is different than treating the court remanded abuser/family. Additionally, different types of agencies may treat referrals from particular sources, thereby further fragmenting the service delivery system (Weidman, 1986).

The clinician must also be aware of the distinctive beliefs and values of the family she is treating. In particular, a person's ethnicity shapes one's thinking, feelings, and behavior (McGoldrick, 1982). Just as the intergenerational cycle of violence is a factor strongly associated with family violence, ethnicity is transferred from generation to generation and is suggested to be related to family violence (Witt, 1987). One's cultural background influences one's gender role definition, one's definition of what is and is not acceptable in relationships, how conflict is resolved, and what defines "violence" (Tellis-Nayak & O'Donoghue, 1982). In order to help a family stop violent behavior, the clinician must fully understand the families' beliefs within a cultural context.

Finally, a crucial component in the theory-treatment loop is the beliefs, values, and experiences of the clinician. Clinicians, also have been socialized into specific gender patterns and beliefs. Even simply using the terms "victim" and "abuser" points to a dichotomy of responsibility which may not be helpful in treating an abusive system. A therapist's particular beliefs about the nature of domestic abuse may influence the subsystem with which she chooses to empathize and work. While work with subsystems is necessary and legitimate (Weidman, 1986), it does not address the responsibility of all members of the system, family, and service providers included, to provide safety and reach a healthier state of existence.

THE INTEGRATIVE SYSTEMS APPROACH

As stated earlier, several theorists have begun to provide integrative theoretical and treatment approaches to address the issue of domestic violence. Goldner *et al.* (1990), for example, describe their perspective on volatile family attachments as a "doubled vision" which includes gender and violence and men and women; and a "double stance" including feminist and systemic perspectives.

These clinicians attempt to stay away from an either/or position in favor of a "both/and" position in order to move away from blame. At the same time, this dual stance allows the acceptance of the assumption that gender inequality is a social reality and that women who are beaten by men are their victims. Similarly, while violence is viewed as an expressive act, it is also seen as a willful strategy of intimidation.

Goldner (1992) also addresses the reality of the high rate of reunion of violent couples, as well as the issue of the role of conjoint or couples therapy in treating the volatile relationship. Goldner (1992) suggests that "when they the couple choose couples therapy over other forms of treatment, they are enacting their problem—they are stuck together in a confusing relationship and are paralyzed" (p. 58). She discusses her position that while she accepts this form of treatment, she also recognizes that this systemic position has consequences of which the therapist must be aware. In particular, the therapist must recognize that at times she must act as "agents of social control" (p. 58), a distinct role from that of the therapist doing therapy.

Weidman (1986) describes a conjoint family therapy program designed to "end violent behavior and to encourage growth in families" (p. 211). Weidman asserts that there are two needs with respect to the current paradigm for treating families experiencing domestic violence. First, there is a need for a more collaborative, and cooperative relationship among the various service providers with the goal of a better integration of services. Second, Weidman asserts that an integrated treatment approach is needed to address the fact that many families experiencing domestic violence remain together. In addition, an integrated treatment approach is needed, he asserts, to address the intergenerational nature of domestic violence.

Weidman (1986) describes a program which includes men's groups, women's groups, children's groups, and conjoint therapy. All members of the system are engaged in creating specific "violence avoidance plans." Goldner *et al.* (1990), Goldner (1992), and Weidman (1986) submit that the acceptance of conjoint therapy makes a clear statement that the volatile nature of the family relationship is a systemic problem.

A CONTEXTUAL VIEW OF MARITAL VIOLENCE

Our discussion of volatile relationships between marriage partners will attempt to integrate the varied views and approaches summarized above. In order to understand the violent relationship, we will first discuss the normal progression of events in the formation and development of a marriage. From this, we will establish a context in which to place volatile attachments. Finally, we will suggest a paradigm of therapeutic decision-making and strategies that flow from our model.

To begin, a statement about our beliefs on this topic: Violence is unacceptable behavior unless used in self-defense in protecting one's physical survival. Violence is an unacceptable and unsuccessful means of conflict resolution in *all* relationships (spousal, parent–child, peer relationships and relations among religious groups, racial groups, ethnic groups, and nationalities). Violence and oppression beget violence and oppression, sooner or later.

The following facts and paradoxes point out that violence in marriage is one of the most compelling yet challenging psychological and societal issues:

1. An estimated 1.6 to 2 million women are the targets of domestic violence in the U.S. each year.

2. Approximately one-fourth of battered women report that they experience violence with their men prior to marriage or cohabitation. Violence typically occurs *after* sexual intimacy is established in the relationship (Walker, 1984, 1991).

3. Follow-up studies of battered women who seek refuge and safety in women's shelters report that within a short period of time, 49–60% of these women return to their violent partners.

4. A relatively low percentage of victims and batterers seek treatment on their own.

5. Many spouse abuse situations involve alcohol and substance abuse. (If this is the case, treat this first. Therapy cannot proceed with active addiction unattended.)

Let us place these alarming facts in context. Almost all couples begin their relationship in a *State of Idealization* (or "fusion"). This state is characterized by seeking completion for one's imperfections in the partner—looking to the other to repair the wounds left from our families-of-origin (Bowen, 1978; Nadelson, Polonsky, & Mathews, 1984).

The central developmental task for all of us is to progress through the individuative process (process of differentiation), i.e., becoming a fully responsible, functioning Self. We all fall short and find someone who, we think, will fill the gap. All of us, to some degree, "escape from self" (DSM

III-R lists the various options). In the beginning, we experience unconditional love, protection, and security. We "fall in love."

For couples where battering occurs, the desperation and need for repair is on a high order. Spouses in such relationships typically come from families-of-origin where violence was a means of dealing with conflict between spouses and coercion was the dominant mode of childrearing. They come from families-of-origin where a woman's sense of individuation is squashed and where a man's ownership of emotional neediness and vulnerability is disqualified.

These women and men leave (or escape from) home in search of a partner who can heal deeply felt wounds. The greater the internal emotional pain, the greater the idealization of the partner selected.

Following idealization, shortly, or after the passage of time, all marriages experience a letdown—an awareness that one's partner cannot deliver this reparative bond. The relationship enters a state of "disillusionment and disenchantment" (Nadelson, Polonsky, & Mathews, 1984). This is inevitable, as the Idealization stage has been an interlude in the journey of individuation. On a deeply emotional level, a "truth" is experienced: *we cannot achieve emotional completion through another human being.*

The most common conclusion for each spouse during this Disillusionment Phase is that one's unhappiness is *caused by* the newly experienced imperfections of the partner. This results in externalization or projective identification (Scarf, 1987; Scharff, 1992), the externalization of what is intolerable to the Self, i.e., that one is incomplete or in need of emotional repair.

Some couples can move beyond the state of Disillusionment and approach a stage of Acceptance (Jacobson, 1993), i.e., a view of reality that includes the acceptance of imperfection in one's mate and ownership of self-responsibility for emotional growth and individuation. Many couples, however, get stuck in the Disillusionment phase and attempt to "resolve" their discomfort by rejecting the external "cause" of their unhappiness by getting divorced (approaching 50% of marriage population) or becoming remarried (high failure rate for second marriages). Other couples stay together, but remain resigned to a life of anger, misery, codependency, and dysfunctionality—the violent marriage being a polarized version of this choice.

The drama of disillusioned/dysfunctional couples appears to revolve around some common themes. First, in dysfunctional marriages one (or both) partners are threatened by too much closeness or too much distance. Most typically, the husband's complaint is, "I need my space." Conversely, the wife may complain that "he's never home," operating from a base of abandonment fears. (These positions can be interchanged between the genders. However, the examples given seem more typically based on societally defined gender roles; (Fogarty, 1978–1983). Often this proximity-distance struggle is played out via tolerance, or lack thereof in perceived sameness and distance between marital partners.

The second theme in dysfunctional marriages is a struggle with marital hierarchy and power. Egalitarianism is an alien concept based on experience from families-of-origin (and partially fostered by societal definitions of gender). The hierarchy in a marriage is organized around issues of adult responsibility (Bepko & Krestan, 1985). Dysfunctional couples seem more polarized in male-entitled/oppressor, female-selfless/subservient extremes.

The resultant of these themes, especially for violent couples, is a man who "escapes from self" (individuation) via an internal prohibition against his "softer side" and who exerts tight control interpersonally. This man is drawn to a woman who does not feel entitled to selfhood and "escapes" the individuative journey by subverting her existence and defining herself via her relationship to others. The fragile sense of Self for men and women in these marriages is cemented by their bond to one another. It is this desperate bond that keeps these couples together despite daily lives filled with misery and pain.

TREATMENT ISSUES AND CHOICES

Based on our understanding of the intrapsychic nature of individuals who are in violent relationships as well as the interpersonal dynamics of such couples, we offer the following guidelines and considerations regarding treatment.

Treatment Goals. The hoped-for outcome of treatment is psychological empowerment for both partners. Movement of each spouse back on the path of individuation and away from "escape from self-development" is fostered. It is our firm belief that the more greatly defined and internally stable the partners are, the less the need for violence to address disputes. The hope is to have two mature functioning adults who will either decide that their marriage can proceed in a healthy fashion, *or* who decide that it is not healthy for their marriage to continue.

Safety First. The clinician needs to make sure that the physical safety of the partners is addressed. At the outset, escape routes, a network of friends and relatives that serve as a source of refuge, need to be in place. If necessary, agents of social control (police/shelters/courts) will be employed in order to enforce safety and protection. This should begin to provide some sense of empowerment and personal control and entitlement for both victim *and* batterer.

Assess for Alcohol and/or Drug Abuse. A careful evaluation regarding alcohol and drug abuse is necessary at the outset. The clinician needs to be aware of the tendency of addicted personalities to deny and minimize in this arena. When there is active drug and alcohol abuse and when the clinician suspects such activity, referral for treatment that addresses these issues is indicated before work on marital violence can proceed. Psychotherapy with an active abuser of drugs and alcohol will prove to be counterproductive.

Respect the Marital Bond. As indicated earlier in this article, the intensity of the bond in these couples is reflective of the effort to preserve a sense of Self (albeit fragile) at all costs. The clinician needs to fully respect this bond and the "illogic" (at least on a surface level) that, despite the battering, most of these couples choose to remain together. As a result, the treatment will likely need to encompass work with each spouse and their interaction as a couple (Goldner, 1992).

The approach to the integrated model of treatment will employ systems thinking in its most comprehensive form. Our belief is that all components of the family system, as well as the system itself, require treatment. In addition, the influence of our multicultural, multiethnic society will need to be included in treatment considerations. Feminist theory, regarding the necessary egalitarian relationship between the genders provides the context in which the goal of individuation for all family members must be cultivated.

It is our belief that an internal state of powerlessness contributes to the likelihood of the eruption of violence. Being part of a minority group in one's society, being an immigrant or refugee and having limited economic opportunities are significant factors in influencing a person's sense of personal adequacy or power (Breunlin, Schwartz, & MacKune-Karrer, 1992). Perceptions about the use of violence are certainly influenced by cultural norms and the belief system regarding these norms that are promulgated by each family. As individuals and families experience chronic stress and ongoing frustration and view their environment as not within their direct influence and impact, there is a tendency to handle daily events like marital disputes via impulsive, "immediate problem solutions" such as coercion which can escalate to violence (Hines, 1989; Minuchin, Montalvo, Rosman, & Schumer, 1967).

Successful and unsuccessful marriages can be differentiated not by the occurrence of disagreement but how the spouses *handle* their disagreements via communication skills and problem-solving strategies (Markman, Floyd, Stanley, & Lewis, 1986). When spouses originate from different cultures and/or religious background, many basic differences in beliefs, experiences, negotiating life cycle events, etc. are built into their marital "package" (McGoldrick, 1989). If these couples lack the skills to appreciate and reach empathic understanding of these differences, arguments will ensue and escalation is likely.

An integrated systems model, in ideal form, would need to encompass the following:

Treatment of the Victim. After the establishment of entitlement to, and plans for, physical safety, the victim will be seen in individual treatment. This therapy will explore current themes that likely will include need for intense closeness and control in relationships, relationship to self characterized by self-punishment, and relationship to others characterized by subversion of one's own needs. In addition, the deeply embedded, self-protective function of holding on to pain, termed "accusatory suffering" (Seagull & Seagull, 1991), must be respected and explored fully with the victim. Participation in support groups of peers and/or 12-step programs can enhance the treatment process.

Treatment of the Batterer. As a parallel to the treatment of the victim, work with the batterer will combine individual and group therapies. A focus on behavior, most specifically, anger control, will need to be prominent. Understanding the client within current and historical contexts, will be essential. Group treatment can be a powerful means of fostering safety in self-disclosure (Guerin, Fay, Burden, & Kautto, 1987; Waring, 1990) for male batterers who tend to guard against the experience and expression of vulnerability at all costs.

Treatment of the Couple. As each spouse untangles their internal web of pain and suffering that contributes to the cycle of violence, working directly with the couple, at least sporadically (perhaps monthly) can help to point the couple toward healthier functioning. Working together, in session, to "deconstruct the violent moment" (Goldner, Penn, Sheinberg, & Walker, 1990) and "surrender" to the nonproductive phases of anger that are inevitable in marriages. Reframing "rage" to an inner sense of powerlessness and helping the couple to hear each other's deep emotional pain without the externalized blame and accusations can gradually promote a bond that transforms discord into empathy. It is via couples' treatment that the ability of each spouse to take an "I" position in an unthreatened manner will develop. Most often, it is helpful to have the victim interrupt the long-standing pattern of emotional pursuit (Fogarty, 1978–1983) of her spouse. Disengaging emotionally and maintaining her own position will tend to create a "transitional state" (Fineberg & Walter, 1989) wherein the couple will feel "emotionally separated." It is from this transitional state that the spouses, empowered with a growing stance of individuation, will be able to gradually make a mature, informed, nondefensive decision regarding their marriage. If the marriage is to continue, it will do so under new, healthier conditions. If a decision is made to move toward dissolution and divorce, a grieving period, followed by mature acceptance by each partner, will more likely follow.

As indicated earlier in this paper, it will be very important for the clinician to take a careful history regarding cultural, religious, and ethnic background of the partners. If the spouses are able to begin to comfortably experience their differences, it will be timely to pursue an in-depth exploration of cultural differences within the marriage and between the marriage and the majority culture. Talking and listening to one another about these core differences can have a major impact on reducing externalization and enhancing empathy, which, in turn, will eventually eliminate the tendency to resort to coercion and violence.

Treatment of Children. It is of utmost importance for clinicians to be sensitized to the needs of the children of violent couples. Ideally, ongoing, individual relationships should be established with the clinician(s) in order to maintain effective reality testing, prevent or defuse triangulation and enmeshment in parental conflict, and, as with the parents, keep the child(ren) on *their own* individuative track. Children, too, can benefit from group treatment involving peers with similar struggles. If possible, children exposed to domestic violence should be followed by clinicians throughout the life cycle so as to guide their development and reduce the high risk of intergenerational transmission of choosing violence as a means of coping with internal and interpersonal conflict.

It is hoped that the integrated systems model presented in this article can point the way toward a comprehensive treatment for the complex pattern of marital violence. The greater the range of conceptual understanding on the part of clinicians and the greater the range of therapeutic interventions available for the entire family, the greater the likelihood of successful treatment for more of these families in need.

REFERENCES

Bepko, C., & Krestan, J. (1985). *The responsibility trap: A blueprint for treating the alcoholic family.* New York: The Free Press.
Berliner, L. (1990). Domestic violence: A humanist or feminist issue? *Journal of Interpersonal Violence, 5,* 128-129.
Bowen, M. (1978). *Family therapy in clinical practice.* New York: Jason Aronson.
Breunlin, D. C., Schwartz, R. C., & MacKune-Karrer, B. (1992). *Metaframeworks: Transcending the models of family therapy.* San Francisco: Jossey-Bass.
Davies, D. (1991). Intervention with male toddlers who have witnessed parental violence. *Families in society: The Journal of Contemporary Human Services, 72,* 515-524.
Fineberg, D. E., & Walter, S. (1981). Transforming helplessness: An approach to the therapy of "stuck" couples. *Family Process, 28,* 291-300.

Fogarty, T. F. (1978–1983). The distancer and the pursuer. *Compendium II. The best of the family.* New York: Center for Family Learning.

Gelles, R. J. (1980). Violence in the family: A review of research in the seventies. *Journal of Marriage and Family, 41,* 873-885.

Goldner, V. (1992). Making room for both/and. *The Family Therapy Networker, March/April,* 55-61.

Goldner, V., Penn, P., & Walker, G. (1990). Love and violence: Gender paradoxes in volatile attachments. *Family Process, 29,* 343-364.

Gorney, B. (1989). Domestic violence and chemical dependency: Dual problems, dual interventions. *Journal of Psychoactive Drugs, 21,* 229-238.

Guerin, P., Fay, L., Burden, S., & Kautto, J. (1987). *The evaluation and treatment of marital conflict.* New York: Basic Books.

Hines, P. M. (1989). The family life cycle of poor black families. In E. Carter and M. McGoldrick (Eds.), *The changing family life cycle* (pp. 513-544). New York: Allyn and Bacon.

Jacobson, N. *The delicate balance: Change and acceptance in couples therapy.* (1993). The Networker Symposium. Washington, D.C.

Jennings, J. L. (1990). Preventing relapse versus "stopping" domestic violence: Do we expect too much too soon from battering men? *Journal of Family Violence, 5,* 43-60.

Kuhn, T. S. (1962/1970). *The structure of scientific revolutions.* Chicago: The University of Chicago Press.

Markman, H. J., Floyd, F. J., Stanley, S. M., & Lewis, H. C. (1986). Prevention. In N. S. Jacobson and A. S. Gurman (Eds.), *Clinical handbook of marital therapy* (pp. 176-196). New York: Guilford.

McGoldrick, M. (1982). Ethnicity and family therapy: An overview. In M. McGoldrick, J. K. Pearce, and J. Giordano (Eds.), *Ethnicity and family therapy* (pp. 3-30). New York: Guilford.

McGoldrick, M. (1989). Ethnicity and the family life cycle. In E. Carter and M. McGoldrick (Eds.), *The changing family life cycle* (pp. 70-90). New York: Allyn and Bacon.

McGregor, H. (1990). Conceptualizing male violence against female partners: Political implications of therapeutic responses. *Australian and New Zealand Journal of Family Therapy, 11,* 65-70.

Minuchin, S., Montalvo, B., Rosman, B. L., & Schumer, R. (1967). *Families of the slums.* New York: Basic Books.

Nadelson, C. C., Polonsky, D. C., & Mathews, M. A. (1984). Marriage as a developmental process. In C. Nadelson and D. Polansky, (Eds.), *Marriage and divorce* (pp. 127-141). New York: Guilford.

O'Leary, K. D., & Vivian, D. (1990). Physical aggression in marriage. In F. D. Fincham and T. N. Bradbury (Eds.), *The psychology of marriage: Basic issues and applications* (pp. 323-348). New York: Guilford.

Roberts, A. R. (1987). Psychosocial characteristics of batterers: A study of 234 men charged with domestic violence offenses. 2, 81-93.

Sakai, C. E. (1991). Group intervention strategies with domestic abusers. *Families in Society: The Journal of Contemporary Human Services, 72,* 536-542.

Scarf, M. (1987). *Intimate partners: Patterns in love and marriage.* New York: Ballantine.

Scharff, J. (1992). *Projective and introjective identification and the use of therapist's self.* New Jersey: Jason Aronson.

Scher, M., & Stevens, M. (1987). Men and violence. *Journal of Counseling and Development, 65,* 351-355.

Seagull, E. A., & Seagull, A. A. (1991). Healing the wound that must not heal: Psychotherapy with survivors of domestic violence. *Psychotherapy, 28,* 16-20.

Tellis-Nayak, V., & O'Donoghue, G. (1982). Conjugal egalitarianism and violence across cultures. *Journal of Comparative Family Studies, 13,* 277-290.

Walker, L. E. (1991a). *The battered woman syndrome.* New York: Springer.

Walker, L. E. (1991b). Post-traumatic stress disorder in women: Diagnosis and treatment of battered woman syndrome. *Psychotherapy, 28,* 21-29.

Waring, E. M. (1990). Self-disclosure of personal constructs. *Family Process, 29,* 399-413.

Weidman, A. (1986) . Family therapy with violent couples. *Social casework: The Journal of Contemporary Social Work, 67,* 211-218.

Witt, D. D. (1987). A conflict theory of family violence. *Journal of Family Violence, 2,* 291-301.

Young, G. H., & Gerson, S. (1991). New psychoanalytic perspectives on masochism and spouse abuse. *Psychotherapy, 28*(1), 30-38.

7

Aggression Among Inner-City Minority Youth: A Biopsychosocial Model for School-Based Evaluation and Treatment

Elizabeth Brondolo, Caren Baruch, Elizabeth Conway, and Lawrence Marsh

The aggressive behavior of severely emotionally disturbed (SED) students presents a significant management problem for schools. Aggressive behavior disrupts classrooms, impedes learning, and places students at risk for physical and psychological injury. Although aggressive behavior in schools is becoming more prevalent, there have been few comprehensive programs designed to deal with this problem. This article provides a description of a comprehensive school-based evaluation and treatment program serving inner-city minority emotionally disturbed youth; it describes a multicomponent school-based treatment program conducted with SED children between the ages of 6 and 19 years. The program included three major components: intensive case management, social skills training, and a token economy. Program descriptions, evaluation data, and clinical recommendations are presented.

INTRODUCTION

The aggressive behavior of severely emotionally disturbed (SED) students presents a significant management problem for schools. Aggressive behavior disrupts classrooms, impedes learning, and places students at risk for physical and psychological injury (Abikoff & Klein, 1992; Sturge, 1982).

Although aggressive behavior in schools is becoming more prevalent, there have been few comprehensive programs designed to deal with this problem. This article provides a description of a comprehensive school-based evaluation and treatment program serving inner-city minority emotionally disturbed youth. In the first section, a model for evaluating aggressive students is presented. The model integrates recent findings on the importance of biological, psychological, and social factors in the development and maintenance of aggressive behavior. In the second section, a multifaceted treatment program is described. This program included intensive case management, social skills training, and a token economy. Preliminary evaluation data are also included.

EVALUATION

Aggressive behavior is multi-determined and influenced by biological, psychological, and social factors. Some "biological" variables change the threshold for aggression by affecting the student's irritability, sensitivity, or capacity for emotional control. Psychological variables more directly affect the students capacity for social problem solving, and include cognitive development, language functioning, and social skills. Social variables affect access to emotional and instrumental resources, and include family structure, socioeconomic status, ethnicity, school resources, and school culture. Variables considered important for evaluation are presented in Table I.

Physical and Mental Health

A child's physical and mental health may affect his/her sensitivity to threatening stimuli or increase irritability. Untreated, many conditions can create more significant problems or result in behavioral difficulties which would not have emerged had early and effective treatment been available. For example, if a low level problem, such as a chronic ear infection, is inadequately treated it can lead to hearing loss and subsequent language impairments. In addition, there are certain medications, such as those commonly used for asthma that can cause irritability as well (Physician's Desk Reference, 1992).

Major psychiatric conditions can also change the threshold for aggression and decrease the capacity for emotional control. For example, attention deficit disorder with hyperactivity (ADHD) is a relatively common childhood disorder associated with increased impulsivity, emotional lability, and decreased social competence (Werry, Reeves, & Elkind, 1987). Students with ADHD are at risk for aggressive behavior and conduct disorder

Table I. A Guide for Evaluating Biopsychosocial Determinants
of School-Based Aggressive Behavior

BIOLOGICAL VARIABLES
   Factors which increase irritability or decrease
   emotional control.

   Poor general health, chronic infections
   Exhaustion
   Malnutrition
   Some medications
   Psychiatric disorders (ADHD, depression, psychoses)
   Neurological disorders, head injury
   Access to medical/psychiatric care

PSYCHOLOGICAL VARIABLES
   Factors which affect problem-solving competence.

   Expressive and receptive language functioning
   Level of cognitive development (pre-operational,
      concrete, etc.)
   Level of moral development
   Specific limitations in abstract reasoning
   Social skills
   Trigger situations/emotions
   Cultural differences in communication style

SOCIAL VARIABLES
   Factors which affect access to resource for
   emotional and instrumental support.

Family resources
   Family and extended family resources
   Financial resources
   Coercive processes

School-based resources for managing aggression
   Coercive processes
   Procedures for managing aggression
   Personnel and physical plant resources

School-based resources for developing prosocial behavior
   Clarity of goals for prosocial behavior
   Programs for developing social skills
   Resources for rewarding prosocial displays

(Abikoff & Klein, 1992). The presence of ADHD can be determined through the use of checklists completed by teacher and parents. Examples are Conner's Teacher Rating Scales (Conners, 1989) and the Attention Deficits Disorders Evaluation Scale (McCarney, 1989).

Untreated ADHD children are often rejected by their peers and judged by teachers as deficient in social competence (Landau & Moore

1991). In addition, the disorganized behavior of children with ADHD can elicit disorganized behavior from non-affected peers (Landau & Milich, 1988). If an ADHD child is in a class with other children who have relatively poor emotional control, the classroom management problems can be exacerbated.

Childhood depression is another disorder which may increase the risk for aggressive behavior since it is associated with irritability and impaired concentration. It is important but difficult to identify depression in children (Kendall, Cantwell, & Kazdin, 1989). In some cases the pattern of vegetative symptoms does not emerge in the same manner as it does for adults. There may be an atypical pattern of symptoms in which the student displays periods of hysterical crying or prolonged agitation interspersed with periods with more stable moods. Inquiring about a family history of mood disorders or substance abuse disorders and/ or using a scale like the Children's Depression Inventory (Beck, 1978) can help identify childhood depression.

Psychotic disorders, such as childhood schizophrenia are not necessarily linked to more aggressive behavior (Eggers, 1978). However, if schizophrenia and other psychotic disorders are not adequately treated, the resulting cognitive and emotional disorganization may promote acting out or leave the child more likely to be targeted for aggression by others. Disorders which increase paranoia or suspiciousness may also increase the potential for violence.

Some brain injuries can also be associated with increased aggressive behavior (Lewis, Shanok, Grant, & Ritvo, 1983). The effects of brain injury can be subtle and appear long after the initial insult. Only recently have investigators begun to recognize that the pattern of deficit associated with a given head injury may change over time and produce subtle defects in social skills.

The risk of receiving poor or no treatment for medical and mental health problems are greater in poor or minority populations. While physical and mental health variables have been grouped under the "bio" section of this biopsychosocial model, it is clear that social forces can exacerbate or attenuate their affects. For example, the incidence of health problems is greater among impoverished and some minority youngsters (Otten, Teutsch, Williamson, & Marks, 1991). Medical and psychiatric problems are more likely to go unrecognized or ineffectively treated in minority or impoverished communities (Ruiz, 1990). We have seen numerous cases of children with significant language disorders who were receiving no or minimal language therapy because their difficulties had been misidentified as primarily psychological or social in nature (e.g., resistant to authority, shy, bilingual, etc.).

A variety of factors may contribute to these assessment and treatment failures. For example, poor or predominantly minority communities may have fewer reasonable health care facilities available to them. Individuals may not seek care because they lack health insurance or the money to pay the transportation and other costs (e.g., child care) associated with visits to a health facility (Hoagberg *et al.*, 1990).

Additionally, ethnic groups differ in their use of health-related services, for example, Cuban-Americans seek prenatal services at a significantly higher rate than do Black Americans (House of Representatives, Committee of Energy and Commerce, 1984). These differences may be a function of beliefs about the role of professional health care providers. Individuals may not understand or trust instructions delivered by health-care providers from a different ethnic group (Becker *et al.*, 1992). Furthermore, poorly educated or non-English speaking parents may be ineffective advocates for their children and be unable to adequately inform a physician about their children's condition or unable to explain their concerns about a recommended course of treatment. In addition, health care providers may be unaware of the cultural differences in the nature of the doctor–patient interaction. Racial discrimination may also make some health care providers more likely to dismiss conduct problems as stemming from social conditions or poor parenting, rather than adequately evaluating the contributing role of medical or psychiatric conditions. Finally, like many parents, they may be confused and may deny the existence of a problem, when symptoms primarily appear in one setting (e.g., school) and not at another (e.g., home).

These problems are exacerbated when health care providers do not adequately consider cultural and socioeconomic contributions to poor treatment adherence. It's not necessarily appropriate to assume that clients understand and then reject a course of action. It may be necessary to work closely with families whose ethnic background or social-economic status make it more likely that they will have difficulty understanding or trusting health care providers.

Although, it is critical to be sensitive to issues of the over-diagnosis of psychiatric disorders and over-prescription of medication, it has been our clinical experience and that of others that the African-American and Latino students served in these inner-city schools were not adequately diagnosed or treated (Serafica, Schwebel, Russel, Issac, & Myers, 1990). The stressful circumstances associated with racism and poverty put these students at greater risk for the development of psychiatric conditions and/or substance abuse. The level of everyday strain and lack of resources often make it difficult for them to gain access to medical and psychiatric care on a regular basis. These youngsters may also be at greater biological risk because their mothers lacked prenatal care or were substance users during pregnancy.

It may be necessary to obtain outside mental health services for the student if the school does not have a psychiatrist and/or a physician on staff. These services may come from community mental health or medical facilities, church or other voluntary organizations. Lists of catchment area resources and their fees and hours are usually available from the intake coordinators of the local community mental health center. In many states, the Office of Vocational Rehabilitation and the Department of Labor have lists of vocational training programs which may be appropriate for SED students.

Psychological Variables

In this section, variables including linguistic competence and cognitive functioning are reviewed. These variables impact on problem solving ability, and students may be at risk for aggressive acting-out if they have poor language and cognitive skills. Expressive or receptive language disorders can increase the risk for aggressive behavior (Hirschi & Hindelang, 1977; West, 1982). Children who have subtle defects in comprehension may appear resistant or noncompliant, while those with in expressive language difficulties may be unable to use verbal mediation to solve social problems. These language deficits can occur in the absence of more obvious articulation deficits, and recognition of articulation deficits does not necessarily mean that other language difficulties have been adequately identified.

Mental health professionals may focus on the contributions of biological, psychodynamic, or familial factors in the determination of expressive difficulties, while paying less attention to neuropsychological or medical problems. For example, in one school a 15-year-old Black male with a history of severe abuse and neglect and a diagnosis of conduct disorder rarely spoke and had been characterized as resistant to psychotherapy. One day while conducting a "spelling bee game," the observer discovered that the student could not systematically distinguish among consonants like "b" and "g." His case records were complete with numerous details of psychological trauma which could potentially account for his resistance to speaking with others, but the alternative hypothesis that he had a receptive language dysfunction needed to be considered as well.

Specific cognitive deficits and the level of cognitive development have implications for the types of interventions employed to increase prosocial skills and decrease aggressive behavior. Many psychotherapeutic interventions depend on higher level cognitive abilities, requiring clients to be able to abstract a general principle related to a variety of situations to recognize similarities among situations and to realize that similar strategies can be used in a variety of situations (e.g., "I always act out when someone makes fun of me, because it reminds me of how my grandfather used to humiliate me," "Fighting with my teacher is similar to fighting with my dad, uncle, etc."). Some forms of psychotherapy also assume that the clients can use insight and verbal knowledge to guide their behavior. However, this level of abstraction and verbal problem solving may be difficult for students with limited verbal IQ or overall IQ. Recent evidence suggests that multiple neuropsychological deficits, including problems in executive functions are present in children with conduct disorder (Aronowitz et al., 1992).

Empathic perspective taking, a core component of many social skills training programs may also be difficult for students who are still functioning at a preoperational level of thinking (Dodge, 1985). Cognitive egocentrism may limit the student's ability to view the world or to take another's perspective. Students may be able to briefly articulate understanding (given enough prompting), but be unable to generate perspectives on their own or to recall strategies without prompts. Specifically cognitive distortions may increase risk for acting aggressively. For example, aggressive students as compared to non-aggressive students are more likely to interpret the nonverbal behavior of their peers as expressing hostility (Dodge, 1985). Aggressive children are more likely to interpret situations as threatening and are less likely than normals to generate solutions and strategies to interpersonal problems and to develop means–end analyses (Dodge, 1985; Lochtzman, White, & Wayland, 1991).

Students may lack basic social skills, including making eye contact, taking turns, asking questions, self-disclosing that are necessary for problem-solving discussions. Through some of our social skills exercises, we discovered that students had significant difficulty in accurately role playing different emotions. Even when they were trying to act out "happy" or "interested," they looked angry or agitated. Several studies have identified deficits in social problem solving and interpersonal skills among aggressive youth (Dodge, 1985; Kazdin, 1987). For example, aggressive children are less likely than normals to defer to authority (Freedman, Rosenthal, Donahue, Schlundt, & McFall, 1978). In addition, cultural differences in both verbal and nonverbal expressive behavior may also impact on the outcome of a problem-solving exchange. There is some evidence that Blacks use less eye contact and have subtle differences in gesturing style in comparisons to Whites, and that these differences result in Blacks being judged as more hostile and less trustworthy than Whites in some circumstances (Fugita, Wexley, & Hillery, 1974; Word, Zanna, & Cooper, 1974). Students may be misinterpreted by others of a different ethnic group, and may not have the ability to negotiate through these differences.

A quantifiable evaluation of children's social competence can be made with instruments such as the Social Skills Rating System (Gresham & Elliot, 1990). The SSRS is completed by teachers and the children. The children are rated on a variety of social skills such as turn taking, cooperating, sharing materials, etc.

Social Variables

Families can provide both emotional and instrumental support. However, often the capacities of the families of SED impoverished minority youth are severely strained. Of the 43 students attending at the start of the school year, only seven lived with both biological parents. However, many students were able to identify members of an extended network of family and friends whom they turned to for emotional support.

The influence of parenting style on the development of antisocial behaviors has been well researched (Kazdin, 1985; Patterson, Reid, & Dishion, 1992). Coercive communication and inconsistent discipline have been identified as key variables mediating aggression and other antisocial acts. The effects of coercive behavior are exacerbated when families are under stress (Patterson et al., 1992). Parents who are isolated, overwhelmed, or depressed may be less likely to be consistent and follow through in disciplining their children. Patterns of coercive communications are difficult to evaluate however, inquiring about methods of discipline is one step toward identifying communication patterns.

Similarly, aggressive behavior is more likely to occur in school when there are limited resources to manage the behavior and when consequences for this behavior are not clearly defined (Patterson, 1982). When evaluating the school's resources for deterring aggressive behavior, the variables to consider include: the total staff to student ratios, the number of crisis staff, the crisis management training offered, and the availability and location of facilities (rooms, mats, etc.), facilities for restraining or detaining an aggressive child. When evaluating the clarity and scope of policies for managing aggressive behavior the variables to consider include the procedures for documenting incidents, the specific consequences which follow particular acts of aggression (e.g., time out for verbal abuse, school suspension for weapon possession, etc.), and the provisions of counseling and support for staff involved in managing aggressive incidents.

The development of prosocial behavior is made possible when the expectations are explicit, good role models are available, and the rewards are desirable and achievable. Methods of developing prosocial skills can be informal (e.g., role modeling, media) or formal (e.g., social skills training, problem-solving classes). When evaluating the school's capacity to reward prosocial behavior the variables to consider include the existence of a token economy or award programs and the degree to which participation in recreation or other pleasurable activities is made contingent on the display of desired behaviors.

In summary, characteristics of the student and his/her environment can influence the display of aggressive behavior. Mental and physical health and their capacity for effective problem solving can influence the extent to which aggression versus other strategies are used to resolve conflicts. School and community policies and resources also govern the choice of conflict management strategies. A thorough evaluation of the variables may assist in understanding and controlling a student's aggression.

MULTIFACETED INTERVENTIONS

The goal of the interventions described below was to enable the students to move to a less restrictive educational environment. These students had been assigned to a highly restrictive placement because they were unable to function in a regular classroom or a special education classroom in a regular education school. Their behavior was either too aggressive or too withdrawn, and their ability to perform classroom activities was significantly impaired.

The intervention included programs aimed at the child, the classroom, the school and the community. Specifically, the three components of the program included: intensive case management (ICM), social skills training (SST), and a token economy. In the following section a description of the students and the school will be presented, followed by a description of the programs, the measurement tools, and the available evaluation data.

The programs described in this section were implemented in a private school in New York City when the first author served as Director of Clinical Services. Students were assigned to the school by the Committee for Special Education when one of the following two conditions was met: (1) the students handicapping conditions were sufficiently severe that no appropriate public school program existed, or (2) an appropriate program existed, but no placement would be available within the time frame legally required for placement. Students attending the school had a primary classification of emotionally disturbed (usually SIE VII), and could have a secondary classification of speech/language impaired or learning disabled.

During 1990-1991, 43 students were in attendance at the beginning of the year and 57 by the end of the year, with attendance fluctuating due to rolling admissions and discharges. Of the 43 students attending from the beginning of the year, all but two were mandated for group counseling and were therefore eligible for participation in the SST program described below. All students participated in the ICM, and the token economy. Evaluation data were collected from students who were attending as of the start of the school year and who were mandated to receive group counseling.

Students ranged in age from 6–21 years, with a Lower School serving students from 6–12 years ($n = 29$) and an Upper School (housed in the same location) serving students between 13–21 years ($n = 12$). Of the 41 students enrolled at the end of the year, 36 were male; 14 students were Latino, 22 were African-American, three students were of mixed descent (White/Latino), one student was White, and one was Asian. A combination of state and city funds supported tuition, and most students were receiving Medicaid. Detailed data on socioeconomic status is not available, although most students were living in impoverished homes. Of the 41 students, seven students came from homes in which they lived with both their biological mother and father. The remainder lived with a single parent and or a combination of relatives and friends, foster care or group homes. Consistent with the notion that verbal information processing deficits play a role in conduct problems, the average VIQ was 73 for the students while the mean PIQ was 85. Forty percent of the student had PIQs which were at least ten points higher than their VIQ. This provides some indirect support of the association between a deficit in verbal ability and aggressive behavior. Students were assigned to classrooms with student:teacher: paraprofessional ratios of either 6:1:1 or 10:1:1.

Treatment Outcome Measures

The outcome measures needed to be brief and easy to administer since the primary responsibility of the clinicians was to provide clinical services and not to conduct research. The students' prosocial behaviors and problem behaviors were assessed via teacher ratings on the Problem Behavior Checklist-PBC (Quay & Peterson, 1983) and the Social Skills Rating Sheet-SSRS (Gresham & Elliot, 1990). The PBC was administered at baseline, midyear, and end of the year while the SSRS was administered at midyear and end of year because we did not discover this valuable tool until then.

Behavioral measures of aggressive and disruptive behaviors were obtained by counting the number of behavioral referrals written for each student. Behavioral referrals were written by any member of the school staff in response to severe verbal abuse or physical aggression or significant property destruction. These referrals were reviewed by the principal, clinical, and crisis staff, and then placed in the students school file. The decision to document an incident was at the discretion of the staff member, and documentation tended to be reserved for more serious infractions. These data are probably the most accurate measure of the number of times a student got into serious trouble in school but, they also are confounded by differences among staff in training and experience. In addition, these referrals had to pass through so many hands before they were finally entered into the students' record that they were subject to getting misplaced or lost. Despite these difficulties, there are data on the validity of these behavioral referrals. The total number of behavioral referrals was related to the teachers ratings of Externalizing behavior on the SSRS) (mid-year: $r = .43$, $p < .07$; mid-year to end year:time 3: $r = .48$, $p < .01$).

The acquisition of social skills was assessed using a Social Skills Test, developed by the authors. Details of the test are presented in the section describing the social skills training. Testing was conducted at three points during the year. Baseline data were collected during October and November, mid-year evaluation were completed in March and April and the end of year evaluation was completed in May and June. The initial measures do not reflect a true baseline since the programs had been piloted from the middle of the previous school year.

Intensive Case Management Interventions (ICM)

Intensive case management (ICM) was conducted by certified social workers, who had caseloads of 15–20 students, and who were supervised by a clinical/school psychologist. Case managers were assigned to two or three classes, and were responsible for the clinical care for the students in these classes and consultation with teachers and paraprofessionals serving these students. Case managers were also responsible for developing and maintaining relationships with families and outside service providers.

The goal of the ICM program was to identify and remediate the determinants of dysfunctional behavior (either externalizing or internalizing disorders) on a case-by-case basis. To evaluate the presence of a psychiatric or medical condition, case managers would conduct individual interviews and classroom observations, and consult with teachers, families, and outside therapists. If a more formal data collection mechanism was required, case managers conducted formal behavioral observations or obtain questionnaires data from teachers.

One of the most critical functions of the case managers was to develop a network of service providers, therapists, and psychiatrists who could provide necessary treatments for the students. The psychiatrists were asked to complete forms detailing the behaviors targeted for treatment and the expected main and side effects of any medications prescribed. These sheets facilitated communication by structuring the frequent follow-up phone contacts between case managers and psychiatrists. This frequent phone contact helped insure that positive medication effects were maximized and negative effects were minimized. Parents, who often felt unable to insure effective administration of medication on their own felt reassured by the knowledge that the school and the physicians were in close contact.

The case managers also maintained close relationships with families. However, students came from all five boroughs of the city, making it difficult to work in person with families so that most contact occurred over the phone. The focus of the contact was essentially positive, with case managers reporting to the parents any progress in Social Skills Training or the token economy. It was our observation that most families of emotionally disturbed students receive overwhelmingly bad news about their children and feel ineffective in managing their children's behavior. Our goal was to increase the families willingness to work with their children by increasing their sense of hopefulness and pride. An example of the case management system follows. If a child was suspected of having ADHD, the case manager might observe the child in class and in individual session, ask the teacher to complete a Conner's Teacher Rating Sheet (Conners, 1989), and interview the family either in person or over the phone. If the student appeared to have a significant number of symptoms, plans for a psychiatric evaluation were developed. The case manager then provided the psychiatrist with ongoing reports on the child's progress (usually once a week or once every two weeks). If the parents were unable to come to the school, contact was made over the phone, and if necessary, the case manager accompanied the students to the psychiatric appointments at one of several local clinics. If medication was prescribed, it was often administered in school to facilitate compliance and insure careful monitoring of main and side effects. Case managers consulted with teachers regularly to monitor progress, using point sheets, Behavior Rating scales, anecdotal data, and classroom observations to form impressions about the child's progress. The psychiatrist and family were consulted at regular intervals to keep them informed about progress and to coordinate other behavioral interventions implemented at home, school, and clinic. (Details about the medication administration program and associated consent forms are available from the first author).

To evaluate the effectiveness of these frequent contacts with family members and outside service providers, case managers were asked to log all calls to outside service providers and families. These data served as the independent variable in a standard multiple regression with frequency of behavior problems during the mid-year period as the dependent variable and frequency of behavior problems during the baseline period as an additional independent variable. The frequency of the calls served a significant predictor of the reduction in behavior problems from time one to time 2 (Adjusted $R^2 = .30$, t for call frequency, $t = -2.02$, $p < .05$). This suggests that efforts to coordinate care, even if they consist only of limited phone contacts with family and outside health care providers, may be of importance in facilitating a decrease in aggressive behavior.

Social Skills Training — "Put Your Feelings Into Words"

Social skills are seen as "socially acceptable learned behaviors that enable the person to interact with others in ways that elicit positive responses and assist in avoiding negative responses from them" (Cartledge & Milburn, 1980). Social skills programs have attempted to remediate social skills deficits in children with a wide variety of difficulties (Schneider & Byrne, 1985). These skills are important for children to acquire because students with positive social behavior generally have a higher rate of academic success and are more liked by their peers (Cartledge & Milburn, 1986).

Social skills training has been found to be most effective in changing children's social behavior (Schneider & Byrne, 1985). In addition, training has been found to be more effective for withdrawn rather than for aggressive children (Schneider, Rubin, & Ledingham, 1985). This may be because withdrawn children are more cooperative during training than aggressive children so that they are more likely to actually learn the skills.

A number of social skills programs have reported significant success (Combs & Slaby, 1977; Conger & Keane, 1981; Urbain & Kendall, 1980). The most powerful technique in social skills training has been the direct reinforcement of appropriate social behavior (Schneider & Byrne, 1985). Programs such as Shure and Spivack (1978) have used cognitive problem-solving techniques to teach children to improve their interpersonal skills. Blechman (1991) developed a program for improving students skills in self-disclosure and facilitative listening as a method for increasing social competence. The work described below is based on the programs developed by Blechman and colleagues.

The goal of the "Put Your Feelings Into Words" social skills training program was to provide students with prosocial alternatives for distress-evoking situations. The program provided instruction in four basic skills: identifying and labeling feelings, recognizing other people's feelings, generating strategies for handling conflict situations, and facilitative listening.

Program Structure. The program was offered to all students who were mandated by the Committee on Special Education for group counseling and was conducted during these group counseling periods. The groups consisted of 3–5 members and were co-led by two case managers or a case manager and the psychologist.

The structure of the groups was well established with each group beginning with the recitation of the group rules (no verbal abuse, no physical abuse, participate and "Put your feelings into words"). Then a brief exercise called "Two Feelings for Today" was performed. In this exercise, the students had to identify two feelings that they had during that day and to identify the situation which evoked the feelings (e.g., "I felt angry when I didn't get called on," "I felt happy when I got to school to see my teacher"). Students were able to look at the "feeling board," if they needed assistance labeling their feelings. Students received points for correct answers and were fined points for inappropriate behavior.

Materials. The materials used in the group included a "feeling board," a large oaktag board which listed 30–40 different feeling words (happy, sad, etc.). These boards were located in all therapy rooms, and most classrooms as well. Other materials included a deck of "feeling cards," each of which contained a different feeling word, a deck of "situation cards" each of which contained a description of a common situation (e.g., getting in a fight with my brother, a teacher yelling at me for something I didn't do). These situations were derived from informal conversations with students in which they were asked to come up with common situations which evoked different feelings.

Program Exercises

Feeling Words. Students were asked to each take a turn reading one word from the "feeling board" and telling about a recent time when they experienced that feeling, (e.g., "I was frustrated when I didn't get a prize for the day"). Variations on the game included having the feeling words listed on cards and each student would draw a card on each turn. For non-reading students, a smaller number of words was used and teachers or case managers read the words to the students. Students continued taking turns until all "feeling words" had been read.

This task initially proved difficult for the students, in part because many did not know all the vocabulary and because they were very embarrassed or reluctant to acknowledge feeling some of the emotions on the list (e.g., sad, hurt, nervous, guilty). This exercise was included in many sessions to provide consistent structure, repeated practice, and to desensitize students to their discomfort about verbalizing emotions.

Feeling Recognition. In this task, students looked at pictures of people experiencing different emotions. These pictures were taken from magazines or available photographs. Students were asked to identify the emotion using one of the words on the "feeling board," and when possible, to identify possible explanations for the feeling (e.g., "he's sad and embarrassed because he just fell off his bike").

Feeling Charades. In this exercise students were handed a card with a feeling word listed on it and asked to act out the feeling while others tried to identify the feeling being displayed. Although we were unable to videotape these exercises, it was surprising to us how difficult students found these tasks. Even when attempting to display positive emotions, they often looked angry or depressed.

Identifying Situation. Students were given cards describing common situations and asked to identify the feeling they might have in these situations. For example, my teacher yells at me when I didn't do anything.

Identifying Strategies. Students were given cards describing situations and asked to provide a prosocial strategy for handling that situation (e.g., "my teacher yells at me for something I didn't do, I'll tell her calmly how I feel and what happened"). Students would also role play some of these strategies.

Facilitative Listening. In this task, one student was assigned the role of the speaker and the other the role of the listener. The Speaker was assigned a topic, and was instructed to describe his or her thoughts and feelings in response to the topic. The Listeners' role was to ask questions or make appropriate comments to enable the Speaker to continue talking. Listeners received credit for facilitative questions and remarks (e.g., "tell me more about what happened, how did you feel"). Speakers received credit for appropriate use of "feeling words" or motivational statements (e.g., "I did that because I wanted to get even"). The conversational dyads generally lasted 1–3 minutes.

Measures. To evaluate the students performance on the social skills training program, a structured interview test was constructed and administered individually by the student's case manager or by the psychologist. The test consisted of five tasks: (1) listing feeling words and putting them into personalized sentences (LISTFEEL); (2) identifying situations evoking a set of different emotions (angry, bored, sad, happy, nervous) (SITUATION); (3) generating strategies for managing a subset of the situations listed in task two (STRATEGY 1); (4) generating strategies to a set of

Table II. Mean Number of Social Skills Acquired over the
School Year[a]

	Time of year	
	Baseline	End-of-year
Social skills		
Feeling words	$m = 7.11$ SD = 4.36	$m = 11.07$** SD = 5.68
Situations	$m = 9.97$ SD = 5.10	$m = 12.14$* SD = 4.82
Strategies	$m = 10.09$ SD = 7.25	$m = 14.54$** SD = 8.31
Facilitative listening	$m = 7.57$ SD = 6.07	$m = 9.86$** SD = 8.10

[a]Significance of paired t-tests comparing beginning (baseline)
to end of the year.
*$p < .05$.
**$p < .005$.

standard situations (STRATEGY 2); (5) generating facilitative comments or questions to a set of standardized remarks (FACILITATE). Answers to these tests were scored by two raters (students from St. John's University) who were blind to the students' identity and the frequency of his/her conduct problems.

Results. The data suggest that the students were able to acquire the skills taught. The mean number of feeling words reported increased from baseline to end of the year. The effects were similar for identification of situations, strategies, and the use of facilitative listening skill (Table II).

The students' performance on the social skills tests was related to the teacher's rating of their social behavior. Specifically, students' end of the year scores on the externalizing dimension of the SSRS were negatively correlated with their end of the year scores on the social skills task evaluating the ability to identify situations ($r = -.48, p < .05$) and to generate strategies ($r = -.61, p < .01$). In addition, scores on the strategies component of the social skills test were also negatively correlated with the attention problems subscale of the PB checklist (mid-year score: $r = -.54$, $p < .05$) and the hyperactivity scale of the SSRS ($r = -.50, p < .05$). In contrast, scores on the feeling words subscale were positively correlated with mid-year global social competence ($r = .43, p < .05$) and academic competence ($r = .67, p < .001$). Scores on the strategies subscales were positively correlated with global social competence and more specifically with cooperativeness ($r = .39, p < .04$) and self-control ($r = .59, p < .005$).

Table III. Standard Multiple Regression Analyses

Variable	Stand. coeff.	SE	t	p value
a. Increase in the use of strategies were associated with decrease in the teacher's rating of externalizing behavior				
Externalizing at mid-year	.63	.18	3.5	.004
Strategies at mid-year	.07	.02	.38	.71
Strategies at end-of-year	−.40	.002	−2.16	.05
b. Increase in the use of facilitative listening skills were associated with increase in teacher's rating of self-control				
Self-control at mid-year	.91	.10	8.2	.0001
Facilitative listening at mid-year	.02	.01	−.21	.84
Facilitative listening at end-of-year	.29	.00	2.6	.03
c. Increase in the use of strategies were associated with increase in teacher's rating of self-control				
Self-control at mid-year	.84	.06	11.9	.0001
Strategies at mid-year	−.08	.00	−11.05	.312
Strategies at end-of-year	.43	.00	6.7	.0001

In the limited subsample of students for whom we had complete data, it appears that the acquisition of social skills was associated with a decrease in teachers' reports of students' externalizing behaviors and an increase in teachers' reports of student's self-control as measured by the SSRS. To test these effects, a standard multiple regression analysis was employed with end-of-year scores on teacher ratings as the dependent measure. End-of-the-year social skills scores served as the independent variable and mid-year teacher ratings and mid-year social skill scores were entered into the regression as control variables. Complete data are available for 16 students. Increases in the use of strategies predicted decrease in teacher ratings for externalizing behavior when controlling for mid-year externalizing ratings and strategies scores (Adj. $R^2 = .57$, $p < .001$) (Table III).

Similarly increases in the use of facilitative listening skills predicted changes in teacher ratings of student self-control while controlling for mid-year self-control ratings and mid-year facilitative listening scores (Adj. $R^2 = .83$, $p < .0001$). Similar effects were found when strategy scores served as independent variables (Adj. $R^2 = .94$, $p < .0001$).

However acquisition of any social skills was unrelated to changes in behavioral referrals.

Clearly, these are very limited data and the volume of missing data requires that the findings be interpreted with caution. However, given the difficulties of acquiring these data, it is encouraging to find even slim evidence for the effects of a very basic social skills training program. The limited findings are consistent with other reports in the literature in which investigators have reported difficulty with the maintenance and generalization of effects. Combined treatments including parent training and social problem-solving training appear to offer more chance of success (Kazdin, Siegel, & Bass, 1992).

Clinical Issues. The students in this school were sufficiently volatile, that many sessions passed before groups were reliably spent on the social skills exercises rather that on behavior management and crisis intervention. The behavior management program for the groups consisted of a simple point system. Students received points for correct answers and appropriate behavior. They lost points for verbal or physical aggression or the inability to take turns. Points earned during the group were applied toward the students participation in the school token economy. Points were also used to determine who received a small treat (a cookie or candy) at the end of the group. Students who were unable to comply with group rules and were sufficiently disruptive that they prevented others from learning were removed from the session and taken to the "crisis" or time out room. Unfortunately, we did not collect systematic data on time spent on task or number of disruptions per group (largely because we were busy managing these conflicts). It would be instructive to know in more detail how long it takes before the routine of the group begins to take hold, and the number of behavior problems occurring within the group begins to decrease.

To make "Put Your Feelings into Words" part of the school culture, the skills learned in the group were also reinforced through weekly meetings in each classroom. These meetings were essential for two reasons. First, they provided an opportunity to make these skills part of the ongoing class process and not simply an isolated training program. While we recognized and publically acknowledged that the skills we taught might not be part of the culture of the street (i.e., the neighborhoods from which these students came), these skills were part of the culture of the school. Students were able to gain recognition and rewards for using these skills in school.

In addition, exposing teachers to the progress also enhanced the probability that the teachers would respond sensitively to the students' attempts to express their feelings in words. We asked teachers to participate in the exercises and discussions, identifying and labeling their "Two feelings for the Day." The teachers were often just as embarrassed as the students were, and it was fun for the students to be able to prompt the teachers to use different feelings and show off their own skills. When the class discussion turned to more general topics, we continually had students use the "feeling board" to help them articulate their concerns and needs.

In summary, the data suggest that these SED students can learn basic skills in labeling feelings and generating strategies for handling interpersonal conflict. These skills are related to teachers' perceptions of the children's social competence and externalizing behavior, although the level of skill is not directly related to the incidence of actual problem behavior as measured by behavior referrals. It is possible that the effects of treatment would have emerged over a longer period of time. Alternatively it is also possible that our measures were insensitive to qualitative changes (i.e., intensity or duration of aggression). Future research should employ more direct and sensitive measures of qualitative changes in interpersonal problem-solving, since direct observation of children's interactions may be the most sensitive method (Schneider & Byrne, 1985).

A Token Economy—Learning Readiness Training

The third level of intervention used in this school was a token economy, called "Learning Readiness Training" (LRT). Token economies have been effectively used in a variety of settings including hospitals, schools, residential treatment programs, etc. (Masters, Burish, Hollon, & Rimm, 1987). In these programs students typically earn points for exhibiting desired behaviors and lose points for inappropriate behaviors and are able to redeem the points for a variety of rewards. The goal of "Learning Readiness Training" was to provide the support necessary for the student to function in an academic classroom. LRT provided a system of external rewards and punishments for the development of these skills.

The program was created jointly by the clinical and educational staffs, through a series of training meetings led by the clinical director (psychologist) and through classroom consultations conducted by members of the clinical staff. Although a rough program was in place within a week of the school year beginning, it took an additional 6 months for a fully functioning schoolwide program to emerge. The program was a straightforward token economy, so that details of the program are presented only briefly below. The remainder of the discussion will focus on clinical and consultation issues which emerged during the design and implementation phases.

The program ran in every classroom, and each class picked their own goals—most of which were common to all members of a class. Examples of goals included, "stays in seat during academic lessons" or "participates in class discussions appropriately." Students were assigned points for the performance of the goals. In the case of the older and less disruptive students, points were assigned each period (every 45 minutes). For younger, more disruptive students, points were assigned every 10–15 minutes, depending on the severity of the behavior.

Student could also be fined (lose points) if they exhibited specific negative behaviors, including verbal or physical aggression. Each class had 3–6 positive goals for which they could earn points, and 1 or 2 "fineable" behaviors for which they could lose points.

To help integrate the social skills training program with the token economy, all classes had "Put Your Feelings into Words" as a goal. Students received credit for meeting this goal if they were able to verbally express feelings in an appropriate manner or were able to work throughout a period without a significant outburst.

Students could redeem their points for gifts and privileges. Two school stores (one for the upper level students, and one for the lower level students) provided the rewards. Rewards included small gifts such as baseball cards, pens, costume jewelry, etc. For upper school students, rewards included more expensive items including Nintendo cartridges and clothing. The point system was constructed so that each student could earn a maximum of 15 cents each day toward any particular goal. Therefore, it would take a weeks worth of perfect behavior to earn a toy worth about 75 cents (e.g. pack of baseball cards or a little doll, etc.). Upper school students might need to work several months to earn an expensive gift. All prizes were chosen and ordered from catalogs or neighborhood stores by the students. The costs of running both stores was approximately $900 over the course of the year.

One day each week students were able to use their points to participate in a schoolwide recreational activities program. Students had to meet specific point targets to be eligible to chose from a variety of fun activities. Students not meeting the goals were assigned to a study hall.

Point sheets were collected by the clinical staff each week, and many classes also sent home copies of these sheets. Since goals were changed whenever mastery became evident (or failure became clear), it was difficult to use these points as data to evaluate the program. No formal evaluation of this program, independent of other programs, was conducted.

Clinical and Consultation Issues

There were a number of clinical issues which arose as we implemented the token economy schoolwide. These issues were addressed in-service workshops and individual consultation meetings with the teachers and para-professionals. Identifying and remediating problems was an ongoing process, and provided an opportunity for teachers, clinical staff, and students to collaborate on a common goal. Some of the issues raised are listed below.

Setting goals for the students proved to be one of the most difficult and important steps in establishing the token economy. Teachers worked hard to identify specific, achievable, positive, and measurable goals. This step was critical because it helped teachers and students focus their attention and concentrate their efforts. Teachers often wanted to include too many goals, correctly pointing out that each of the children had numerous skill deficits. However, choosing a long series of goals or too high a standard of behavior defeats the intervention, since it left students and teachers frustrated. It proved to be better to build on success, by having students experience mastery at one or two achievable goals.

A variety of faulty beliefs appeared to undermine the goal-setting efforts. Teachers sometimes were pleased by improvement in one area, but still said, "That's fine, but what about all these other problems.". Teachers believed that if they focused on one or two goals, they were essentially giving permission to the student to fail in the other areas. Some teachers also feared that rewarding limited success (i.e., the achievement of the first two goals) would undermine the student's efforts to achieve further success. In other cases teachers expressed concerns that if they didn't immediately choose perfect performance as the goal then they were providing permission for the student to perform in a substandard way. Teachers also had difficulty feeling comfortable putting other, non-priority goals on the "back burner." They had concerns that they would be criticized by parents or administrators if they made discretionary choices about how to focus their attention.

Another faulty belief held by many teachers, and students as well, is the belief that there was one factor motivating all the bad behavior. Teachers often believed that students were behaving badly because they were distressed over some unresolved conflict with their parents or some trauma. They hoped that if this trauma was resolved psychologically (e.g., through psychotherapy), all bad behavior would simultaneously disappear. Many of our students had experienced significant trauma, (i.e., loss of a parent, child abuse, rape, etc.) so it was not unreasonable to suspect that these episodes had emotional sequelae. However, these events were also often associated with conditions, such as poverty and neglect which left students socially unskilled as well as depressed and unmotivated. This lack of social skills and emotional control often hindered the students ability to work through their feelings about the specific incidents that had occurred. To help address some of these faulty beliefs more specifically, we continually encouraged teachers to view social skills training and the token economy as methods for getting the student "therapy ready" as well as "classroom ready." We emphasized the need to identify those conditions under which students were able to demonstrate self-control and social or academic competence. Teachers and case managers were continually asked to answer the question: "What support and guidance does the students need to consistently exhibit good self-control in this situation?" This helped increase the likelihood that staff would respond effectively to students' aggression and not excuse it as a function of distress.

The next challenge was establishing procedures for insuring consistency and integrity in assigning points. As Patterson *et al.* (1992) have pointed out, a coercive process often exists between antisocial children and their families. This same process emerged between students and teachers. For example, when a student failed to perform a particular desired behavior, the teachers would sometimes assign the students points despite the failure, because the student would begin whining or screaming or throwing objects when he/she understood the teacher was not going to give the points. Initially, students would escalate their aggressive behavior in attempts to force the teachers to give them points. All school staff wished to avoid these confrontations, and this avoidance was completely understandable. However, when students were allowed to coerce teachers into giving them "something for nothing," it undermined the effectiveness of the point system.

To help limit some of these negative consequences, it became important to ask "What support do teachers and other school staff need so that they are able to assign points consistently and fairly?" The answer to this question proved to be complex. The most important element in effective assignment of points seemed to be planning and preparation. The steps involved included (1) identifying goals worthy of attention and commitment, (2) anticipating problems in the students' ability to adhere to these goals (including anticipating violent behavior), and (3) assembling and assigning the manpower and resources to allow enforcement of the objectives.

The planning required can best be illustrated with an example. Once a week, students could "turn in" their points for participation in a variety of positive activities (e.g., going to the park, Nintendo, etc.). Initially, when students did not earn their points or when they were closed out of a desired activity, they would become violent. Weekly demonstrations including chair throwing, fist fights, accompanied the sign-up time for students who did not earn the rewards. Since it was critical to use point redemption time as an opportunity to enforce the value of points (and not allow students with no points to go on activities), we developed a system of structure and support to accommodate the children's needs.

Activity sign-up and point redemption activities were conducted by a senior person at the school (the first author) to emphasize its importance. The psychologist was accompanied by a team of crisis managers who went from class to class to provide physical and moral support to the teachers as they read off the point records. Students who were disruptive during this period were automatically sent to study hall and had other consequences imposed. Study halls were manned by effective school crisis counselors, who were also provided repeated support by the clinical staff. In this way, the appropriate and needed support was available, so students could learn that the rules were genuine and important and that the points had value. This was a time-consuming process, but a valuable lesson for the students.

The Big Picture

Did we make a difference? Did the students get better, i.e., less aggressive, better able to maintain themselves in the classroom, more likely to be able to perform in less restrictive settings. The answer is complicated. On a day-to-day basis we took delight in any sign of improvement, a day with fewer fights or a child who talked about his feelings. Overall, it is clear that some children benefitted substantially from our programs, and the limited data which was available helped clarify our successes and failures. Developing data driven evaluation procedures is crucial since it was easy to confuse establishing rapport with a troubled child with success in reducing aggression. In this section, the results of the program will be reviewed, and some ssues in establishing an outcome evaluation procedure are discussed.

Overall, some students did seem to benefit from our interventions. Of the 29 children on whom we have complete behavioral referral data, 11 showed reductions in the frequency of aggression from the beginning to the end of the year. At baseline, these students had an average of 1.2 serious incidents/week with a range from .18 to 2.5 incidents. At the end of the year these students had an average of .58 incidents/week with a mean reduction of .45 incidents/week so that by the end of the year nine out of 11 students had less than one significant incident/week. This may seem like a small decrease but it was clinically significant in that many of these incidents required a considerable effort of manpower to manage.

Four students displayed no aggressive behavior at baseline and continued to display no aggression at the end of the year. Thirteen students displayed an increase in aggressive behavior. At baseline the students displayed an average of .44 incidents/week (range 0–.95, SD =.30). At the end of the year the students displayed an average of .89 incidents/week (range .1–1.6) with a mean increase in incidents of .6 incidents/week. Data were unavailable from many upper school students who were frequently truant. This program was ineffective in luring these students back to school in any consistent manner, despite intensive attempts.

Since there was no control group, it is difficult to evaluate this outcome, and any conclusions drawn are speculative at best. However, the results may not be as negative as they first appeared, since Bry (1982) who evaluated a multifaceted treatment program for youth at risk for substance abuse and employed a prospective design with students randomly assigned to treatment and control groups, points out that even in the presence of intensive interventions these students deteriorate, but they do not deteriorate as quickly or as intensely as untreated students. Halting a decline may be a reasonable goal.

As we examined the "improvers" and "decliners" several trends emerged. Again, we do not have data to support these claims, they are simply observations based on clinical judgment. Among the students who demonstrated a decrease in behavioral referrals over the course of the year, 7/11 were students for whom the intensive case management system had resulted in effective and appropriate changes in medication. That is, as a result of collaboration between the case managers and the students family and outside service providers, the students was either placed on medication or had his/her medication regimen changed. This is not to imply that the medication alone is responsible for the change in behavior. The change in regimen would not have occurred without careful and persistent intervention by the case managers. In addition, the involvement of the case managers may also have inspired hope in the families and the outside services providers, encouraging them to renew their efforts to help the particular child.

In contrast among the 11 children who deteriorated over the course of the year, the following issues emerged. Four of these children were older, and were members of the upper school. Only one of the "improvers" was in the upper school and he was one of the youngest students there. It may be that older children require an more intensive or residential programming to assist them in improving. In addition, the 11 children who deteriorated had initial behavior referral scores which were lower than the 11 children who improved. One possibility is that while our energies were focused on the children most in need, the other children declined or became more aggressive in an attempt to direct attention to them.

Six of these students had significant mood components to their disorders. That is, they frequently displayed severe outbursts of despair and rage, although they were not depressed on a daily basis. It was difficult to effectively treat the depressive component to these children's difficulty. It may be that as more effective anti-depressant medications become available for use with children, some of these disturbances will attenuate. For three of these children their deterioration may have been linked to serious problems involving custody and placement. These were ongoing issues for many students, and highlight the importance of a stable home life (no matter what the composition of the home is) in establishing social and academic competence.

Procedures for evaluating program effectiveness are critical. Dodge (1985) reported that observations of children's social interactions provide the best measure and most robust measures of social skills training programs; however, systematic observational data is difficult to obtain in a setting primarily devoted to clinical care. It may be more useful to obtain a questionnaire which measures basic social skills and academic competence and administer this four times a year. These data can be easily scored using many different computer programs. Keeping track of significant incidents (either using behavior referrals or checklists) may also be an easy way to measure those behaviors most likely to prevent a child from succeeding in a new less restrictive program.

Ongoing feedback and evaluation is critical for program success. This feedback may provide the motivation for students to continue making good efforts and will help justify the expense and programming of the intensive efforts required to make progress with this difficult group of students.

In sum, comprehensive care is demanding but appears to pay off, at least for some students. Students who received more intensive intervention benefitted more than students receiving less. One tentative conclusion is that the schoolwide programs, although useful, are insufficient on their own to produce changes in severely disturbed behavior. These programs must be accompanied by intensive case management programs. Yet even with relatively small caseloads, 15–20 students, it was difficult for the case managers to provide the needed levels of support for every student and every family. When they devoted their efforts to a particular case, and worked hard to coordinate care, their efforts paid off.

CONCLUSIONS

The multiple needs of minority, impoverished SED students require intensive, persistent efforts. A range of biopsychosocial factors may contribute to aggressive behavior and clinicians need to be sensitive to the possibility that factors which promote aggression are different in populations of different socioeconomic status or ethnic backgrounds. Remediation of these difficulties may require interventions from a host of agencies and support systems including child protective services, a mental health agency, a medical center, the students' family and continuous consultation with school staff. Programmatic, schoolwide interventions such as social skills training programs and token economies provide a structure for encouraging these students to develop emotional control and prosocial abilities. These programs are demanding, in terms of time, money, and resources. However, given the costs of the consequences for the failure to treat adequately (i.e., incarceration or hospitalization), it seems appropriate to channel resources into facilities such as schools which have the opportunity to succeed.

REFERENCES

Abikoff, H., & Klein, R. (1992) . Attention deficit hyperactivity and conduct disorder: Comorbidity and implications for treatment. *Journal of Consulting and Clinical Psychology, 60,* 881-892.

Aronowitz, B., Liebowitz, M., Durlach-Misteli, C., Frenkel, M., Mosovich, S., Garfinkle, R., DelBene, D., Cohen, L., Rubin, L. (November 1992). *Neuropsychiatric and Neuropsychological Findings in Conduct Disorder and Attention Deficit Hyperactivity Disorder.* Paper presented at the Meeting of the NY State OMH Research Conference, Albany, NY.

Beck, A. T. (1978). *Children's Depression Inventory-BDI.* San Antonio, Texas: Psychological Corporation, Harcourt Brace Jovanovich.

Becker, D. M., Hill, D. R., Jackson, J. S., Levine, D. M., Stillman, F. A., & Weiss, S. M. (Eds.) (1992). *Health behavior research in minority populations: Access, design, and implementation,* Washington, D.C.: NIH Publication.

Blechman, E. (November 1991). *Communication skills for conduct-disordered youth.* Institute presentation at the Association for the Advancement of Behavior Therapy, New York, N.Y.

Bry, R. H. (1982). Reducing the incidence of adolescent problems through preventive intervention: One and five year follow up. *American Journal of Community Psychology, 10,* 265-276.

Cartledge, G., & Milburn, J. (Eds.) (1980). *Teaching social skills to children.* New York: Pergamon.

Combs, M. L., & Slaby, D. A. (1977). Social skills training with children. In B. Lahey and A. Kazdin (Eds.), *Advances in clinical child psychology.* New York: Plenum.

Conger, J. C., & Keane, S. P. (1981). Social skills intervention in the treatment of isolated or withdrawn children. *Psychological Bulletin, 90,* 478-495.

Conners, C. K. (1989). *Conners' Rating Scales Manual.* North Tonawanda, NY: Multi-Health Systems.

Dodge, K. A. (1985). Attributional bias in aggressive children. In P. C. Kendall (Ed.), *Advances in cognitive behavioral research and therapy* (Vol. 4). Orlando, FL: Academic Press.

Eggers, C. (1978). Cause and prognosis of childhood schizophrenia. *Journal of Autism and Childhood Schizophrenia, 8,* 21-35.

Freedman, B. J., Rosenthal, L., Donahue, C. P., Schlundt, D. G., & McFall, R. (1978). A social-behavioral analysis of skills deficits in delinquent and nondelinquent adolescent boys. *Journal of Consulting and Clinical Psychology, 46,* 1448-1462.

Fugita, S. S., Wexley, K. N., & Hillery, J. M. (1974). Black–White differences in nonverbal behavior in an interview setting. *Journal of Applied Social Psychology, 4,* 343-350.

Gresham, F. M., & Elliot, S. N. (1990). *Social skills rating system.* Circle Pines, MN: American Guidance Service.

Hirschi, T., & Hindelang, M. J. (1977). Intelligence and delinquency: A revisionist view. *American Sociological Review, 42,* 571-587.

Hoagberg, B. L., Rode, P., Skovholt, C. J., Oberg, C. N., Berg, C., Mullet, S., & Choi, T. (1990). Barriers and motivators to prenatal care among low-income women. *Social-Science and Medicine, 30,* 487-495.

Kazdin, A. E. (1987). *Conduct disorders in childhood and adolescence.* Newbury Park, CA: Sage.

Kazdin, A. E., Siegel, T. C., & Bass, D. (1992). Cognitive problem solving training and parent management training in the treatment of antisocial behavior in children. *Journal of Consulting and Clinical Psychology, 60,* 733-747.

Kendall, P. C., Cantwell, D. P., & Kazdin, A. E. (1989). Depression in children and adolescents: Assessment issues and recommendations. *Cognitive Therapy and Research, 13,* 109-146.

Landau, S., & Milich, R. (1988). Social communication patterns of Attention-Deficit Disordered boys. *Journal of Abnormal Child Psychology, 16,* 69-81.

Landau, S., & Moore, L. A. (1991). Social skills deficits in children with Attention-Deficits Hyperactivity Disorder. *School Psychology Review, 20,* 235-251.

Lewis, D. O., Shanok, S. S., Grant, M., & Ritvo, E. (1983). Homicidally aggressive young children: Neuropsychiatric and experimental correlation, *American Journal of Psychiatry, 140,* 148-153.

Lochtzman, J. E., White, K. J., & Wayland, K. W. (1991). Cognitive-behavioral assessment and treatment with aggressive children. In P. C. Kendall (Ed.), Child and Adolescent therapy. *Cognitive behavioral procedures.* New York: Guilford Press.

Masters, J. C., Burish, T. G., Hollon, S. D., & Rimm, D. C. (1987). *Behavior therapy: Techniques and empirical findings.* New York: Harcourt Brace Jovanovich.

McCarney, S. B. (1989). *The Attention Deficits Disorders Evaluation Scale Technical Manual Home Version.* Columbia, MO: Hawthorne Educational Services.

Otten, M. W., Teutsch, S. M., Williamson, D. F., & Marks, J. S. (1991). The effect of known risk factors on the excess mortality of Black adults in the United States. *Journal of American Medical Association, 263,* 845-850.

Patterson, G. R. (1982). *Coercive family process.* Eugene, OR: Castalia.

Patterson, G. R., Reid, J. B., & Dishion, T. J. (1992). *Antisocial boys* (Vol. 4). Castalia Publishing Co: Eugene, OR.

Physician Desk Reference (1992). Montvale, NJ: Medical Economics Company.

Quay, H. C., & Peterson, D. R. (1983). Interim manual for the Revised Behavior Problem Checklist (1st ed.). Coal Gables, FL: University of Miami.

Ruiz, D. S. (Ed.) (1990). *Handbook of mental health and mental disorder among Black Americans.* Westport, CT: Greenwood.

Sarafica, F. C., Schwebel, A. L., Russel, R. K., Issac, P. D., & Myers, L. B. (1990). (Eds.) (1990). *Mental health ethnic minorities.* New York: Praeger.

Schneider, B. H., & Byrne, B. M. (1985). Children's social skills training: A meta-analysis. In Schneider, B. H., Rubin, K. H., and Ledingham, J. E. (Eds.), *Children's peer relations: Issues in assessment and intervention* (pp. 175-190). New York: Springer.

Schneider, B. H., Rubin, K. H., & Ledingham, J. E. (1985). *Children's peer relations: Issues in assessment and intervention,* New York: Springer.

Shure, M. B., & Spivack, G. (1978). *Problem solving techniques in childbearing.* San Francisco, CA: Jossey-Bass Publishers.

Sturge, C. (1982). Reading retardation and antisocial behavior. *Journal of Child Psychology and Psychiatry, 23,* 21-31.

Urbain, E. S., & Kendall, P. C. (1980). Review of social-cognitive problem-solving interventions with children. *Psychological Bulletin, 88,* 109-143.

U.S. House of Representative, Committee of Energy and Commerce. *Infant mortality rates: Failures to close the black-white gap.* March 16, 194. U.S. Government Printing Office. Washington: 1984.

Werry, J. S., Reeves, J. C., & Elkind, G. S. (1987). Attention deficit, conduct, oppositional and anxiety disorders. I. A review of research on differentiating characteristics. Journal of the *American Academy of Child and Adolescent Psychiatry, 26,* 133-143.

West, D. J. (1982). *Delinquency: It's roots, careers, and prospects.* Cambridge, MA: Harvard University Press.

Word, C. O., Zanna, M. P., Cooper, J. (1974). The nonverbal mediation of self-fulfilling prophecy in interracial interaction. *Journal of Experimental Social Psychology, 10,* 109-120.

8

The Abused and Neglected Foster Child: Determinants of Emotional Conflict and Oppositional Behavior

Beverly Greene and Daniel Pilowsky

Behavioral and emotional problems have been observed in emotionally vulnerable children in foster care under certain circumstances. A common pattern involves the unpredictable appearance of a previously absent or unavailable natural parent. Such an occurrence precipitates the reawakening of the child's ambivalent feelings toward both natural and foster parents as well as their fears of abandonment. This frequently leads to behavior that is oppositional and difficult to manage. If the foster parents find the child's behavior unmanageable, and if they are not provided with appropriate professional support during this difficult period, a crisis often follows that precipitates the child's removal from the foster home. Individual, familial, and systemic contributions to this dilemma are discussed. This article emphasizes the origins and nature of the intrapsychic dilemma faced by these children. Particular emphasis is placed on the manifestations of a conflict of loyalty, in the child, and its relationship to the oppositional behavior of these children in foster care. Additional considerations include the impact of inconsistent parenting, abuse and neglect by the natural parents, the assumption of a parental role by the child and a concomitant renunciation of the child's dependency needs, as well as an examination of the role of the foster parent's fantasy of what it will be like to parent a traumatized child.

INTRODUCTION

We have observed on an inpatient psychiatric service, a significant number of children in the midst of an emotional crisis that had emerged while they were in foster placement. A common antecedent to these crises was the unexpected appearance of a natural parent who had been chronically or intermittently unavailable to the child. These children were placed in foster care following abuse, neglect, and/or abandonment by a natural parent. The unexpected appearance of the natural parent and the ensuing demand for filial love places these children in a painful dilemma. They are torn between their feelings for foster parents and natural parents.

It is suggested that an intrapsychic conflict occurs and that it is frequently expressed in oppositional behavior and impairments in the child's functioning. This constellation of problems causes severe strains in the foster parent–child relationship. The child's intrapsychic conflict and its behavioral consequences constitute the focus of this article. A detailed understanding of this dilemma and its sequelae may be helpful in addressing and hopefully preventing the resulting crisis and the problems many of these children encounter in foster care.

To fully appreciate the child's dilemma we must briefly discuss the complex systems interacting with the foster child. In addition to the child, they include the natural (now absent parents), foster parents, and the foster care system.

THE ABSENT PARENT

The absent parent is a natural parent' in the cases we have observed, who is minimally and inappropriately involved with their child, while the child is in foster care, and who appears at unpredictable times. The parent's behavior prior to the child's placement in foster care was deemed either abusive or neglectful to a degree that it was perceived by child welfare authorities to put the child's safety at risk. This resulted in the child's removal from the parent's care. We observed that "absent parent's" make repeated promises to the child of future regular visits, which they do not keep or keep intermittently at best. This experience recreates the child's sense of abandonment and mistrust of adults. Jackson and Westmoreland (1992) note a range of circumstances that can increase the probability that a child will perceive the environment as uncertain and unsafe. Those circumstances include: irregular contact with natural parents; both the lack of stable figures with whom to identify and the confusion about names and residences which often accompanies multiple foster home placement; transient and unstable peer relations all increase the probability of the child's perception of the environment as uncertain and unsafe (Jackson & Westmoreland, 1992).

THE FOSTER PARENT

Although the psychological status of the foster parent is a crucial element in the child's adjustment, it receives little attention. National data suggest that most foster parents are married and have or have had children of their own (Carbino, 1980). We may assume that they have preconceived notions and expectations about parental and child roles. The nature and extent of their preconceived notions about parent and child roles may make it difficult for them to understand the complex and intricate loyalty conflicts that a foster child must work through to adjust. Most foster parents are middle-aged, blue collar, and lower middle class (Carbino, 1980). These households often provide more structure, discipline, and expect more compliance than the often chaotic households of origin. While the majority of foster parents are white, nonwhite children are more likely to be placed in foster care than white children (Stenho, 1982). Currently, 30–33% of all children in foster care are African American (Jackson & Westmoreland, 1992). If we assume that most white foster parents prefer white children, then we can presume that it may be more difficult to place children of color, extending the period of time that they spend in interim or multiple placements and institutions. Jackson and Westmoreland (1992) note that African American children who are placed in white foster homes face additional challenges as well. Mullender and Miller (1985) observe that African American children frequently do not reveal experiences of racism to their white foster parents, thus leaving children to unravel these painful and confusing experiences alone. It is also noted that African American families and communities play an important role not only in buffering the climate of racial hostility that their children encounter but of preparing them to address racial hostilities as well (Greene, 1992; Jackson & Westmoreland, 1992). The absence of these important role models and their capacity to transmit adaptive skills in this area is significant. Our sample observations are based on two African-American children.

THE FOSTER CARE SYSTEM

Perhaps the major purpose of foster care is to provide children, some of whom have experienced trauma in the context of disorganized or unsafe family systems, with an important respite from these circumstances. It may also offer the family an opportunity to organize itself so that it may be more responsive to the child's needs. Jackson and Westmoreland (1992) note however that foster care alone is not sufficient to help children whose placement is a result of abusive or neglectful family circumstances. This is consistent with our experience of the children observed in the hospital setting. It would seem that many of these children's difficulties in foster care would be predictable given the circumstances surrounding their placement, i.e., severe abuse and/or neglect.

Unfortunately, despite good intentions, this system is not always free to carry out its mission unencumbered. One hallmark of the foster care system, besides overburdened agencies and discouraged child care workers, is its inability to be free to respond solely to the needs of the child or even the best interests of the child's natural family. This system must satisfy the demands and requirements of many other agencies whose cooperation is a legal and practical necessity. A slow and inefficient court system may frequently preclude efficient and speedy placement, leaving children in limbo for months or years at a time. Their resulting emotional turmoil is predictable. Budget constraints and other problems may interfere with getting therapeutic interventions to children and their families before the child exhibits symptoms of severe pathology.

THE EMOTIONALLY VULNERABLE CHILD

Emotionally vulnerable children are more affected by developmental failures than children who do not share this vulnerability. We labeled children as emotionally vulnerable if the events that take place before their placement in foster care include neglect, maltreatment, and inconsistent parenting. These events are likely to have negatively influenced their development (Egeland, Sroufe & Erickson, 1983; Jackson & Westmoreland, 1992; Martinez-Roig, Domingo-Salvany, Llorens-Teral, & Ibanez-Cacho, 1983; Kunkel, 1983; Steele, 1986). We are aware that many additional factors, such as the age of separation from natural parents, the presence of other significant adults and support systems in the child's life, the child's temperament and intellectual abilities can also contribute to how detrimental these effects may be to a given child (Cicchetti & Rizley, 1981; Jackson & Westmoreland, 1992).

THE INTRAPSYCHIC IMPLICATIONS OF INCONSISTENT PARENTING

In a pioneering study of maternal deprivation, Spitz (1946) established that lack of human contact for infants results in major impairments in their development. It is noted that emotional inconsistencies of parents or caretakers and inappropriate interactions have a negative impact on a child's ability to form meaningful relationships (Bowlby, 1973; Egeland & Sroufe, 1981; Jackson & Westmoreland, 1992; Kinard, 1980; Steele, 1986).

Ainsworth (1978) believes attachment is instinctual but observed different qualities of attachment among different people. Ainsworth's conclusions were based on observations of many children and their parents before, during, and after separation. When anxiety in the interaction is observed before separation, two different outcomes are noted. In one, the child rarely cries when separated from the mother and avoids her when reunited. This is called anxious attachment-avoidant type. In the second outcome of anxious attachment intense distress is observed on separation, however it is followed by ambivalence on reunion. This response is referred to as anxious attachment-ambivalent type. The cause of "anxious attachment" is ascribed to parents who are late, inappropriate, insensitive, or unresponsive to appropriate signals sent by infants. Similar problems in attachment have been observed in abused and neglected children (Blanchard & Main, 1979; Egeland & Sroufe, 1981; George & Main, 1979; Hyman & Parr, 1978; Steele, 1986). Instead of meaningful relationships, these children may establish "need fulfilling" part-object relationships to whomever instantly gratifies their wishes, evoking fantasied images of the "good mother" (Burland, 1980).

A requirement for appropriate ego development is the successful negotiation of the symbiotic stage of development. Differentiation cannot successfully take place if no firm attachment has ever existed. What can occur is an unstable, brittle attachment borne of chronic dissatisfaction (Steele, 1986). For many of these children a reliable and consistent dyad and/or family constellation has never existed, thus impairing the emergence of a differentiated ego from its inception. Even if differentiation has been achieved, healthy psychological development may be hampered by the unavailability of consistent objects. As a result of these difficulties, healthy psychological development may be impaired in a variety of areas. Such impairments may include a compromised ability to successfully develop a capacity to form stable and meaningful relationships (George & Main, 1979; Jackson & Westmoreland, 1992; Kinard, 1980; Lampshear,1985). Self-esteem, ego functions associated with good reality testing, and cognition may suffer, and control over destructive wishes and fantasies may deteriorate as well (George & Main, 1979; Jackson & Westmoreland, 1992; Kinard, 1980; Kunkel, 1983; Lampshear, 1985; Martinez-Roig, 1983; Reid, Taplin & Lorber, 1981; Steele, 1986).

THE ABSENT PARENT REVISITS

Both day to day caretaking and the very labeling of foster parents as "parents" as opposed to "custodians" creates the confusing illusion of a permanent alliance for the child and sometimes for the foster parent. A caretaker, after caring for a child beyond a certain period may experience themselves and be experienced by the child as the psychological parent (Goldstein, Freud, & Solnit, 1973). This situation becomes complicated when the foster parent experiences him or herself as only a temporary caretaker but the child experiences the foster parent as a psychological parent or *vice versa*. Dissonance in the expectations of the foster parent and the foster child, and the dissonance between their expectations and the agencies plans for the child adds another level of woe to all involved.

While foster children may want and need a stable alliance between themselves and their foster parents, they may actively struggle against this alliance. Their rejection of this alliance may be rooted in their need to preserve the appearance of allegiance to their natural parents. This delicate equilibrium is often intensified and threatened by the statements or actions from natural parents to "reclaim" the child's loyalty. This presents a particular problem for emotionally vulnerable children who may not be able to extricate themselves from the resulting emotional confusion. Children who are forced to behave with a maturity that exceeds their developmental capabilities may be particularly vulnerable. A phenomenon of this type is reflected in the following two case illustrations.

CASE ILLUSTRATIONS

In the two case illustrations that follow, children were separated from a natural parent, who was seriously neglectful or abusive. We observe that the parent's neglectful behavior prior to the separation results in the child's adoption of inappropriate levels of responsibility for both their parent and themselves. We presume that both factors serve as significant sources of difficulty between the child and subsequent caretakers.

DEBORAH

Deborah is a short, attractive, articulate 9-year-old African American female. She was admitted to an Inpatient Child Psychiatry Service following an attempt to jump from a fifth floor window "because I was mad at my foster mother." This patient, in her fifth foster home within 1 year, had a history of temper tantrums, running away from foster homes and stubbornly refusing to comply with the requests of adult caretakers.

Deborah was removed from her natural mother's care 1 year before her hospitalization, after she was sexually assaulted by one of her mother's associates. Since Deborah was unsupervised at the time, her mother was deemed neglectful by Family Court.

Deborah's natural mother had a 10-year history of drug and alcohol addiction, multiple physical and emotional problems, was often incapacitated, and could not adequately care for her. Instead, Deborah often took care of her mother, thus reversing the normal parent–child roles.

Visits between mother and child were conducted under the supervision of an agency caseworker. Deborah's mother frequently failed to keep promised visits, leaving Deborah frustrated, disappointed, and angry. When she did visit, she was either glad to see Deborah or was rejecting and punitive toward her. On at least two occasions, Deborah's mother greeted her with "I'm sick of you, you only cause me trouble..." Deborah ran to a corner crying while her mother followed screaming at her. At other times she would greet Deborah enthusiastically with promises of regaining custody, and suggestions that Deborah was not properly cared for in the foster home.

During her hospitalization Deborah frequently verbalized the fear that her mother would be in danger during her absence. She appealed to staff members with a sense of desperation that she must be allowed to return to her mother "because she needs me...I have to take care of her." Deborah reported an incident in which her home was burglarized and her mother "had been taking drugs and couldn't get up...and he locked me in the bathroom." Occasionally she reported that her mother "fell over the stove" while trying to cook "after she was taking drugs." However, when staff or her therapist attempted to confront her with her mother's limitations, she would vehemently deny that she had ever said these things. She would blame staff members or herself for having "caused trouble...lying on my mother." At these times she became agitated, verbally and physically assaultive toward staff and peers, and threatened "I'll cut my throat... cut my arms... I'll kill myself." This impulsivity and poor judgment in emotionally provocative situations and the propensity to become self-destructive was consistent with observations of many of these children.

Initially, Deborah presented herself in an excessively ingratiating manner, until she was denied something. At that point, she became enraged, and threatened or attempted to harm herself. It was felt that Deborah's inability to openly express her anger at her mother led to her need to conceal that anger, direct it toward herself or at inappropriate figures with an intensity that the precipitating event did not warrant. She appeared to need a substitute fantasy of a faultless mother. This too was striking in the face of her quick assumption of the adult role with peers and authority figures on the unit. She frequently told staff members that she believed that behaving badly would get her "thrown out of my foster home and then they'll have to send me back to my mother." In this regard she was similar to many children we observed. She also verbalized ambivalent feelings toward her foster mother, saying that while she was cared for and treated well in her foster home that she could not "love my real mother and foster mother both at the same time."

In summary, we are presented with a "parental" child who idealized her neglectful natural mother, disparaged her foster parents and assumed responsibility for her mother's care and condition. This occurred while the natural mother was simultaneously inconsistent and inadequate in her emotional and physical availability to Deborah; she blamed Deborah for her problems; made unrealistic promises of reunion; and overtly disparaged the child's foster parents. Her mother's behavior reinforced Deborah's maladaptive illusions.

MARY

Mary is a charming and appealing 6-year-old African American female who was admitted to an Inpatient Child Psychiatry Service after setting a devastating fire in her foster parent's home.

Mary, the oldest of two children, was born to a drug addicted mother. She was placed in foster care at the age of 4, after her mother was found neglectful by Family Court. Mary and a sister 2 years younger were routinely left alone by the natural mother for long periods of time. Mary was somehow able to feed herself and care for her younger sister when the mother was absent.

The placement in the first foster home lasted only 5 months. The first foster parents requested Mary's removal because she refused to follow instructions, was defiant and consistently "talked back" to them. In the second foster home she displayed the same type of defiant behavior toward foster parents, but she was also "cute" and ingratiating toward them. They tolerated her behavior until Mary set a major fire in their home. In school and in the home, her oppositional, defiant behavior kept her in direct conflict with adults.

In both the hospital and the foster home this little girl was very ingratiating toward the staff and authority figures as long as her wishes were complied with. If anyone attempted to set limits on her behavior, she changed, in seconds, from a cute, sweet little girl to a defiant, angry child, who cursed adults with fury. During an interview Mary told the interviewer that she was happy to play with him. A few minutes later she wanted to play with the interviewer's phone. She was told to play with the toys instead of the phone. Mary said to him in a state of uncontrollable anger, "I hate you... there is another Doctor in this place... he is much nicer than you."

We can see how Mary learned to mistrust adults and care for herself while living with an unreliable and neglectful mother by assuming an adult role. When placed in foster care, she continued to mistrust the ability of adults to care for her and defied them. She was unable to depend on caring adults because she saw them as unreliable and potentially hateful. Her refusal to relinquish the inappropriate adult role resulted in a conflict between Mary and her new adult caretakers. It is also clear that she saw caring adults as need satisfying objects. She was ingratiating with her foster parents and doctors as long as they complied with her wishes. Mary became defiant and even hateful when they did not. Her image of the "good parent" could not be sustained when she was mildly frustrated.

Sometime after Mary was placed in foster care, her mother visited her. She led Mary to believe that she would soon return to her care. The mother also told the foster care agency that she would attend a drug rehabilitation program. She did not follow through on either promise, and she rarely visited Mary. We believe that her inconsistent visits and broken promises contributed to Mary's conflicts, thus exacerbating her defiance and confusion.

DETERMINANTS OF OPPOSITIONAL BEHAVIOR

A question arises as to the determinants of the oppositional behavior displayed by these and children like them following their placement in foster care. Abused and neglected children are known to manifest maladaptive behaviors from infancy (Egeland et al., 1983; George & Main, 1979; Jackson & Westmoreland, 1992; Kent, 1976; Kinard, 1980; Lampshear, 1985; Reid et al., 1981; Reidy, 1977; Steele, 1986). George and Main (1979) described abused toddlers who tended to be aggressive toward their peers and caretakers. The two children previously described certainly manifested those behaviors. They had also assumed parental roles. We suggest that there is a connection between the parental roles played by these children before placement and the oppositional behavior manifested during placement. The parental roles they played before placement intensified the emotional vulnerability of these children and played a major role in the oppositional behavior displayed in the foster homes. Before explaining the connection between parental roles and oppositional behavior, we will briefly discuss the concept of the parental child.

Minuchin and Fishman's (1981) conceptualization of the parental child is one in which a child is delegated authority by a responsible adult for the purpose of taking care of a younger child or children in the adult caretaker's absence. This term may be extended to children who do not have a responsible caretaker and are forced to care for themselves and/or younger siblings and perhaps an irresponsible adult. Younger siblings often become resentful and oppositional with a parental child as a caretaker. When this becomes a problem, Minuchin (1981) reestablishes the authority of the parent and tries to increase the involvement of older siblings with age appropriate peers.

Minuchin (1981) describes some advantages of the role of parental child for the parents and for the child, however there are some potential problems. There are differences between the parental child whose authority was legitimately delegated and the parental child who assumes this role as a means of survival when caretakers abdicate their responsibility. Whether the child is being asked to parent a younger sibling or to parent a caretaker, when either is done out of the caretaker's abdication, the defensive tasks may be similar. These children attempt to adopt the role of appropriate adult caretakers themselves, a role that they cannot execute successfully. In their attempt to adopt this adult role, they must deny what they really are, dependent children who require caretaking themselves (Steele, 1986). Once required to assume the mantle of "adulthood" prematurely, their dependency needs become alien and unacceptable given the often correct assumption that those needs will be frustrated. This alienation from appropriate dependency needs begins to interfere with these children's ability to comply with the limits set by new authority figures.

These children have learned from their experiences that authority figures are unreliable and unable to meet their needs. It is therefore adaptive when living with incompetent natural parents for these children to attempt to take care of their own needs. They are often encouraged by their parents to take care of themselves, younger siblings, and often the parent(s) as well! It would be surprising if any child did not apply this rationale to new situations.

We have observed in these children, after placement in foster care, an ingratiating, manipulative quality that barely conceals their underlying anger and contempt for the authority figure. When the foster parent, or other authority figures, instantly gratifies the child's wishes, the child appears very grateful. When they do not, the destructive fantasies and wishes lurking under the surface are unleashed. The unsuspecting foster parent, who has seen a compliant and ingratiating child, and who feels that they are being a good caretaker is puzzled when faced with an insolent, defiant youngster.

Another complication of this situation is the child's need to idealize the natural parent (Main & Goldwyn, 1984). The more neglectful the parent, the more intense this compensatory idealization may be because the degree of the child's unconscious rage is related to the level of unconscious idealization. Intermittently the realization of the natural parent's limitations may become conscious to the child and may be expressed verbally with some anger attached to it. Jackson and Westmoreland (1992) observe that therapy may be most useful to these children at such times as they may escape, albeit temporarily, the burden of demonstrating their loyalty to their natural parent by not expressing anger or criticism toward them. Our observations are consistent with these findings. This may be the only time the child's anger is directed at the appropriate object. Usually the anger is displaced onto objects of lesser significance. If the child is in placement, an overdetermined target for this anger is the foster parent. The dangers of expressing this anger toward the natural parent, who may have already abandoned the child physically or emotionally or threatened to do so, include the child's fear of having their destructive and angry wishes for the parent realized.

Another reason for the child's idealization of the natural parents may rest in the child's inability to tolerate or understand his/her own ambivalent feelings. This ambivalence may be a concept that a young child does not yet have the cognitive apparatus to understand nor the emotional maturity to withstand. Therefore, these children cannot cope with what to them appear to be powerful, mutually exclusive feelings for the same parent. For these children, to justify continuing to love and feel attached to a parent who hurts them, they must deny the hurt and when that is not possible, blame themselves or others (Main & Goldwyn, 1984; Kunkel, 1983). For a child, there may appear to be only two alternatives. One is to stop loving the parent and experience the pain of doing so, which is untenable. The other is to deny the parent's shortcomings and maintain the idealized image of that parent.

A number of factors may leave these children with difficulty tolerating positive feelings for a natural parent and a foster parent simultaneously. Such factors would include the child's ambivalence about their natural parent, the child's own emotional and cognitive immaturity, and the degree of emotional pain inflicted by the natural parent. For these children, experiencing affection for the natural parent and the foster parent may imply a blatant betrayal of the natural parent. In our experience, most children avoid this at all costs. They pay dearly for this avoidance in terms of self blame, denial of reality, and behavior that often precipitates alienation by the foster parents and other benevolent adult figures.

To maintain their precarious psychological alliance with a natural parent via the idealization of that parent, these children must at least consciously disparage the foster parent. To view the foster parent as competent would require these children to confront the incompetence of the natural parent and their subsequent angry feelings toward that parent. There are other consequences involved in confronting the real as opposed to the idealized image of the natural parent (Kunkel, 1983).

These children may experience parental failure as if it were a result of their own deficiencies and not their parent's deficiencies. The idealized parental image may serve the purpose of preserving the child's illusion that there is a competent parent who is in control. If forced to acknowledge the absence of such a parent, the child may have to consciously experience the absence of responsible figures in his/her life. The absence of any such figure for a child may represent the ultimate fear and despair, particularly for a child who is filled with rage. Here, these children are left alone in a situation where there are no apparent limits, or supports, only their own frightening impulses.

A present danger is that the child's disparaging fantasy of the foster parents may become a self-fulfilling prophecy. The foster parents, who have their own fantasies of being nurturing figures, are left with a child who is temporarily unavailable for nurturing. This leaves all parties feeling frustrated and deprived. We have discussed some factors that may render these children unreceptive to nurturance (Kunkel, 1983).

Spitz (1946), Mahler (1975), Bowlby (1969), and others (Egeland & Sroufe, 1981; Kinard, 1980; Steele, 1986) suggest that the capacity for a trusting relationship is a function of having experienced consistent or "good enough" parenting early in life (Egeland & Sroufe, 1981; Hyman & Parr, 1978; Kinard, 1980; Kunkel, 1983; Lampshear, 1985; Steele, 1986; Winnicott, 1965). There may be many reasons for the natural parent's failure to provide "good enough parenting." Since children who are constitutionally vulnerable or difficult have a higher risk of parental difficulties, such as neglect and maltreatment, they are also at higher risk for placement in foster care. Therefore, it is not surprising to find that children placed in foster care may have a higher percentage of constitutional difficulties that they also bring to the foster parent.

A typical example may be a child who is constitutionally difficult, has suffered inadequate or abusive parenting and is placed with foster parents. The foster parents have their own fantasies of nurturing and rescue, but the child mistrusts, disparages, and therefore frustrates them. If the foster parent cannot tolerate this combination or if they are inadequate to the task, this child will be subjected to yet another experience of parental failure. The intermittent appearances of natural parents, who reinforce the disparagement of foster parents make the latter outcome even more likely.

In this context, oppositional behavior patterns may arise serving multiple functions. They may serve as the child's test of the foster parent's commitment; the hope that the behavior will precipitate rejection by foster parents and lead to a fantasied reunion with the idealized natural parent; the maintenance of loyalty to his/her natural parent; displacement of anger at the natural parent onto the foster parent; and for maintaining an abusive rejecting parent–child interaction and perpetuation of his/her negative self-image (repetition compulsion) (Steele, 1986).

A foster parent's rejection of the acting out behavior and request to have the children removed from the home confirms the child's negative self-image. This situation, the idealization of and fantasies of reunion with the natural parents are reinforced. In this instance, these fantasies may represent the child's last hope of being reunited with the natural parents, making it even more difficult to prepare them for a new foster placement. This has been illustrated in the case of Deborah.

RECOMMENDATIONS

Adequate screening and subsequent mandatory training of foster parents is essential. They must be helped to gain insight into their own motives and needs, and how they may expect many of those parenting needs to be frustrated by many of the children in their care. Specifically, they must understand the loyalty conflict of the foster child and the ways that it may predispose the child to disparage the foster parent. It must be made clear that this disparaging behavior is not a reflection of the foster parent's true parenting abilities or necessarily of the child's true feelings for them. Further, foster parents must be helped to appreciate how damaged and empty many of these children are, and how brittle and unmalleable their egos may be to the environmental, physical, and psychic assaults of life. They must be able to tolerate giving much consistent nurturance to an apparently "ungrateful, insolent child" who cannot for some time, return that love and affection consistently, if at all.

Agencies must provide assistance to foster parents in the form of counseling and ongoing support when these predictable frustrations mount and a crisis with the child results. Training in child management and behavior modification and support for the stressors inherent in taking care of these children may be useful as well.

Work with the natural parents is essential to helping them understand the impact of their behavior on their child. While parental visitation is important to the child's emotional development there are circumstances when it can be harmful. Involvement of all parties in visitation arrangements, particularly until a certain regularity of contact can be established may be helpful. In the context of the agency's attempts to work with the natural parent, if there are continued failures to keep appointments and old destructive patterns that seriously undermine the child's adjustment persist, suspension or termination of visits should be considered but always with the awareness of the importance of the natural family to the child and *vice versa*.

Institutional staff members and foster parents must avoid fueling the child's fantasies of reunion with the inconsistent natural parent, despite the natural parent's promises. This is often difficult when the nature of court outcomes are uncertain. Childcare workers must understand and recognize how their own history of relationships with their own parents or children may predispose them to wish to reunite or separate children from their natural parents in ways that are inappropriate to their client's situations.

Finally, it is important that these children be helped to understand the conflicts of loyalties they experience and its ultimate impact on their behavior.

ACKNOWLEDGMENTS

The authors would like to thank Dr. Dorothy Gartner, Dr. Sam Tsemberis, Dr. Mahin Hassibi, and Dr. Eli Messinger for their thoughtful comments and suggestions in the preparation of this paper.

REFERENCES

Ainsworth, M. D., Blehar, M., Waters, E., & Wall, S. (1978). *Patterns of Attachment: A psychological study of the strange situation,* New Jersey: Lawrence Erlbaum & Associates.
Blanchard, M., & Main, M. (1979). Avoidance of the attachment figure and social emotional adjustment in day care infants. *Developmental Psychology, 15,* 445-446.
Bowlby, J. (1969). *Attachment and loss, Vol. 1: Attachment.* New York: Basic Books.
Bowlby, J. (1973). *Attachment and loss, Vol. 2: Separation.* New York: Basic Books.
Burland, J. A. (1980). A psychoanalytic psychiatrist in the world of foster care. *Clinical Social Work Journal, 8,* 50-61.
Carbino, R. (1980). *Foster parenting: An updated review of the literature.* New York: Child Welfare League of America.
Cicchetti, D., & Rizley, R. (1981). Developmental perspectives on the etiology, intergenerational transmission, and sequelae of child maltreatment. In R. Rizley, & D.

Cicchetti (Eds.), *New directions for child development: Developmental perspectives in child maltreatment.* San Francisco: Jossey Bass.

Egeland, B., & Sroufe, L. A. (1981). Attachment and early maltreatment. *Child Development, 52,* 44-52.

Egeland, B., Sroufe, L. A., & Erickson, M. (1983). The developmental consequence of different patterns of maltreatment. *Child Abuse and Neglect, 7,* 459-469.

George, C., & Main, M. (1979). Social interactions of young abused children: Approach, avoidance, and aggression. *Child Development, 50,* 306-318.

Goldstein, J., Freud, A. & Solnit, A. J. (1973). *Beyond the best interest of the child.* New York: The Free Press.

Greene, B. (1992). Racial socialization as a tool in psychotherapy with African American children. In L. Vargas & J. Koss-Chioino (Eds.), Working with culture: *Psychotherapeutic interventions with ethnic minority children* (pp. 63-81). San Francisco, CA: Jossey Bass.

Hyman, C. A., & Parr, R. A. (1978). A controlled video observation study of abused children. *Child Abuse and Neglect, 2,* 217-222.

Jackson, H., & Westmoreland, G. (1992). Therapeutic issues for Black children in foster care. In L. Vargas & J. Koss-Chioino (Eds.), *Working with culture: Psychotherapeutic interventions with ethnic minority youth* (pp.43-62). San Francisco, CA: Jossey Bass.

Kent, J. A. (1976). A follow up study of abused children. *Journal of Pediatric Psychology, 1,* 25-31.

Kinard, E. M. (1980). Emotional development in physically abused children. *American Journal of Orthopsychiatry, 50,* 686-696.

Kunkel, B. E. (1983). The alienation response of children abused in out of home placement. *Child Abuse and Neglect, 7,* 479-484.

Lampshear, V. S. (1985). The impact of maltreatment on children's psychosocial adjustment: A review of the research. *Child Abuse and Neglect, 9,* 251-263.

Mahler, M.A Pine, F. & Bergman, A. (1975). *The Psychological birth of the human infant: Symbiosis and Individuation.* New York: Basic Books.

Main, M., & Goldwyn, R. (1984). Predicting rejection of her infant from mother's representation of her own experience: Implications for the abused-abusing intergenerational cycle. *Child Abuse and Neglect, 8,* 203-217.

Martinez-Roig, A., Domingo-Salvany, F., Llorens-Terol, J., & Ibanez-Cacho, J. (1983). Psychological implications of the maltreated child syndrome. *Child Abuse and Neglect, 7,* 261-263.

Minuchin, S, & Fishman, H. C. (1981). *Family therapy techniques.* Cambridge, MA: Harvard University Press.

Mullender, A., & Miller, D. (1985). The ebony group: Black children in White foster homes. *Adoption and Fostering, 9,* 33-40, 49.

Reid, J. B., Taplin, P. S., & Lorber, R. A. (1981). A social interactional approach to the treatment of abusive families. In R. Stuart (Ed.), *Violent behavior: A social learning approach to prediction, management, and treatment.* New York: Brunner Mazel.

Reidy, T. J. (1977). The aggressive characteristics of abused and neglected children. *Journal of Clinical Psychology, 33,* 1140-1145.

Spitz, R. A., & Wolf, K. M. (1946). Anaclitic depression: An inquiry into the genesis of psychiatric conditions in early childhood. *Psychoanalytic Study of the Child, 2,* 313-342.

Steele, B. F. (1986). Notes of the lasting effects of early child abuse throughout the life cycle. *Child Abuse and Neglect, 10,* 283-291.

Stenho, S. (1982). Differential treatment of minority children in service systems. *Social Work, 27,* 39-45.

Winnicott, D. W. (1965). *The maturational process and the facilitating environment.* New York: International Universities Press.

9

Multicultural Perspectives on Counseling Survivors of Rape

Clare G. Holzman

The dominant Euro-American culture is a rape-prone culture, as defined by Sanday. Within that culture, rape is both a tool and a consequence of interlocking systems of oppression based on race, ethnicity, class, and sexual orientation. The impact of rape on an individual survivor can only be fully understood in the context of the survivor's own culture, religious beliefs, and experience as an immigrant or refugee. Issues of race, culture, class, and sexual orientation influence every step in the counseling of a rape survivor. Knowledge about the client's culture is essential if accurate assessment and culturally appropriate service are to be provided. Specific examples of the impact of these issues are presented. Ways in which the cultural values implicit in the crisis counseling model may conflict with the client's values and needs are examined.

INTRODUCTION

The focus of this paper is on cultural issues that we need to be aware of in counseling rape survivors in culturally heterogeneous urban areas in the United States. To put those issues in context, rape is first considered from a broader perspective. Peggy Reeves Sanday (1981) surveyed anthropological data on the prevalence of rape in 156 cultures throughout the world and over about 4000 years of human history. She identified rape prone societies, "in which sexual assault by men on women is either culturally allowable or largely overlooked (p. 15)" and rape free societies, in

165

which "the act of rape is either infrequent or does not occur (p. 15)." Forty-seven percent of the societies she studied were rape free; only 18% were rape prone. Sanday found that rape prone societies were characterized by "a social ideology of male dominance (p. 24)," a high level of interpersonal and intergroup violence, and sexual separation, or "the presence of structures or places where the sexes congregate in single sex groups (p. 24)."

Three points about Sanday's findings are relevant to this discussion. First, they demonstrate that rape is not an inescapable aspect of human nature; Sanday found more rape-free societies than rape-prone societies. Second, the dominant Euro-American culture of the United States is a highly rape-prone culture, both in terms of the incidence of rape and in terms of the cultural configuration described by Sanday. According to the Uniform Crime Statistics compiled by the FBI, the number of rapes and attempted rapes reported to the police in 1991 was 106,593 (Federal Bureau of Investigation, 1992). Since less than 10% of rapes are reported (Russell, 1982), the number of rapes and attempted rapes that actually occurred in that 1 year alone can be estimated at well over a million. Estimates of the percentage of American women who will experience a rape or an attempted rape at some time in their life range from 15% to 46% (Lundberg-Love & Geffner, 1989; Russell & Howell, 1983).

In addition to the factors examined by Sanday, there are a number of other features of contemporary Euro-American culture that support a high incidence of rape (Bourque, 1989; Burt, 1980; Lottes, 1988). These include:

(1) The linkage of aggressive, violent behavior with the very definition of masculinity, and of compliance and gentleness with the definition of femininity.

(2) The belief that women frequently say no to sexual advances by men when they really mean yes, that they want the man to persist in spite of their spoken objections and physical resistance, and that they find the use of force by a man sexually stimulating.

(3) The belief that it is impossible to sexually penetrate a woman against her will, so that by definition rape is impossible.

(4) The belief that once a man is sexually aroused, he loses the ability to control his sexual behavior, and that therefore it is the woman's responsibility either to avoid arousing him or, if she does arouse him, to provide him with sexual release.

(5) The cultural institution of dating, in which a man and a woman who hardly know one another go off alone together, unchaperoned. This arrangement, combined with the beliefs I have just described, is clearly a script for date rape, and it is not surprising that surveys on college cam-

puses find that over 27% of college women experience rape or attempted rape (Koss, Gidycz, & Wisniewski, 1987).

The third point suggested by Sanday's findings is that the dynamics of rape involve the ways in which power and violence are structured by a particular culture, not just the psychodynamics of individual perpetrators or victims. In the United States today, that structuring takes place not only on the basis of gender, but also on the basis of race, ethnicity, class, and sexual orientation. Rape is both a tool and a consequence of an interlocking system of oppressions based on these factors (Collins, 1993; Davis, 1981). Institutionalized differences in power influence who can rape whom and get away with it, and what happens to the rape victim in the aftermath of the rape. And rape or the threat of rape is one way of intimidating and demoralizing people and thereby reinforcing their subordination. Now that mainstream institutions are endorsing multiculturalism, there is a tendency to talk about "difference" and "diversity" as if they were just an interesting source of variety, and to ignore power differentials and oppression. To understand rape, it is necessary to understand to how racism, classism, and heterosexism impact on rape survivors.

Those who have the least power in a society are the most vulnerable to rape (Bourque, 1989; Hindelang & Davis, 1977; Sorenson & Siegel, 1992). This vulnerability may be based on the victim's economic dependence on the perpetrator, on the knowledge of both parties that the victim will not be believed or that the perpetrator will not be punished by the criminal justice system, or by other factors that restrict the victim's freedom to resist or to hold the perpetrator accountable for his actions. Melanie Kaye/Kantrowitz (1992) writes:

> Poor women have less choice about housing, less police patrol and less reason to believe in police protection, less money to drive cars or take taxis instead of using public transportation, less possibility of refusing night jobs, or jobs which include sexual harassment or generally expose us to unsafe conditions. Women of color, frequently poor, are often exposed to abuse in dangerous neighborhoods and in demeaning jobs. Women surviving on women's wages—single women, lesbians—are frequently poor. Perceived as unprotected because "man-less," we are particularly vulnerable to abuse by men, especially if we live outside our own cultural or racial community: outsider women are marks, and visible lesbians are doubly outsiders (pp. 17-18).

An upper middle class employer can get away with sexually assaulting a working class employee who desperately needs the job. Not only does she risk being fired if she resists, but they both know that even if she reported the rape, a jury would be less likely to convict him than if he were a janitor (Deitz & Byrnes, 1981). Undocumented immigrants are even more vulnerable: not only is their economic situation precarious, but they cannot turn to the police or other institutions for help without risking being deported, often to places where their lives will be in danger. Disabled women are three times as likely to be raped as able-bodied women; often the perpetrator is their caregiver, on whom they are physically dependent (Burstow, 1992; Sobsey & Tanis, 1991). Rapists consciously target the most vulnerable potential victims. People who challenge the system of power and privilege are also targeted as a way of reasserting dominance. This is a major factor in the rape of lesbians and gay men. The clinical relevance of this analysis is that information about the cultural supports and power dynamics of rape can be very helpful to a survivor who is trying to understand why the rape happened and who may be feeling personally responsible.

The impact of rape on an individual survivor can only be fully understood in the context of the survivor's own culture. For the counselor, the process of becoming knowledgeable about a wide range of cultures is a never-ending one. Some good places to start are the textbooks by Monica McGoldrick and her colleagues (1982), by Pedersen (1985), and by Devore and Schlesinger (1987). Another good place to start is with ourselves. The more we know about our own culture, the less likely we are to think its particular customs and beliefs are cultural universals. We also need to become aware of the racial and ethnic stereotypes of others that we harbor, so that we can work at modifying them, or at least correcting for them in our work (Pinderhughs, 1989). Workshops on unlearning racism and ethnocentrism are widely available now, and are an essential part of basic competence as a counselor or therapist.

IMPACT OF CULTURAL DIFFERENCES AND STEREOTYPES IN THE RESPONSE TO RAPE

As we acquire more information about cultures other than our own, it is important not to let that information become a new set of stereotypes. There is a great deal of diversity within what we may think of as culturally homogeneous groups. The term "Asian," for example, applies to people from China, Cambodia, India, and a large number of other culturally and linguistically distinct countries. In addition to national differences, there are regional differences, religious differences, class differences, differences between urban and rural populations, and differences in the extent to which the indigenous culture has been modified by colonialism and economic imperialism. In the United States, people from the same country of origin may differ widely in the extent to which they have retained their traditional culture and ties to an ethnic community, or have become assimilated into the dominant culture. There are also individual differences among people who may be identical on all the dimensions named, as we can readily see by thinking about the variability within our own families. In working with an individual survivor, we can never assume that what we have heard or read about his or her culture of origin applies to this person's individual experience. It is important for us to have the information so that we will be prepared to hear and understand what the client tells us, but we also have to be prepared to revise our thinking based on what we hear.

The following are examples of ways in which a particular cultural context influences a rape survivor's experience of and response to rape. For African-American women, the cultural context of rape always includes the history and legacy of slavery, in which African-American women were systematically raped both as a means of increasing the supply of slaves and as a way of reinforcing White supremacy (Carby, 1987; Collins, 1993; Davis, 1981; Hall, 1983; Hooks, 1981; Wyatt, 1992). As an attempt to justify this process, an ideology of the sexual promiscuity of African-American women was promulgated. It was maintained that it was impossible to rape an African-American woman because she was never unwilling. This stereotype is still with us. African-American women walking down the street are routinely assumed to be prostitutes both by civilian males and by the police. An African-American woman who reports a rape to the police is also likely to be assumed to be a prostitute, and therefore, in the eyes of the police, either a willing participant or undeserving of concern. Even if she is not assumed to be a prostitute, there may be an assumption that she was a willing participant rather than a victim.

Closely linked with the legacy of the sexual exploitation of African-American women is the legacy of the lynching of African-American men accused of raping White women (Collins, 1993; Davis, 1981; Hall, 1983). Both are based on a stereotype that Africans are characterized by animal-like, unrestrained sexuality. There is extensive evidence that African-American men accused of rape are more likely to be arrested and convicted, to receive longer sentences, and to be sentenced to death than White men accused of the same crime (Bradmiller & Walters, 1985; Feild, 1979; LaFree, 1980). When an African-American woman is raped by an African-American man, she may want him to be punished, but she may also be reluctant to turn him in to a racist criminal justice system. These are issues that need to be recognized and validated by a counselor who is helping her to consider her options.

Institutionalized sexual exploitation may also be an issue for Southeast Asian women who may have been victimized by the extensive use of that region for sex tourism, for so-called rest and recreation for American military personnel, and as a source of mail order brides (Enloe, 1989). Just as African-American women are stereotyped as sexually promiscuous,

Asian women are stereotyped as exotic, submissive, and totally devoted to pleasing men.

In many traditional cultures, a woman who loses her virginity because of a rape is regarded as irreparably soiled and devalued, so that no one will want to marry her (Kanuha, 1987; Van Boemel & Rozee, 1992). In some cases she may be expected to marry the rapist, because economic survival outside of marriage is seen as impossible and the rapist is the only possible partner. A woman who is raped may also be seen as bringing great shame on her entire family, and may be expected to keep the rape a secret for their protection.

Religious beliefs about sexuality, about guilt and punishment, and about divine purpose are also factors in a woman's recovery after a rape. Young (1993) has written about the messages embedded in Roman Catholic stories about women who achieved sainthood by choosing to die rather than submit to rape. A Catholic woman who makes a different choice may feel afterward that she has committed a sin. A Catholic woman who becomes pregnant as the result of a rape may suffer extreme conflict over whether to have an abortion. Orthodox Jewish women have to contend with Talmudic teachings that in some cases assign blame to the rape victim because it is assumed that she should have cried out and that if she had cried out, she would have been rescued. Women who are subjected to sexual acts that are forbidden by their religion may feel even more guilty and defiled than other women do. Some religious women suffer greatly because they feel that God would not have allowed them to be raped unless they had done something terrible to deserve it. Or, if they hold onto their conviction that they do not deserve that kind of punishment, then they struggle to reconcile the fact of the rape with their belief in a just and merciful God. Some women feel guilty because they are feeling rage and hatred toward the rapist, and their religion forbids these emotions and prescribes forgiveness; they may benefit from hearing that most women do feel rage and hatred at some point, and that forgiveness comes much later, if ever. Counselors need not pretend to share a survivor's religious beliefs, but do have to be respectful of them, validate her concerns as real and serious, and support her in her struggle to find some resolution that works for her.

Religious beliefs can be a source of conflict for rape survivors, but they can also be a source of comfort. Even a counselor who is unfamiliar with the tenets of a client's religion, or unsympathetic to them, can help the client to think about what her religion has to offer in this regard. Buddhism, for example, teaches that everything that happens, no matter how painful, happens for a purpose and provides an opportunity to learn a larger lesson (Kanuha, 1987). There may be specific rituals of healing or purification that a survivor can take part in, or she may want to create a ritual of her own. Often it can be helpful for her to talk to a spiritual leader of her own faith about the assault, but she should be cautioned to look for someone she has reason to think will be compassionate rather than rigid and judgmental. She may have to approach more than one person before she finds the right one. Whether she chooses to make use of these options will depend, of course, on whether the religious beliefs of her heritage continue to be meaningful to her personally. Even people who have broken with their religious heritage, however, sometimes turn back to it in times of crisis.

Cutting across membership in a particular culture is the immigrant experience *per se*. Recent immigrants are likely to be struggling with multilayered issues of loss, including loss of status, loss of economic security, loss of familiar surroundings, loss of a whole network of support from friends, extended family, and familiar institutions. Just the energy that it takes to communicate in an unfamiliar language is a constant source of stress. The experience of rape is then superimposed on coping mechanisms that may already be strained to the breaking point. Furthermore, in many cultures, the level of shame associated with rape is such that the survivor feels that she cannot turn to family or friends for help. One intervention that can be effective is to help the rape survivor to make contact with women's organizations within her own community that are dealing with issues of violence against women, where she can obtain support in her own language from people who know her culture well. On the other hand, she may prefer to seek counseling outside her community because she can be sure she will not be seen by anyone who knows her or her family. The survivor's own preferences should be the determining factor. If a referral is made, it is important to do it in a way that does not convey the impression that the counselor is not willing to take the trouble to communicate across the difference in cultures.

Related to but not identical with the immigrant experience is the refugee experience. For women who are refugees from war-torn countries or from extreme political persecution, the context of rape may be the unmitigated horror of wartime atrocities and/or torture, of which rape is often a part (Bowen *et al.*, 1992; Chester, 1992). Barbara Chester, who established the Center for Victims of Torture in Minneapolis, reports rates of extreme sexual violence at 40–60% among women torture victims from Southeast Asia and Latin America. According to Chester, some women who have been tortured are afraid to seek treatment because if it is known that they were tortured, it will be assumed that they were also raped. Some may seek counseling for extreme, chronic post traumatic stress disorder. For others, who may have been coping successfully for some time, a new sexual assault, or the perceived threat of such an assault, may trigger reactivation of extreme symptoms. Not only recent refugees, but women whose trauma dates back to the fall of South Viet Nam a generation ago or to the Holocaust in Europe two generations ago, may still be carrying the scars of that trauma. These women learn from experience that few people are able to listen to the explicit details of what has been done to them, and so they will not talk about it unless the counselor demonstrates some awareness of the issues and a willingness and capacity to face them.

Issues of race, culture, class, and sexual orientation influence every step in the counseling of a rape survivor. The very concept of rape is shaped by culture (Bourque, 1989; Williams, 1984; Wyatt, 1992). It is only in the last few years that marital rape and date rape have begun to be recognized as rape in the United States, and that recognition is still not widespread. If a woman does not define what happened to her as rape, she will not go to a rape crisis program for help with it, and she may not mention it if she seeks counseling for problems such as depression, anxiety, or sexual dysfunction. For some women, realizing that what happened to them was in fact a rape can help them to make sense out of the experience and their reaction to it. Others will resist re-defining the experience as a rape because the cultural or personal meaning that they attach to the term rape is intolerable. It is not necessary for a survivor to acknowledge that she was raped to begin the process of recovery. It is important for her to hear that however she chooses to name what happened, it is normal for her to be experiencing intense and lasting distress about it.

Other cultural factors will also influence whether or not a survivor will present herself to us for counseling. Shame will prevent some survivors from telling anyone at all about the rape. In communities where gang violence is prevalent, and where the rapist may be a member of a gang, the survivor may fear retaliation if she tells anyone about the rape. Avis Ridley-Thomas, the founder of the Rosa Parks Sexual Assault Crisis Center in Los Angeles, talks about the pressure on African-American women to live up to their image as tough and able to take anything, which can make it difficult for them to admit that they need counseling. Some cultures frown on turning to anyone outside the family or the community for help with problems of any kind (Matthews, 1993). If the rapist is a member of the same community as the survivor, there may be concern about bringing discredit on the community; the more endangered the community perceives itself to be, the more powerful a factor this is (Kaye/Kantrowitz, 1992). A lot will also depend on the nature of the setting where you work, and whether it is perceived as welcoming and offering culturally appropriate services to members of a particular community. Furthermore, some survivors will not be able to afford the fees, or to take time off from work, or even to pay for the transportation or childcare costs involved in seeking counseling.

Survivors who do get to our offices for counseling will be carrying out their assessment of us as we are making our assessment of them. If we do not match their concept of a competent, knowledgeable professional who is capable of understanding their circumstances, they will not come back. They may make veiled references to sensitive issues to see whether we pick up on them and how well we handle them. There are things they will not tell us unless we ask, but if we ask too soon or too bluntly, or if we make inaccurate assumptions, they will pull back. For example, a Lesbian may talk about her partner's reactions to her rape without using any pronouns; if we assume that the partner is a man, she may conclude that it is unsafe to disclose her sexual orientation to us.

The optimum physical distance between two people, the pace of verbal exchange and of silences, the degree of formality expected in a professional relationship, the amount of eye contact, the amount of emotional expressiveness all vary from one culture to another. Knowledge about culturally appropriate behavior is important both so that we can adapt to our client's needs and accurately interpret her behavior. An Asian woman who is emotionally reserved is not suffering from blunted affect and she may be experiencing a great deal of inner turmoil, but she is doing her best to maintain her dignity (Ward, 1988). A Latina woman who expresses emotion freely should not be diagnosed as a hysteric on that basis. On the other hand, real psychopathology should not be written off on the basis of cultural stereotypes. If we are not familiar enough with the range of appropriate behavior within a particular culture, we may have to seek consultation with someone who is.

I have already mentioned some of the ways in which cultural attitudes influence how a rape survivor interprets her experience, and how they shape the response she receives from her family and community. Several studies have investigated cultural differences in attitudes toward rape among different racial and ethnic groups in the United States. The findings are complex and sometimes contradictory, but in general, African-Americans and Hispanics seem to be more likely to endorse rape myths, more likely to blame the victim for the rape, and less likely to regard a sexual encounter as a rape (Bourque, 1989; Feild, 1978; Fischer, 1987; Giacopassi & Dull, 1986; Williams, 1984). Bourque (1989) found that the factors that most strongly influence whether a scenario is considered to be a rape differ with race and gender. White women are most influenced by whether force was used; African-American men are most influenced by whether the victim resisted. All of these differences affect the level of support a woman can expect in the aftermath of a rape as well as how she herself interprets the experience and whether she blames herself.

INTERVENTION BIAS IN THE RAPE SITUATION

Prompt and appropriate medical attention is important for every woman who has been raped. Even if there are no obvious physical injuries, she may have sustained internal injuries that she is not aware of. She should also be treated for the prevention of sexually transmitted diseases, and she should have a pregnancy test immediately after the rape and again 6 weeks later. The medical examination is also where important physical evidence is gathered in case she decides to press charges against the rapist. The best place to have all this done is at a hospital emergency room that has been designated as a rape crisis unit. The cost of treatment is covered by Crime Victims Compensation, so most hospitals will treat a woman even if she has no insurance and cannot pay in advance. There is no legal requirement that the hospital report the rape to the police, but some hospitals do it routinely unless the woman is very assertive about wanting her confidentiality maintained. If a woman is fearful of having the police notified, a phone call to the hospital emergency room to find out their policy can be reassuring. Some women will feel more comfortable seeing their own physician or going to a clinic in their own community, and some will refuse medical treatment entirely. Although counselors have a responsibility to explain the reasons for seeking medical attention, they should not pressure a woman who decides otherwise.

Unfortunately, hospitals are not immune to racism, classism, ethnocentrism, or heterosexism, and awareness of these factors may discourage some women from seeking medical care or may result in their receiving insensitive or inappropriate treatment. Women of color may find that they are assumed to be indigent and uneducated, and their questions and concerns may not be treated with the same respect as those of White, middle class women. Trained translators are often unavailable. Stevens and Hall (1990) have described negative experiences encountered by Lesbians seeking health care. These include ostracism, invasive questioning, mistreatment of partners, improper referral to mental health services, and derogatory comments. Gynecological care is a particularly problematic area for Lesbians: intrusive questioning about sexual activity, use of birth control, and the possibility of pregnancy often force women to disclose their sexual orientation when they do not feel safe doing so. Eighty-four percent of the women interviewed said they were reluctant to seek health care because of the likelihood of negative experiences.

Another decision a rape survivor confronts is whether to report the assault to the police. One reason for reporting is that crime victims compensation is only available if the rape has been reported. Crime victims compensation can cover medical and other expenses, lost income, and even long-term, private psychotherapy, although reimbursement can take as long as 2 years. Some survivors feel empowered by doing everything they can to see that the rapist is punished. Others want to protect other women from being victimized. On the other hand, there are valid reasons for deciding not to report the rape, including fear of mistreatment by the police, the traumatic nature of the pre-trial and trial procedures, and lack of optimism that justice will be done. White, middle class women in particular may have unrealistic expectations that the police will question them courteously, that police protection will be available if the rapist threatens them with retaliation, and that the rapist will be arrested, tried, convicted, and sentenced to jail. In reality, only about 4% of reported rapes terminate in that outcome. African-American, Asian, and Latina women are less likely to report a rape to the police than are White women (Feldman-Sommers & Ashworth, 1981; Wyatt, 1992).

It may be helpful to separate the decision about reporting to the police from the decision about whether or not to press charges against the rapist. Reporting secures the survivor's right to crime victims' compensation and puts the incident on the record. The survivor can then postpone the decision about whether to press charges. As with the decision about medical care, the counselor's role is to help the survivor to explore the available options and their possible consequences and to help her to make her own decision about what to do.

Many survivors want to make major life changes after a rape, either to increase their safety or to escape from an environment that is associated with the assault and triggers symptoms of post traumatic stress syndrome. Racism or poverty may seriously limit the options that are open to them. Employment discrimination may make it difficult to change jobs. Discrimination in housing and the lack of low-cost housing may make it impossible for a woman to move out of a high-crime neighborhood or even out of the apartment in which she was raped. Survivors who live in New York City housing projects can apply for an emergency housing transfer, but they have to demonstrate that they are at high risk of being attacked again by the same assailant; just the fact that the projects are a dangerous place to live is not enough to give them a priority over all the other people who want a transfer. Psychological factors, such as an inability to sleep at night in the same apartment where you were raped, are not taken into account. Poverty may also limit a woman's ability to nurture herself in the ways she needs in the immediate aftermath of a rape. She may not be able to get a paid leave of absence from work, or to afford to take time off without pay.

For women living in poverty, basic needs may have to take precedence over dealing with the rape. Matthews (1993) reports that at the Compton YWCA rape crisis program, women come for help finding emergency housing, food, or a job, and only when those issues have been addressed will they mention that they have also been raped.

IMPACT OF VALUE DIFFERENCES IN COUNSELING
RAPE VICTIMS

There are certain values that are deeply imbedded in Euro-American culture, and therefore in our model of rape crisis counseling, which may be very different from the values of our clients or inappropriate to their life circumstances (Pedersen, Fukuyama, & Heath, 1989). One such cluster of values has to do with individual autonomy and independence vs. interdependence with family and community. Euro-American, and especially Anglo-American, culture has developed the ideal of the self-determining, inner-directed, autonomous individual to an extreme that is quite rare among cultures. Advice to a client that encourages her to assert herself more, to put her own needs first, to do what she feels is right regardless of what others think, and so on, can be totally unacceptable to her in terms of her own values and, if she attempts to follow it, can put her in severe conflict with people whose support she needs. We also need to be careful about diagnosing a survivor as overly dependent or enmeshed with her family or masochistic or codependent when she is in fact behaving in culturally appropriate and adaptive ways.

The Euro-American emphasis on individual autonomy may also clash with cultural values of deference to authority: male authority over women, the authority of elders, and so on. Van Boemel and Rozee (1992), who work with Cambodian refugee women, describe having to win the approval of the eldest male in the family before the women would participate. The East Los Angeles Rape Hotline, which serves a Latino community, found they had to include men in their services to gain credibility in the community (Matthews, 1993).

Another cluster of values has to do with open and direct communication vs. discretion, tact, reserve, and indirect and implicit ways of expressing something. In many cultures, the direct, explicit style of communication valued by Euro-Americans would be experienced as rude, intrusive, and insensitive. Kanuha (1987) recommends using indirect methods such as metaphor and third-party references when talking to Southeast

Asian women about sexual assault. Much time may have to be spent on establishing trust before a woman is ready to disclose an assault. Mollica (1986) found that 95% of his Cambodian psychotherapy patients had been raped, but it took an average of 3 years before they talked about it (Van Boemel & Rozee, 1992).

The value our model of counseling places on openness and communication also influences our recommendations to survivors about telling people about the rape. We tend to view open communication as an essential part of a relationship, and secrets as inherently damaging. However, a survivor may know that telling friends, family members, or other members of the community will have consequences far worse than the consequences of living with her secret. Feldman-Summers and Ashworth (1981) found that White women were more likely than Asian, African-American, or Latina women to tell their husband, boyfriend, or lover about a rape.

Open communication of negative emotions such as anger is encouraged by our model of counseling, but may be inappropriate for clients whose culture values the preservation or restoration of harmony. This value can be very adaptive in small, contained, highly interdependent communities that cannot afford to be torn apart by conflict. Some survivors genuinely do not feel anger at the rapist, or are not comfortable expressing it even to a counselor. We should not give them the message that this is abnormal or that they can only recover if they get in touch with their anger. If a woman is feeling anger, it is important to validate that as normal and appropriate, but she may have very little support in her community for the open expression of that anger or for directly confronting the rapist. Our role may be to help a woman to explore culturally appropriate ways of channeling her anger, or providing a safe space in which she can express it.

Differences in values can create an ethical dilemma for the counselor. Our professional ethics codes require us to put the best interests of our client first. They also require us to be respectful of the client's culture. This becomes a problem when her culture subordinates her best interests to the best interests of the group, or has a different view of what really is in her best interests. There is no simple solution to this dilemma. One point to keep in mind is that the client has to live with herself and in her own community. Another is that depending on her degree of assimilation to the dominant culture, the conflict of values may exist within her, not just between her values and ours. We are not serving her if we try to choose for her, either in the direction of defying cultural values or of deferring to them. We can be most helpful by helping her to identify the conflicting pulls she is experiencing, to explore the costs and benefits of her various options, and to find solutions that work best for her.

One final point about how our model of crisis counseling may be inappropriate for many of our clients. Michelle Fine (1983-1984) points out that current psychological theories stress taking control of one's life circumstances as the hallmark of successful coping with crisis. However, this model is applicable only to people with sufficient power and privilege to have some degree of control over those aspects of their life circumstances that are causing their problems. The specific kinds of control recognized by the model are unlikely to be effective for people with little social power. Fine writes that "trusting social institutions, maximizing interpersonal supports, and engaging in self-disclosure are strategies most appropriate for middle class and affluent individuals whose interests are served by those institutions, whose social supports can multiply available resources and contacts and for whom self-disclosure may in fact lead not only to personal change but to structural change (p. 256)." For people with little social power, effective coping strategies may include "ignoring advice to solve one's problems individually [,] . . . rejecting available social programs as inappropriate to one's needs, or recognizing that one's social supports are too vulnerable to be relied on (pp. 250-251)." She adds that "establishing strategies to survive, when change is unlikely, needs to be recognized as acts of control (p. 252)." Too often, the active coping strategies of clients who have little social power are misinterpreted as passivity and giving up. She illustrates this by examining her interaction as a rape crisis counselor with an impoverished African-American woman in a hospital emergency room. The client refused to speak to the police, turned down the offer of an appointment with a counselor and did not intend to tell her friends or family about the assault. Her experience was that talking about her problems just made things worse by keeping them in her thoughts when nothing could be done about them. She feared that if her brothers or her mother's boyfriend found out about the rape, they would kill the rapist, and she did not want them going to jail. Her social worker was the person who had taken custody of her children away from her, not someone she would choose to confide in. "Resisting social institutions, withholding information and preserving emotional invulnerability emerged as her strategies for maintaining control (p. 256)."

CONCLUSION

To summarize, in order to be effective counselors for rape survivors, we need to understand how racism, classism, and heterosexism are intertwined with the power dynamics of sexual assault and with the institutions to which survivors turn, or choose not to turn, for help. We need to understand the cultural context of our clients' lives, the meaning of sexual assault within that context, and the cultural circumstances and values that influence the options available to them as they go through the recovery process. Although we cannot be experts on the culture of every client we see, we can be sensitive to the fact that cultural factors are undoubtedly operating, and open to learning what they are. We can recognize our own biases as products of our own culture, and refrain from imposing them on our clients. We can listen for conflicts that result from living simultaneously in the dominant Euro-American culture of the United States and the client's home culture, and help to make these explicit. We can encourage clients to seek out the sources of support and healing within their own cultures. And finally, we can trust our clients to make the choices that are right for them.

ACKNOWLEDGMENTS

The author wishes to thank William Dycus for assistance with the literature search for this paper.

REFERENCES

Bourque, L. B. (1989). *Defining rape*. Durham, NC: Duke University Press.

Bowen, D. J., Carscadden, L., Beighle, K., & Fleming, I. (1992). Post-traumatic stress disorder among Salvadoran women: Empirical evidence and description of treatment. *Women and Therapy, 13*, 267-280.

Bradmiller, L. L., & Walters, W. S. (1985). Seriousness of sexual assault charges: Influencing factors. *Criminal Justice & Behavior, 12*, 463-484.

Burstow, B. (1992). *Radical feminist therapy: Working in the context of violence*. Newbury Park, CA: Sage.

Burt, M. R. (1980). Cultural myths and supports for rape. *Journal of Personality and Social Psychology, 38*, 217-230.

Carby, H. V. (1987). *Reconstructing womanhood: The emergence of the Afro-American woman novelist*. New York: Oxford University Press.

Chester, B. (1992). Women and political torture: Work with refugee survivors in exile. *Women and Therapy, 13*, 209-220.

Collins, P. H. (1993). The sexual politics of Black womanhood. In P. B. Bart and E. G. Moran (Eds.), *Violence against women* (pp. 85-104). Newbury Park, CA: Sage.

Davis, A. Y. (1981). *Women, race, and class*. New York: Random House.

Deitz, S. R., & Byrnes, L. E. (1981). Attribution of responsibility for sexual assault: The influence of observer empathy and defender occupation and attractiveness. *Journal of Psychology, 108*, 17-29.

Devore, W., & Schlesinger, E. G. (1987). *Ethnic-sensitive social work practice* (2nd ed.). Columbus, OH: Merrill.

Enloe, C. (1989). *Bananas, beaches, and bases: Making feminist sense of international politics*. Berkeley, CA: University of California.

Federal Bureau of Investigation (1992). *Uniform crime reports for the United States (1991)*. Washington, D.C.: Government Printing Office.

Feild, H. S. (1978). Attitudes toward rape: A comparative analysis of police, rapists, crisis counselors, and citizens. *Journal of Personality and Social Psychology, 36,* 156-179.

Feild, H. S. (1979). Rape trials and juror decisions: A psychological analysis of the effects of victim, defendant, and case characteristics. *Law and Human Behavior, 3,* 261-284.

Feldman-Summers, S., & Ashworth, C. D. (1981). Factors related to intentions to report a rape. *Journal of Social Issues, 37,* 53-70.

Fine, M. (1983-1984). Coping with rape: Critical perspectives on consciousness. *Imagination, Cognition and Personality, 3,* 249-267.

Fischer, G. J. (1987). Hispanic and majority student attitudes toward forcible date rape as a function of differences in attitudes toward women. *Sex Roles, 17,* 93-101.

Giacopassi, D. J., & Dull, R. T. (1986). Gender and racial differences in the acceptance of rape myths within a college population. *Sex Roles, 15,* 63-75.

Hall, J. D. (1983). "The mind that burns in each body": Women, rape, and racial violence. In A. Snitow, C. Stansell, and S. Thompson. (Eds.), *Powers of desire: The politics of sexuality* (pp. 329-349). New York: Monthly Review Press.

Hindelang, M. J., & Davis, B. L. (1977). Forcible rape in the United States: A statistical profile. In D. Chappell, R. Geis, and G. Geis. (Eds.), *Forcible rape: The crime, the victim, and the offender* (pp. 87-114). New York: Columbia University Press.

hooks, b. (1981). *Ain't I a woman: Black women and feminism* (pp. 22-86). Boston: South End Press.

Kanuha, V. (1987). Sexual assault in Southeast Asian communities: Issues in intervention. *Response, 10,* 4-6.

Kaye/Kantrowitz, M. (1992). *The issue is power: Essays on women Jews, violence and resistance.* San Francisco: Aunt Lute.

Koss, M. P., Gidycz, C. A., & Wisniewski, N. (1987). The scope of rape: Incidence and prevalence of sexual aggression and victimization in a national sample of higher education students. *Journal of Consulting and Clinical Psychology, 55,* 162-170.

LaFree, G. D. (1980). The effects of sexual stratification by race on official reactions to rape. *American Sociological Review, 45,* 842-854.

Lottes, I. L. (1988). Sexual socialization and attitudes toward rape. In A. W. Burgess (Ed.), *Rape and sexual Assault II* (pp. 193-220). New York: Garland.

Lundberg-Love, P., & Lundberg-Love, G. R. (1989). Date rape: Prevalence, risk factors, and a proposed model. In M. A. Pirog-Good and J. E. Stets (Eds.), *Violence in dating relationships* (pp. 169-184). New York: Praeger.

Matthews, N. A. (1993). Surmounting a legacy: The expansion of racial diversity in a local anti-rape movement. In P. B. Bart and E. G. Moran (Eds.), *Violence against women* (pp. 177-192). Newbury Park, CA: Sage.

McGoldrick, M., Pearce, J. K., & Giordana, J. (Eds.) (1982). *Ethnicity and family therapy.* NY: Guilford.

Mollica, R. (1986). *Cambodian Refugee Women at Risk.* Paper presented at the American Psychological Association Annual Meeting, Washington, D.C. Cited in G. B. Van Boemel and P. D. Rozee (1992). Treatment for psychosomatic blindness among Cambodian refugee women. *Women and Therapy, 13,* 239-266.

Pedersen, P. (Ed.) (1985). *Handbook of cross-cultural counseling and therapy.* Westport, CT: Greenwood.

Pedersen, P. B., Fukuyama, M., & Heath, A. (1989). Client, counselor, and contextual variables in multicultural counseling. In P. B. Pedersen, J. G. Draguns, W. J. Lonner, and J. E. Trimbale (Eds.), *Counseling across cultures* (3rd ed.) (pp. 23-52). Honolulu: University of Hawaii.

Pinderhughes, E. (1989). *Understanding race, ethnicity, and power: The key to efficacy in clinical practice.* New York: Free Press.

Russell, D. E. H. (1982). The prevalence and incidence of forcible rape and attempted rape of females. *Victimology, 7,* 81-93.

Russell, D. E. H., & Howell, N. (1983). The prevalence of rape in the United States revisited. *Signs, 8,* 688-695.

Sanday, P. R. (1981). The socio-cultural context of rape: A cross-cultural study. *Journal of Social Issues, 37,* 5-27.

Sorenson, S. B., & Siegel, J. M. (1992). Gender, ethnicity, and sexual assault: Findings from a Los Angeles study. *Journal of Social Issues, 48,* 93-104.

Stevens, P. E., & Hall, J. M. (1990). Abusive health care interactions experienced by lesbians: A case of institutional violence in the treatment of women. *Resist, 13,* 23-27.

Van Boemel, G. B., & Rozee, P. D. (1992). Treatment for psychosomatic blindness among Cambodian refugee women. *Women and Therapy, 13,* 239-266.

Ward, C. (1988). Stress, coping and adjustment in victims of sexual assault: The role of psychological defense mechanisms. *Counseling Psychology Quarterly, 1,* 165-178.

Williams, J. E. (1984). Secondary victimization: Confronting public attitudes about rape. *Victimology, 9,* 66-81.

Wyatt, G. E. (1992). The sociocultural context of African American and White American women's rape. *Journal of Social Issues, 48,* 77-91.

Young, K. Z. (1993). The imperishable virginity of Saint Maria Goretti. In P. B. Bart and E. G. Moran (Eds.), *Violence against women* (pp. 105-113). Newbury Park, CA: Sage.

Index

Abelson, R., 42
Abikoff, H., 121, 123
Abused and neglected foster children, 149–163
    absent parent, 150–151
    case examples, 154–157
    emotionally vulnerable child, 152
    foster care system, 151–152
    foster parent, 151
    inconsistent parenting, intrapsychic implications of, 152–154
    oppositional behavior, 157–161
    overview of, 149–150
    recommendations, 161–162
    relational dissonance, 154
Adler, G., 38
African-Americans, 69–84
    abused and neglected foster children, 149–163. *See also* Abused and neglected foster children
    anger and, 44
    future research, 83
    inner-city minority youth, 121–148. *See also* Inner-city minority youth
    overview of, 69–70
    prevalence of domestic violence among, 70–71
    rape counseling, 168–174
    stereotyping and, 74–77
    theories of domestic violence, 71–74
    treatment issues, 78–83
    women, 77–78
Aggression
    anger and, 37, 39–40
    defined, 48–50
    diagnosis and, 44–47
    inner-city minority youth, 121–148. *See also* Inner-city minority youth
Ainsworth, M. D., 153
Akbar, N., 9
Alpert, J. L., xvi
American Psychiatric Association, 44, 45
Ammerman, R. T., 19, 21
Anger, 35–67
    aggression and, 39–40
    avoidance of, 36–37, 38
    constructs in, 47–51
    culture and, 42–44

    definitions, 37
    diagnosis and, 44–47
    diagnostic criteria proposed, 51–54
    domestic violence and, 39–40
    emotional scripts and, 59–62
    overview of, 35–36
    physical illness and, 40–42
    psychology and, 37–38
    therapeutic interventions with, 54–59
Anger/hostility disorder, diagnostic criteria proposed, 51–54
Aponte, J., xvi
Arias, I., 39
Aronowitz, B., 127
Asbury, J., 71, 74, 75, 77
Ashworth, C. D., 175, 177
Asian families. *See* Chinese families
Assessment, 3–17
    alternative approaches, 9–15
    Chinese families, 99–100
    overview of, 3–4
    sociocultural factors, 6–9
    study types, 4–6
Attention deficit disorder with hyperactivity, inner-city minority youth, 122–124
Averill, J. A., 37, 40, 46, 47, 48, 58, 60

Bachman, R., 20
Bandura, A., 40
Barefoot, J. C., 42, 50, 51
Barling, J., 39
Barlow, D., 37
Bass, D., 138
Battering, patterns in, 23
Beck, A. T., 43, 50, 124
Becker, D. M., 125
Bell, C., 73, 74, 76
Bepko, C., 114
Bergman, A., 20, 23
Berk, R. A., 39
Berk, S. F., 39
Berkowitz, L., 48
Berliner, L., 107
Biaggio, M. K., 38
Blanchard, M., 153
Blechman, E., 133
Bordin, E. S., 55